MEDIA AND LITERACY

Second Edition

MEDIA AND LITERACY

Learning in an Electronic Age - Issues, Ideas, and Teaching Strategies

By

Dennis Adams   **Mary Hamm**

Charles C Thomas

PUBLISHER • LTD.

SPRINGFIELD • ILLINOIS • U.S.A.

Published and Distributed Throughout the World by

CHARLES C THOMAS • PUBLISHER, LTD.
2600 South First Street
Springfield, Illinois 62704

©2000 by CHARLES C THOMAS • PUBLISHER, LTD.

ISBN 0-398-07031-8 (cloth)
ISBN 0-398-07032-6 (paper)

Library of Congress Catalog Card Number: 99-048808

With THOMAS BOOKS *careful attention is given to all details of manufacturing and design. It is the Publisher's desire to present books that are satisfactory as to their physical qualities and artistic possibilities and appropriate for their particular use.* THOMAS BOOKS *will be true to those laws of quality that assure a good name and good will.*

Printed in the United States of America
CR-R-3

Library of Congress Cataloging-in-Publication Data

Adams, Dennis M.
    Media and literacy : learning in an electronic age--issues, ideas,
    and teaching strategies / by Dennis Adams, Mary Hamm.-- 2nd ed.
      p. cm.
    Includes bibliographical references and index.
    ISBN 0-398-07031-8 (cloth) -- ISBN 0-398-07032-6 (paper)
    1. Audio-visual education--United States. 2. Television in education
--United States. 3. Visual learning--United States. 4. Computer-assisted
instruction--United States. I. Hamm, Mary. II. Title.

LB1043 .A33 2000
371.33'58'0973--dc21

                                        99-048808

PREFACE

There are multiple technologically-intensive literacies found in today's environment: media literacy, visual literacy, digital literacy, networking literacy, and more. All of these competencies influence citizenship. And they can all can be powerful instructional allies. As mass communications, teaching, learning, and literacy take on new meaning in the Information Age, we must be sure that all students have access to literacy in its most powerful forms.

There is a growing acceptance of standards for what students should know and be able to do in core subjects. Many standards projects have been undertaken in recent years. Subject matter organizations have developed these voluntary standards in a way that reflects what we know about content and pedagogy. In all cases, they include information and communication technology. This book references the core standards projects, suggests a mix of media possibilities, and explores ways that multiple literacies connect to the language arts, science, mathematics, the arts, and technology. It also suggests approaches to becoming intelligent media consumers. Although each standards project approaches technology from a somewhat different direction, each focuses on what is being taught, what is being learned, and the mix of media involved. Some of the projects, like science, have supporting supplementary materials to help teachers with the basics of standards-based reform. Others, like the language arts, provide a solid vision but omit sample lessons.

The standards provide a central view of what schools must do to reach national educational goals. Performance standards focus on the nature of proficiency at various levels. Aligning the standards with the curriculum and assessment is a central concern. Opportunity to learn standards suggests what is required for all students to have a fair shot at high achievement. The emphasis here is on subject matter (content) standards and multiple literacies required in a digital world.

At one time literacy was squeezed into an established framework of reading and writing. The meaning has changed as new circumstances and new approaches to teaching have opened up a much wider range of possibilities. The word "literacy" has become almost synonymous with the word "competence." Although we do not push the definition that far, we do agree with writers who refer to technological or scientific literacy without any reference to reading and writing. We also agree that the core subjects and their technological associates will all play a role in tomorrow's elevated concept of literacy.

What will it mean to be literate in the twenty-first century? *Media and Literacy* will attempt to answer that question. It is written in a style that we hope teachers will find accessible. Many practical media-related activities have been included. All of the suggestions here are based on the belief that children can build knowledge (including media knowledge) in ways that connect to their own experiences. This constructivist approach to teaching implies that knowledge cannot be gained simply by absorption through the senses. It is our belief that active thinking, hands-on inquiry, and collaborative doing capitalize on how children learn best.

Children need access to the most powerful technology available so that they can examine reality from many angles and in different lights. As they use media to engage in social, physical, and mental activities, it is possible to visualize new connections and choices. Teachers will continue to guide their students to think critically about the information presented to them by a mix of distant sources and media. When you get connected to the Internet, for example, you have to understand that it can be an empowering medium when used responsibly. When used irresponsibly, it can be a colossal waste of time. Whiz-bang, high-tech skills help. But sound fundamentals like individual judgment, values, and knowledge skills are most important when it comes to handling today's technology.

A healthy irreverence for the established way of doing things often goes hand-in-hand with the ability to think deeply and widely. This applies as much to teachers as it does to students. Everything possible should be done to make tomorrow's schools attractive, pleasant places where imagination, ingenuity, and creativity are valued. Technology can help. But getting millions of teachers who can break new educational ground requires raising the the level of what teaching is all about. More than a third of the teachers working today are expected to retire in the next decade. At the same time, a surge is expected in the number of schoolchildren. To recruit a sufficient cadre of well-educated new teachers will require better pay, more prestige, and much better working conditions. Only then will we get enough teachers who can demonstrate that it is possible to be educated, thoughtful, confident, and action oriented.

CONTENTS

MEDIA AND LITERACY

Chapter 1

MULTIPLE LITERACIES
MEDIA ACROSS THE CURRICULUM

All of our inventions are but improved means to an unimproved end.
–Henry David Thoreau

Social power extends from being able to understand and manipulate the processes used to create messages in the modern world. Being literate now implies having the ability to decode information from all types of media. Here the media literacy umbrella will be extended to cover technological literacy, visual literacy, information literacy, networking literacy, and more. New electronic possibilities hold great promise, but they should be viewed as a means rather than an end. Therefore the core curriculum and subject matter standards are central concerns. As contemporary media converge, the features of multiple literacies will increasingly overlap with each other and with basic subject matter.

This book is an effort to contribute to the conversation about the nature of literacy in today's technology-intensive world. It is our belief that everyone should have access to literacy in its most powerful forms. American children have always spent years mastering elements of traditional literacy systems and learning how to use them fluently. It is time to reach out to new media. The ascendancy of television and the computer are two of the most important technological developments of our time. Now everyone has to go beyond the traditional basics of reading, writing, and calculating. Science, art, and technology are the new kids on the basic educational block. Across the curriculum, today's students have to learn how to understand and create messages through varied experiences with many forms of print *and* nonprint media. In the future, subject matter will be even more closely associated with technology.

As new interlocking technologies increasingly shape our future, it is important to explore the possibilities and the problems. The power of today's information, communications, and networking media requires special attention. But it would be foolish to provide too warm a welcome without more serious thought. Will developing multimedia technology provide a transforming vision and a new awareness? Possibly. But developments have been moving so fast that few have taken the time to consider where we are going or where we might end up.

DRAWING ON A SHARED MEDIA CULTURE

Media literacy cuts across all basic subjects. It involves more than teaching through media, it is teaching *about* and *with* media. As part of an expanded definition of literacy, *media literacy* may be thought of as composing, comprehending, analyzing, and appreciating the multiple print and nonprint symbol systems. From television to Internet web sites, when production is added to the process, it can serve as an integrating force in the classroom.

Today's students live in a world where more and more information is communicated through viewing. The habits of the mind fostered through media interactions really do need to be highlighted. The future may well belong to those who can intelligently see it. Clearly, students in tomorrow's schools will interact with the full range of media possibilities–viewing them all as "texts" to be experienced, appreciated, analyzed, created, and shared. Internet technology puts the world at the student's fingertips. For the first time, active, hands-on learning is available for students all over the world, but buyer beware. Information and disinformation are intertwined.

Students now have to develop the ability to sort out what's worth knowing. They also have to understand how print and nonprint texts function together in the development of thought, knowledge, language, and literacy. Communicating effectively and creating meaning with a multitude of media is becoming an essential part of literacy instruction.

We live in a technological hall of mirrors where it is becoming increasingly difficult to separate reality from virtual reality. Today's media landscape is dominated by solitary obsessions and odd subcultures on the Internet. It is little wonder that the natural world often feels out of joint. The digital revolution has contributed to a sense of cultural vertigo. To function in a media-saturated environment, students need a solid media knowledge base. This means helping students learn how to evaluate their media choices, understand the the underlying values, and use each medium for creative expression.

CHANGING THE SHAPE OF IDEAS

An examination of the recent past and little informed wisdom about the present would certainly help.

> *To understand today you have to search yesterday.*
> –Pearl Buck

No matter how stunning or entrancing, new media will not negate the wisdom of the ages. Nor will it allow us to escape our limitations. All media are simply extensions of ourselves–the good, the bad, and the ugly. The degree to which the imagination is stimulated, deadened, or colonized has always been open to question.

Historically, when a new medium comes along, it changes the shape of ideas and affects the basic nature of human communications. It often changes the way we think. The possibilities of the print media didn't become clear until well after it was on the scene. For example, after Gutenberg turned his wine press into a printing press, it took more than fifty years before an apprentice thought of numbering the pages. More recently, it took a graduate student's term project at MIT to come up with the radical notion of using a computer for word processing. To make a medium come alive sometimes requires a poet. Sometimes it requires a plumber. And sometimes it takes a clever student.

If a technology is not well understood, there is a tendency to either overstate its possibilities or dismiss its promise. Exaggerations in either direction can kill an instructional tool before it has a chance to develop. False prophets betray the promise of new technology. We seem in a constant race between media growing up and the maturity of wise human use.

Only rarely does *anyone* accurately predict the full impact of new technologies. Utopia or disaster? Usually neither one. Seemingly good ideas often go sour. Remember flying cars, picture phones, computers as big as a barn, intelligent robots, and Orwell's vision of *1984*? Words of wisdom, exaggerations, and high-tech flops abound. Something important may eventually happen, but extreme visions of technology's promises and pitfalls rarely come to pass.

The outlines may be blurry, but we can be sure that educational technology and subject matter standards will be part of our educational future. Each core area now recognizes the need to understand and use the whole range of electronic media. The schools realize that they cannot avoid the fact that we live in a technological age. Exactly how information technology is going to be incorporated into the curriculum is still an open question.

We have to accept the fact that as today's communication and information revolution expands, things will happen that cannot be predicted. But before blindly plowing ahead, it would be wise to give serious thought to what the technology will undo—and *what it will do*. On the positive side, how can we make sure that information and communications technology will be used to spark a renaissance in human learning, thinking, and communication?

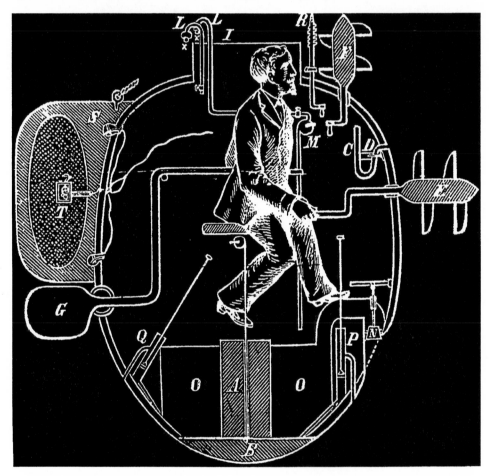

Figure 1.1. A nineteenth century underwater warship, a forerunner of the submarine.

CONSTRUCTING MEANING WITH VISUAL MODELS

The long-term implications of recent changes in educational and communications technology are important, if not frightening. The convergence and increased power of media technologies are causing a major change in societal behaviors, lifestyles, thinking, and learning patterns. With few people monitoring what is going on—and fewer still theorizing about its health—electronic media and it associates may be doing all kinds of strange things to us. The future offers yet more extensions to our sensory organs—electronic eyes, ears, and information navigators. The newer the media, the less we know about it. Some of the findings from reading print and watching television apply; some don't. We need more research on how people are using digital media and Internet technologies. Now is the time to figure out how all of this might be employed to work on our behalf.

One of the problems is that the future is moving upon us faster than anyone thought possible. By the time the results of research on new media come in, the technology has often moved onto another plane. There is only so much we can do much about the fact that before anything like understanding or quality assurance gets developed, the human race is forced to sink or swim in an electronic sea of ideas.

Information and communication technology are bound to have an effect on cognitive and affective development. It is clear that the perception of reality acquired from viewing television is one of the mediating factors in forming personal behavior and social attitudes across age groups. But the level of influence depends on many factors. When it comes to schooling, the power and permanency of what we learn are greater when visually-based mental models are used in conjunction with the printed word.

Every age seeks out the appropriate medium to confront the question of human existence. Ours just happen to be electronic. Many of the charges leveled against new media have been faced by writing and print. New media technologies have the potential to be life diminishing or life enhancing. Like books, television, computers, and the Internet have an effect on our personal values, our educational institutions, our ways of experiencing the world, and how we conduct our lives.

Inferences drawn from sophisticated visual models can lead to more profound thinking. Children often rely on their visual learning even when their conceptual knowledge contradicts it. Verbal explanations, personal experience, and active learning in a real classroom will remain important. But there are times when the video screen can provide potent visual experiences that push viewers to accept what is presented. The moving image has as much power to make our thoughts robust as it does to make them feeble.

Before schools put more resources into buying computers or wiring classrooms for the Internet, we need to identify significant instructional problems that the technology is going to help us solve. The educational goals come first. The next step is to figure out how to apply the technology to our new curriculum standards.

Basic Points to Consider in Technology Planning

- Make teachers' needs a top priority
- It takes time for technology to take hold
- It takes more than technology to change schools
- The pedagogical plan has to come first
- The curriculum should drive the way technology is used
- Keep the focus on specific learning needs
- Pay attention to access and equity.

CYBERPATHS TO INFORMATION AND GRAND ILLUSIONS

There is little question that today's reality is being shaped by electronic information and electronic illusions. Baby boomers are the first TV generation and "generation X" is rapidly becoming the "Net generation." If the future isn't televised, it is bound to be on the Internet. As the commercial TV model takes hold on the Web, it makes teaching with the Internet more difficult. As the Internet turns into a shopping mall, some universities and governmental agencies are turning to an alternative (non-commercial), high-speed, "Internet II." Whatever combination schools end up with, the printed page will remain the best way to convey many forms of information.

Using the media available in his day, Piaget showed how certain notions of time, space, or morality are beyond a child's grasp until certain developmental levels are reached. It is not just vocabulary limitations that impede children when it comes to dealing with adult content. Children seem to lack the fundamental integrative capacities to chunk (group) certain kinds of information into meaningful categories which are obvious to adults. As we become more experienced with visually-intensive media, we get better at selective attention. But young children who have not developed strategies for tuning out irrelevancies may be especially vulnerable to unwanted adult content.

Whatever form the technology takes, children often construct the meaning of television content without consciously thinking about it. They attend to stimuli and extract meaning. How well visually-intensive content is understood varies according to similarities between a child's experiential background and content. Needs, interests, and age are also important.

Students profit from exploring how technologies intrude themselves into their culture and their personal lives. Teachers can raise questions about changes in media technology. Children need an intellectual and moral compass for assessing media. They also need tools for and sorting through the information glut. School-based instruction can make a difference by helping students construct meaning, interpret information, and assess information found on the Internet, TV, and on computer programs. We are just beginning to understand the tremendous impact of things that might, at first glance, seem frivolous.

A note of caution. From time to time we need to be reminded that a little skeptical inquiry about technological miracles is in order. No media is a good substitute for actual developmental experiences with concrete materials or face-to-face collaborative learning. Electronic media has its place, but children need time for play experiences, conversation, and reading.

MASS MEDIA IN THE AGE OF INFORMATION AND SHOW BUSINESS

Does a society really get the mass media it deserves? In recent decades, American journalism has gone a long way towards losing the confidence of its readers and viewers. Caught between new technologies and a heightened concern for profits, information and the news have shifted from a public service to a commercial enterprise. For the last twenty years, a vast technological revolution has transformed the way we get and process information. In the late 1970s, for example, most Americans (over 80 percent) watched one of the evening newscasts on CBS, NBC, or ABC. Now it is less than 40 percent.

The communications market has been fractionalized into dozens or even hundreds of channels. How to attract audience share is the new profit-motivated obsession. "Dumb it down and sleaze it up" doesn't exactly make for high journalistic standards. The simple truth is that whatever debases the culture, panders to violent impulses, or isolates us from one another *degrades the value of a caring social community.*

Although there is enough societal blame to go around, filmmakers, computer gamers, TV producers, and news reporters must all share in the responsibility for desensitizing young people to violence. Internet filters may help. But you can't program a V-chip (TV) to sort the violence out of the local news. Good journalists have always been able to transform their craft into an agent of positive change for the whole society. It is harder than ever, but it is still possible to do more than reflect entertainment values or the worst of our society.

From television to the Internet, every medium borrows from others while taking on momentum of its own. We are just beginning to understand how evolving electronic media systems affect educational, cultural, perceptual, and social organization. The schools need to be involved in helping children become more critical consumers of electronically-produced information. This is a major educational and societal responsibility. Teachers can help children develop a new vocabulary to understand new circumstances. It is time to figure out how to ask the right conceptual questions in a world illuminated by the constant glow of the video screen.

MEDIA SYMBOL SYSTEMS INFLUENCE COMMUNICATION

Although the impact of any medium can be influenced by another, print, film, video, and computers take somewhat different approaches to communicating meaning. Print relies upon the reader's ability to interpret abstract symbols. The video screen is usually more direct. Whatever the medium, thinking and learning are based on internal symbolic representations and the mental interpretation of those symbols.

We live in a complex society dependent on rapid communication and information access. Television, film, computers, and the Internet are rapidly becoming our dominant cultural tools for selecting, gathering, storing, and conveying knowledge in representational forms. It is little wonder that the various standards projects point to the importance of students developing the skills necessary for interpreting and processing all kinds of media messages.

Individuals must learn to use a media's symbolic forms for purposes of internal representation. To even begin to read, for example, a child needs to understand sound-symbol relationships between the letters. They also need the vocabulary and a rich experiential background to comprehend what they are reading. To move beneath the surface of video imagery requires some of the same understandings. But it takes skill to break free from an effortless wash of images and electronically-induced visual quicksand. Serious instruction is required to develop critical media consumers who are literate in interpreting and processing visual images. Media literacy is now a participant in the conversation about subject matter standards.

Each communications medium makes use of its own distinctive technology for gathering, encoding, sorting, and conveying its contents associated with different situations. The technological nature of a medium affects the interaction with its users–just as the method for transmitting content affects the knowledge acquired.

Print or visual representation–unlike direct experience–is always coded within a symbol system. Learning to understand that system cultivates the mental skills necessary for gathering and assimilating internal representations. Children are now involved with television, computers, or the Internet nearly thirty hours a week at home and over seven hours a week at school. This is bound to change the texture of learning.

What a child learns is more affected by what is delivered than by the delivery system itself. In other words, the quality of the programming is the key to the quality of any medium, but different media are more than alternative routes to the same end. Specific media attributes call on different sets of mental skills, and by doing so, cater to different learning styles. The processing of information always takes place and this process always requires skill. The closer the match between the way information is presented and the way it can be mentally represented, the easier it is to learn. Better communication means easier processing and more transfer. Voluntary attention and the formation of ideas can be facilitated by electronic media—with concepts becoming part of the child's repertoire.

New educational choices are being laid open by information and communication technologies. Understanding and employing these technological forces require a critical perspective that interprets new literacies from a unique perspective. We would do well to remember that while certain educational principles remained constant, moving from speech to handwritten manuscripts to print required major changes in teaching and learning.

MASTERING ELECTRONIC MESSAGES

Subject matter standards can give focus to how technology is used in classrooms. As with reading a book, understanding the conventions of electronic media can help cultivate mental "tools of thought." A new medium provides new ways of handling and exploring the world. For example, to fully interpret the action and messages on a video display terminal requires going beyond the surface to understanding the deep structure of the medium. Understanding the practical and philosophical nuances of a medium moves its consumers in the direction of mastery.

Moving around graphics, icons, music, and font sizes may be fun, but students may not be learning anything useful. Seeing an image does not automatically ensure learning from it. The levels of knowledge and skill that children bring with them to the viewing situation determine the areas of knowledge and skill development acquired. As with print, decoding visual stimuli and learning from visual images require practice. Students can be guided in decoding and looking critically at what they view. One technique is to have students "read" the image on various levels. Students identify individual elements, classify them into various categories, and then relate the whole to their own experiences. They can then draw inferences and create new conceptualizations from what they have learned.

Computers, Netcams, camcorders, and the Internet are getting easier to use. VCRs are also moving in that direction. They are no longer as difficult to operate as when they were referred to as "Vague Chance of Recording" machines that blink 12:00. The new ones have at least stopped blinking. Almost every school now has several. Over a quarter of Americans can even videotape their own scenes with a camcorder. These new "video pencils" can transform the landscape of student visual creations.

Planning, visualizing, and developing a production allow students to critically sort out and use video techniques to relay meaning. Young video producers should be encouraged to open their eyes to the world and visually experience what's out there. By realizing their ideas through video production, students learn to redefine space and time, and use media attributes such as structure, sound, color, pacing, and imaging.

New lightweight camcorders and digital cameras attached to the computer makes video photography simple, and the Internet makes "publishing" the results much easier. Sometimes, the more amateur the work, the easier it is to gain insight into how a visual idea can be created. Getting students involved in simple video production or website design also gives them a powerful framework for evaluating, controlling, and creating with electronic media.

Since the field of education seems to be entering a unique period of introspection, self-doubt, and great expectations, theoretical guidelines are needed as much as specific methods. It is dangerous to function in a vacuum because rituals can spring up that are worse than those drained away. As electronic learning devices flood our schools and homes, we need to be sure that their use is linked to good educational practice. A close connection between home and school requires defining educational needs in a more theoretical *and* a more practical way. If practice, theory, and research aren't integrated, then one will get in the way of the others. Good research informs good teaching—and vice versa.

A wide range of intellectual tools can be applied to media production in ways that help students understand social and physical reality. Technology can be an ally in the learning process, or it can be an instrument for subverting human integrity. To avoid the latter, adults and children need to have control over the technology they are using. The authoritarian "read your e-mail or else" type approach has to go. A major characteristic of effective instruction, within a democratic system, is professional autonomy.

Schools teach students to read and write by making sure that they read good literature, tap personal experience, know how to search out information, write for a real reader, and cooperatively edit their material. Now students can "publish" what they write on the Internet. Learning how to "read" and "write" with electronic media can follow a similar pattern.

ANTICIPATING THE CONTOURS OF A VISUAL WORLD

Good teaching means opening students' eyes to things they might not have thought of on their own. It requires tapping into real experience, fantasies, and personal visions. Information technology can serve as a capable collaborator. The combination of thoughtful strategies and the enabling features of electronic tools can achieve lasting cognitive change and improved academic performance.

Print, writing, and hand-drawn pictures have been the cognitive tools that Western culture has traditionally chosen to teach children. Good theoretical and practical techniques have been developed for teaching reading and writing. These understandings will be helpful in dealing with media today—and with possibilities beyond the current technological horizons in education. The information age is on the cusp of the millennium. Are you ready for robotic Internet search engines and voice-activated Web surfing?

Television, computers, and the Internet have taken their place in the classroom as interactive conveyers of information. Teachers and students now have a new set of tools for gathering more selective information and manipulating imagery on video display screens. As print, computers, and video merge, children and young adults can develop explicit metacognitive strategies as they search for data, solve problems, and graphically simulate their way through multiple levels of abstraction. With this mind-eye approach, previously obscure concepts can be presented with greater depth. And they can be made comprehensible to students at an earlier age. In a society that is becoming increasingly impersonal, the next step is adding active hands-on work with peers to the technological mix.

LAYING THE GROUNDWORK FOR MOTIVATED LEARNERS

We are putting together the technological elements needed to give us electronic access to a truly individualized set of learning experiences. To do this right, we need to develop a modern philosophy of teaching and learning that recognizes high-tech realities. For example, electronically connecting the human mind to global information resources will result in a shift in human consciousness similar to the change that occurred when a society moved from an oral to a written culture. The challenge is to provide the intellectual framework and make sure that the possibilities are available for all. New technology might even be able to help us change the tone and priorities of learning in a democratic society. To make this happen our nation must achieve a better balance of its moral, intellectual, financial, and technological capital.

While learning to use what's available today, we need to start building the social and educational infrastructure of the knowledge highways of the future. If educators don't take part in the process, then someone will do it for them. And the results won't be pretty. The ultimate consequences of innovation in electronic learning may be open to question. But the development of basic skills, habits of the mind, wisdom, and traits of character will be affected—one way or another—by the new media technologies.

The Internet can give users fresh, fast, free-associative images that are as much like an action painting that you can feel as they are like printed text that you can intellectually comprehend. When computer simulation is added to this mix, students can enter an electronic environment, build imaginative stories (with print and moving graphics), and bring them to life.

Links to databases have put many libraries or information utilities within windowing distance of a personal computer. Information can be made available in seconds—wherever it resides. This helps break down the barrier between school knowledge and information in the real world. We can now place our cursor on a footnote, click the mouse, and zoom in on a full text (with pictures) of the reference from a distant database. Traveling wisely on such knowledge highways requires students to act more like researchers than traditional learners.

Computer control gives us the ability to move information around as we think—rather than forcing our thoughts to move around as the program does. Now you can connect to the Internet, create a window on your computer-controlled video screen, and selectively hop down a number of database alleys. The Internet is like a library with all of the books dumped in piles on the floor. Today's search engines are blunt devises that are not all that good at cutting through the information glut. Before long we will have much more efficient individualized search engines ("Bots") that roam the vast expanses of cyberspace in search of the specific information that we need.

Television will not be left too far behind. WebTV has been on the scene for several years. Soon we will have artificially intelligent (computer-controlled) high-definition television sets that will present movie quality material according the viewer's preferred presentation style. These artificially intelligent (AI) systems will learn what is of most interest to the viewer and comb extensive databases and networks to assemble video programs. All of this will be possible within the next few years as personal computers become video processing machines.

There are some things that we can be sure about today. For example, if teachers are going to do their share in educational renewal then they need a thorough knowledge of their *subject matter* discipline and the *teaching methods* that characterize effective instruction. They also need the capacity to make critical instructional judgments about communications and information media.

Teachers must be aware of the world's scientific, technological, communication, social, and personal changes. And they must be prepared to respond to them. As we reach for a mobilizing vision there's no need to settle for obvious solutions or accept recent social, educational, or technological limitations. The past, the future, and our expanding knowledge of human beings provide a good set of lenses. Of course, to fully comprehend an uncertain future we may have no choice but to experience it.

SHIFTING HABITS OF THE MIND

What may appear to be trivial in the beginning can end up causing a fundamental shift in human ways of knowing and perceiving. How we create knowledge, how we come to experience products of the mind, and how we communicate is being changed by media technology. This is a very big deal. Use with caution. To paraphrase Jane Austen, *When unquestioned forces go to work on a weak mind they produce every kind of mischief.*

Television has become a major influence on most media in this country. Having been around for half a century (or so) there are some lessons there for the taking. There are many paths to a mistake. On TV the interests of the advertisers usually come before those of the viewer. Information is frequently removed from any realistic social context. In this atmosphere, journalism, politics, and religion are turned into forms of entertainment. Add music, film, and the Internet and you will see American popular culture altering information, communication, and entertainment in cultures around the world.

Understanding how evolving electronic systems affect educational, cultural, perceptual, and social organization means learning how to ask the right conceptual questions. Helping children become critical consumers of electronically-produced information is a major societal responsibility. With all too little thought, imagery-intensive technology is releasing conceptualizing power that is as hard to control as a raging river. For example, the fast pace of a medium like the Internet often leaves little room for personal or social reflection.

What's the difference between technology and a medium? Technology might be thought of as a hardwired creation. A medium is more of a social construct. The same technology can be used in a multitude of ways, depending on the cultural context. The technology of television, for example, can be used as visual wallpaper, a money-making machine, propaganda, trash, or a tool to illuminate learning. Some countries use it one way, some another.

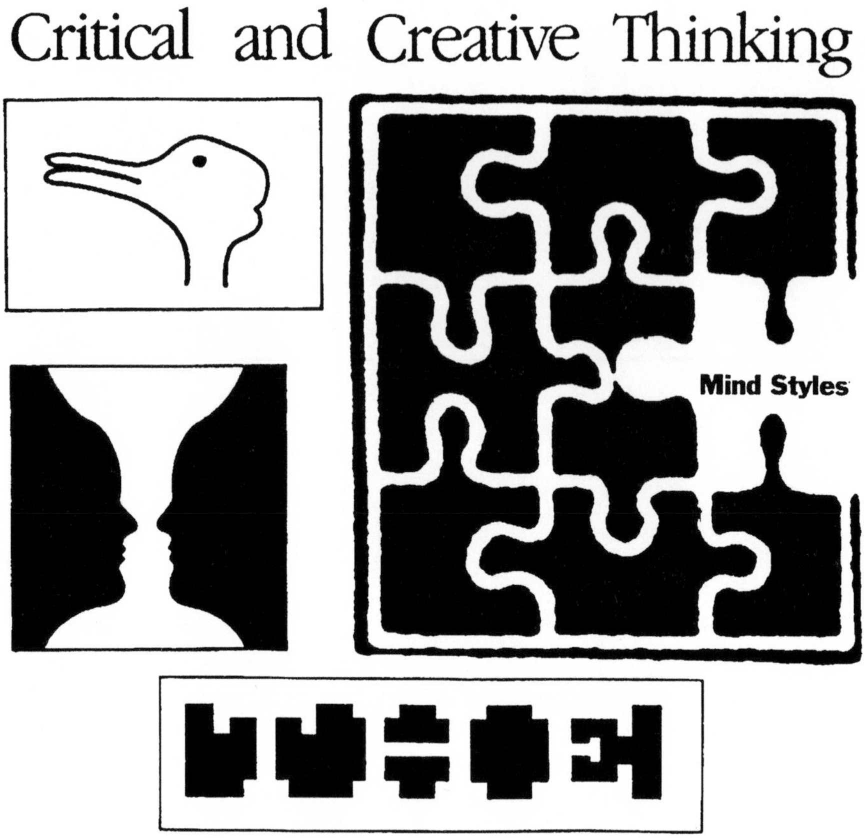

Critical and Creative Thinking

Figure 1.2. Critical and creative thinking.

The full range of electronic media can be anything between an intellectually rich adventure and a manipulative bore. It can rob us of time or empower us with knowledge. Whether it enhances or diminishes life depends on how we shape it.

LESSONS LEARNED FROM COMMERCIAL TELEVISION

Increasing numbers of electronic devices, video applications, and courseware are not neutral. They represent essential characteristics that are already changing the nature of work, recreation, and learning. Television, from its inception, has been a great marketing tool. It sells a synthetic drink as "the real thing" and distorts the classic Beatles song "Revolution" to sell running shoes. Broadcast television has made marketing and its entertainment byproduct the natural format for the representation of experience. Even the local news programs are not presented very seriously—or with much depth "... the world is coming to an end, details at 11." It's not that local or national news programs (unlike advertisements) purposely set out to deceive the viewer. They just do it to get more viewers and make more money.

As network producers point out, there are only 22 minutes to cover the globe. Infusing the news with entertainment values may give some viewers what they want. But what they need for informed decisions is another matter. No wonder the Internet's Matt Drudge says he's a reporter, not a journalist. Define it any way you want, but journalism is becoming something akin to professional wrestling. No pesky editor need apply. A multitude of 24-hour news channels will take anything they can get. Run a rumor on the Internet and everyone seems justified in putting it before the public.

The rash judgments that mainstream electronic journalists make are usually sincere, even though the most shocking events are coupled with music and commercials. We now have an epistemology in which all information is forced to become entertainment to capture and hold the public's attention. The worst values of show business get applied so that the news can capture market share. News stories in quality newspapers have long been viewed as an early draft of history. If electronic "speed journalism" is going to be the first rough draft of history, then today it is badly in need of revision, editing, and good judgment.

The dominant visual format of commercial TV has little tolerance for intelligent argument, guesswork, questioning, or explanation. Substance and logic are often replaced by image, gesture, and the values of merchandising and show business. The very nature of the medium often leaves little to the imagination or intellect—sound cues even tell us which emotion or mood is appropriate.

As society moved from speech to written information, many had a deep suspicion of the rituals surrounding the rarely understood written format. Similar concerns surfaced in the Renaissance movement when movable type technology began to replace the established art of beautiful writing (calligraphy). Each major change resulted in new winners and new losers. Today's electronic media results in similar shifts that go well beyond changes in modes of knowledge acquisition.

In one guise or another, the video screen is becoming a major information and educational delivery system. Today, electronically produced visual imagery is being called upon to play a more fundamental role in thinking, learning, and how we experience products of the mind. The long-running collision among art, commerce, and the public good continues at an intensified pace.

READING IMAGERY

From television to the Internet, visual imagery influences children's view of fact, fiction, and traditional literacy. Film and television entertainment are often viewed as representing social reality in spite of an accumulation of life experiences that suggest the opposite. Children, for example, are able to recognize books as fiction long before they are able to recognize what's real or unreal on TV.

As we create a public that views reading as a distant work-related task, the idea of reading as a natural activity is diminished. We are now a culture where ideas, information, and ways of knowing are more shaped by television than the printed word. One byproduct of this change is that nearly a quarter of American adults, would have trouble comprehending a well-written paragraph. The literacy umbrella may cover a broader range of media, but being illiterate condemns you to the bottom of the economic barrel.

The reading of either print or video imagery involves attention to matters of fact, seeing analogies, drawing inferences, and personally shaping distinctions. The main goal of any medium is involvement. Each builds on its own particular technological base to allow for various forms of synthetic form-making activity in the user's mind. To reach a higher level, the major goal should be to make any medium interesting, involving, and life enhancing.

> *Our way is not a random path...*
> *our way begins from coherent understanding.*
> —Ayi Kwei Armah (West African novelist)

LEARNING FROM THE VOCABULARY OF A MEDIUM

A main purpose of understanding human events or media is to sense alternative human possibilities. Different media have different ways of examining how the world operates. Reading print is particularly good at encouraging the analytic arrangement of information in a sequentially organized manner. It involves conscious effort and requires varying levels of complex skills. Books frequently deal with a topic that appeals to a narrow spectrum of people. In contrast, television has traditionally taken the lowest common denominator approach. But even the common culture of TV is changing as hundreds of narrow-casting channels spring up. Pick your language and specific topic and you might find it on cable or your satellite system.

In contrast to books, TV viewing demands less mental energy or literacy skill for a superficial understanding. It is a much more immediate medium.

For ease of understanding, TV scriptwriters favor short five-to-seven word sentences with limited vocabulary. Shakespeare may have used 25,000 words, but TV scripts try to limit it to about 6,000. Shallow dialogue may help some individuals unfamiliar with the language but hinders more advanced English speakers. Given the universality of American popular culture, it is little wonder that "broken English" has become the lingua franca of the world.

With its truncated vocabulary, and simplistic sentence structure, commercial television shows will—on their own—do little to improve language skills, critical thinking, or mental processing of viewers over the age of ten. The nature of both television and the Internet lends itself to fragmented conversations and escapist entertainment. We know a lot more about television. Watching it does not automatically discourage reading, conversation, and experiential discovery. It does, however, take time away from other activities in which these are embedded. In a late nineties twist of the screw, the Internet started cutting into TV viewing time. Each type of medium has its own agenda and does best with its own kind of content and particular orientation. The advantage to the electronic variety is that it can be an exciting visual introduction to worlds that would otherwise go unseen. Potentially this could provide the highest form of justice to the visible universe.

Children retain certain kinds of material presented by visually-intensive media and tend to comprehend more of what they see than what they read or hear on the radio or on audiotape—and they remember it longer. In addition, children are more attracted to action and sound effects than dialogue. But once that action is viewed, it tends to be remembered. Any medium that provides access to millions of minds has the latent ability to extend literate thought. Unfortunately, because of the commercial nature of American mass media, tapping the possibilities has always been difficult.

Much has been written and discussed about the damaging effects of television for children. But why can't TV serve as an instrument of educational visions? The power for visual learning afforded by this electronic image manipulator should not be underestimated. Television has as much potential of becoming a source of illumination as it has to be a colossal time waster. The fact that a new medium like the Internet is taking on commercial TV values speaks volumes about the influence of television on any promising new medium in America.

Television and its younger associates may promote different mental skills than those developed by reading and writing, but these skills are not always inferior. TV's wide accessibility has the potential for making learning available for groups of children who do not perform well in traditional classroom situations. It can reach children on their home ground—but the most promising place for critical study is in the classroom. Excluding television and other visually-intensive media from the from the schools may actually hurt some learners.

Television has always been an easy target for criticism. But many of the same issues (violence, for example) extend to film, video games, and the Web. Violence in public entertainment is a lethal American issue. It helps shape our character and our lives. Everyone seems to have an opinion about the profusion of violence in the media, but paralysis sets in when it comes to doing much about it. Resolving such dilemmas will require private measures from individuals and large-scale collective efforts. But whatever the programming, critics agree that it has a certain harsh power that is very compelling for large numbers of people.

Figure 1.3. A digitized image including elements from a painting by Ronnie Cutrone.

Media programming can capitalize on the developmental aspects of how children learn and process information. Studies of children's educational TV programs found that visually dramatic techniques can sometimes be very successful in teaching early reading skills. The same may well hold true across electronic media. Visually-intensive media may be more closely matched to the mental processes of beginning readers than print. The video screen can hold a child's attention longer and act as a powerful agent of socialization. Quality educational programming has also proven that it can encourage children to discover their creativity–while giving them the tools to visually restructure subject matter concepts.

With or without information technology, expanded teacher, community, and youth participation is crucial to shaping richer learning possibilities. Learning requires active social involvement and personal mental effort. Transforming TV from a passive to an active medium is essential in tapping its full teaching potential. New educational programs can get children actively involved by sending the child's school (or parents) closely related computer programs and print media. Each medium stands alone–yet relates to the same teaching concept. Innovative educational programming can play to the strength of electronic media and even redefine the boundaries of television, computing, and print.

Don't forget the strong influence of film just because the video screen is where the majority of Americans frequently view movies. But whether it's the theater screen or on the TV set, the dynamics of film are a bit different. The production values are higher, with cameras, lighting, and sound arranged differently. So why is there so much sex and violence these days? It used to be that movie studios made most of their money in the United States. Now they make more overseas. Action pictures are more direct and easier to translate than comedies or dramas. Strong character development, dialogue, and comedy hangs on a thin cultural thread. Literal and descriptive titles often take the place of more subtle metaphors. For example, "Field of Dreams" was viewed in Asia as "Imaginary Dead Baseball Players Live in My Cornfield ". The "Full Monty" becomes "Six Naked Pig Warriers " and "Home Alone III" is sold as "The Little Devil is Master of his Home ". In China "Babe" became "The Happy Dumpling-To-Be Who Talks and Solves Agricultural Problems." [The most common Chinese title for "Babe" was I May be a Pig, But I'm Not Stupid.] "Batman and Robin" was sold under the title: "Come to My Cave and Wear this Rubber Codpiece, Cute Boy."*

---

*Reader beware, some of these titles were reported on the evening news. Some came from Internet sources.

TECHNOLOGY, A MOTIVATOR THAT ALTERS
TIME AND SPACE

America's dissatisfaction with its dominant information medium (television and film) and its dominant educational institution (schools) has become chronic and endemic. Yet faith in education—and technological solutions—continues. We know that education in the future will include technology and begin at an earlier age. And we know that it will continue throughout life. Since it continues throughout life, learning will more often occur outside of traditional settings—in the home, the workplace, and on field trips. Technology will be a partner throughout. We can be sure that human teachers will be needed to provide a variety of learning experiences.

For education to be truly effective, students must be motivated to participate in the world of ideas. Generating intrinsic motivation to learn is all the more important than ever in a period of lifelong learning and technological change. A major goal of education is to motivate students to continue to learn and discover simply out of interest. Other goals include instilling the desire to read, speculate, think differently, and being open to the possibility of being filled with wonder and irony. Technological tools can help by providing a framework to hang ideas on.

Concrete direct experiences in the actual environment are the best teachers. But sometimes the real experience isn't available... or practice is needed first... or the subject is too distant in time and space. A good computer-controlled simulation can really help. Digital media can help students go beyond seeing and hearing to provide opportunities for the actual experience. It is possible to learn about the real world from electronic imagery, computer simulation, and the Internet. Concrete experience does not hold the only key to reality. What's found on the street is not necessarily the best teacher.

In art, science, and many other subjects, the human construction of reality is to some degree an invention. In a good movie, for example, reality is frequently a clever illusion. Concrete experience does not hold the only key to reality. With today's media we have the visual possibilities are right there for the taking. There seems to be at least some truth in the notion that we remember about 10 percent of what we read, 20 percent of what we hear, 40 percent of what we see, and 80 percent of what we hear, see, and do.

There are always unintended side effects to technological and educational progress. The present onslaught of computers and video devices sets forth an unavoidable, if ambiguous, new agenda for teaching, learning, and extending human minds. The technology has the power to motivate students to the point where they do more work on a project simply because it's fun.

Computers, for example, can engage students in enticing projects. But are they learning what's most important? For information technology to assist in the process of revitalizing schooling we must give more attention to instructional programming and creating curriculum-based electronic learning environments. Content and pedagogy do matter. Without intelligent application, even the best electronic media is ineffective.

Chalk on the blackboard is giving way to pixels on a screen. In some school districts field trips now come with digital cameras, laptop computers, and the technological capacity for downloading the material onto school computers for multimedia reports. Multimedia computers with moving video and good graphics certainly spice up a dry subject. But many students get nowhere near the technological possibilities. Access usually depends on a community's wealth and on knowledgeable teachers. In America, excellence rarely connects to equity.

Experience has shown that technologically influenced curriculum works best when the learner is empowered with decision-making authority under the guidance of a knowledgeable adult. Placing instructional innovations in the classroom also requires an appreciation of the individuality and complexity of real youngsters living in a real environment. Clearly, building intellectual autonomy necessitates getting beyond a chalk, talk, and worksheet. And just as clearly, it is adult attention that makes children grow.

NEW MEDIA AND VISUAL LITERACY SKILLS

Discussion over the place of of the "old" and "new" literacies in the curriculum is a vital debate. The struggle is between worthy opponents contending for a larger share of the pedagogical picture. The central question is *what* fraction of instructional time will be spent with *which* communications medium. One thing for sure, visual literacy will be more important than ever.

Visual literacy might be thought of as the ability to comprehend and create visuals in a variety of moving and static media in order to communicate effectively. This involves components of writing, reading, comprehension, visual interpretation, critical evaluation, and production. Images have always been important to learning and its transfer to real world situations. New technology just amplifies the process.

From cave drawings to medieval cathedrals to children's book illustrations, visual imagery has been a major human communication tool. Illustrations, photographs, charts, and graphs increase children's learning of meaningful written and verbal material. Visual thinking and visual rehearsal are effective instructional techniques. Teaching with images can help students focus on lessons, retain information, and improve psychomotor skills. Children who view illustrations may well recall more of a story than students who just listen. Illustrations and their internal representation can improve retention and comprehension. Teachers have long known that visuals help children comprehend unfamiliar vocabulary and add meaning to stories in ways that words alone cannot match.

Effective use of imagery adds interest and enhances student involvement and understanding of the material they are dealing with. Children can also improve comprehension, problem solving, and creativity through internal imaging. The effective utilization of images can help students understand the content of classroom material and remember that information. It is little wonder that the various standards projects attend to visual literacy.

THE FORCE OF POPULAR CULTURE IN AMERICA

As schools become more and more distanced from children's non-school world, television has become the universal curriculum. The sharing of messages through the dominant mass media (television) does not mean that we share the same understandings of the messages. Mass communication is the production and distribution of messages with technological devices. There are some new kids on the block. Still, certain principles hold. Becoming a critical consumer of any medium requires training. Like television, it can entertain us, distract us, *or* settle worthy concepts in our hearts and minds.

Being an intelligent consumer of media implies an understanding of the form and content of media messages. It also implies an understanding of how to place those messages in a context and understanding how the various social, political, commercial forces shape the message. Media literacy involves critical viewing skills and the ability to examine, evaluate, and interpret content. Teachers, parents, and others can take this neglected literacy and develop serious learning activities.

Television, computer programs, and the Internet grow more visually striking and interactive with each passing year. Netcams now let us see who we are dealing with on the Internet. New digital technology allows cameras to view things previously seen only with devices like electron microscopes, or radio telescopes. The digitization of one picture allows the viewer to zoom in or provide three-dimensional imagery of the elements from any angle. Computer graphics can take over from there. Students can "see" what it's like to be in the middle of an atom or looking at the galaxy—where no camera has gone before (or science for that matter). The supremacy of physical proximity is no longer quite as omnipotent. The Internet allows you to reach out to distant places and share.

Whether the imagery is computer generated or produced with a video camera, youngsters can sometimes get closer to understanding with electronic devices as they can with books or through discussion. This is especially true if electronic imagery is coupled with concrete activities. Simulate a dangerous chemical reaction. Then use some real chemicals for something safer. Actual experiments can be viewed at the micro level with new digital cameras, graphically simulated by computer, *and* carried out by students with real chemicals.

DON'T TRAP CHILDREN IN LONELY ARTIFICIAL WORLDS

The Internet has been praised as superior to television and other passive media because it allows users to choose the kind of information they want to receive, and often, to respond to it in chat rooms, E-mail exchanges, or on electronic bulletin boards. The reality is that sometimes we connect and sometimes we don't. It has long been known that television reduces social involvement. The idea that Internet communications can be just as lonely may come as a surprise to many. But virtual relationships can be disembodied and distant when formed in the vacuum of cyberspace. Online study and instructional television may be able to teach certain practical disciplines. However, learning the broader themes of life requires a certain amount of face-to-face interaction with knowledgeable adults and a community of peers.

The problem with much of our current information and communications technology is that it can fill our heads with isolated fragments of facts without providing the social context that would give these facts meaning. This can make life in the world's technological societies a whirl of disconnected general notions and attitudes. Fortunately, there are some positive possibilities. For example, teachers can avoid placing children in solitary confinement by pairing them up on a computer. No one has to be trapped in the sad lonely world out there in cyberspace. Teachers can also take advantage of the computers' proven ability to provide dynamic visual representations of various concepts.

New forms of electronic learning are often more powerful, but they do not necessarily cut children off from reality or from their imaginations. Electronic media does change things. As media technology progresses, the difference between the real (physical) and the unreal will become increasingly blurred. Still, the video screen doesn't have to be escapist. In fact, it has many ways of helping us get closer to hidden realities. The key is putting a human face on our technological marvels.

Figure 1.4. Don't trap students in the artificial worlds.

We would do well to remember that the entire curriculum, no matter how advanced technologically, must be filtered through the mind of the classroom teacher. Machines can never replace well-trained adults. The negative side of this coin is that most comprehensive hi-tech curriculums and advanced classrooms are of little use unless matched by quality teacher preparation. Putting learned thoughts and principles into action requires better teacher and student preparation. When it comes to childhood learning, media technicians, scientists, humanists, teachers, and parents share a common cause in rejecting any medium or technique that cheapen thought. It is equally important for our society to realize that consciously or unconsciously, everyone is involved in the education of children.

An effective medium has the ability to change how we use our senses to process thought and perceive reality. Like traditional reading and writing, it is not a simple matter of decoding symbols, but the construction of meaning. The video image is more vivid than print. And that certainly speaks well to a new generation. In fact, the ease with which the electronic image involves all of our senses is unparalleled in the history of communications. The next step is taking advantage of the latent power waiting to be tapped.

When new electronic means are coupled with effective teaching strategies, speech, writing, print and visual media can all be enhanced. The use of technology isn't about getting away from reading and writing. It's about giving the student a richer, more interactive experience that enhances basic education. Eventually, all successful media become transparent as we lose consciousness of the medium itself and think about what truth it has told us about ourselves and our world. No matter how powerful the technology, learning how to write well, communicate with team members, and speak effectively in public will be part of what we do in school.

By applying their knowledge of effective instruction and using high-tech tools, teachers can help children imagine, create, and reach new thinking and learning plateaus. By using the technological tools of the day and the intellectual tools of their profession teachers can open student minds to subject matter and the potential of promising technology.

> *One should, each day, try to hear a little song, read a good poem,*
> *see a fine picture, and if possible, speak a few reasonable words.*
> —Goethe

EXPLORING THE TECHNOLOGICAL HORIZONS OF EDUCATION

Just as the computer has changed our relationship to television, the Internet is changing both. We are starting to get good enabling programs that allow us to sort through the glut of information. But unlocking the full potential of communications and information technology is out there beyond the technological horizons in education. One thing is for sure: over the next few years a powerful new media synergy will radically change how we think and how we learn.

There is general agreement that information and communication technology can help us reexamine instructional strategies and educational goals. It is just as clear that digital media is becoming increasingly important in education. The various standards projects recognize these developments and point to the need for incorporating electronic media into the core curriculum. Certainly electronic media is becoming a dominating agency of education throughout the world. What isn't clear is exactly how technology will improve instruction and change the day-to-day work of teachers.

Media experiences both inside and outside the classroom can provide access to learning for all students. Our shared media culture can serve as the basis for classroom exploration. The critical factor is always how the technology is used by people. But there is no reason why we can't turn the one-way commercial system of mass media into a two-way process of reflection and discussion. Creative action with one another and with the media itself is key. Still, no matter how interactive and easy to manipulate media images become, it is more important to address the broader issues.

In the twenty-first century individuals must be highly literate, flexible, and capable of finding and solving problems. The days of a highly educated elite and a general population with basic skills are over. Computer-based technology can do most of the repetitive tasks. To remain competitive in a fast changing world societies now have to make sure that the majority of their future citizens are well educated. This will require clear, high standards for all students. And it will require a sustained societal focus on those standards—with clearly recognizable consequences when those standards are not met. Once we have the means and the will, all of our citizens can be educated to their fullest potential. Nothing would be more wonderful for the individual and for the community in which we must all live together.

Technology does not have a magical ability to turn things around overnight. Although it should not be the destination, it can be an effective vehicle for approaching education for understanding. Putting learning first is key to effective use. After you set your goals and standards, it is time to figure out how technology can help you accomplish them. The human component is critical. As new technology expands the perception and learning envelope, asking what's good for children and teachers is always more important than asking what's good for media specialists, techno-enthusiasts, or a high-tech company's profits.

It is best to play to the strengths of a new technology and explore how developments will affect schooling in the years to come. Understanding past literacy efforts helps. For example, we now have a fair understanding of how to teach students about print media, and we have a solid base of knowledge in the area of writing and computation. The challenge now is to learn how newer media can be understood, improve instruction, and help shape a better future.

GREETING THE FUTURE

Past and future technological possibilities provide one set of lenses; our expanding knowledge of human beings another. Research from neuroscience to cognitive psychology is expanding our understanding of how humans learn. As far as technology is concerned, the complexity imposed by software is fading and it is getting easier to use. Before long, you may be able to interact with computers and the Internet much like you interact with people. As the machines use an assortment of tools (like cameras), they will learn to read a frown and other emotions. Eventually they may even take on a some of the characteristics of a good tutor. But no matter how far the technology develops students will always need real teachers for companionship on journeys of discovery and enlightenment.

The old view of teaching as the transmission of content is being expanded to include the management of a vast range of knowledge resources–accessed by a multitude of literacy-intensive technologies. In many respects, teaching is beginning to take on some of the traditional characteristics of the scholar and the researcher–using electronic tools to search vast warehouses of knowledge.

At the very time the teacher's role is becoming more complex, working conditions and poor pay have led to a dangerous shortage of talented people. Subject matter standards help, but schools need a fresh infusion of thoughtful and generous adults who want students to see, think, know, and perform better. Helping young people explore the technologies through which present, past, and future ideas are communicated is a lasting contribution.

As the schools try to greet the future, a new standards-based curriculum is encouraging teachers to help students critically perceive, analyze, interpret, and discover the range of meanings conveyed by print and the electronic media. With a more critical understanding–and new technological links–electronic images can enrich learning. Teachers are beginning to use multisensory approaches that allow the student to see, hear, touch, and apply the concepts taught. This requires a passionate search for meaning and belief with the full range of information and communication possibilities. Whatever the subject, electronic imagery can serve as a helpful collaborator. Just remember, there are as many paths to a mistake as there are to success.

Linking computers with widespread reform is among the most promising ways to use technology. However, technology alone isn't sufficient. New media can contribute to teaching and learning when a curriculum scaffold calculates the potential contribution. Once goals and standards are in place, it is time to figure out how technology-assisted learning can help.

Even if electronic windows are made of refracted glass they can allow students access to images on their own terms. The power to recreate reality through any medium is built on all sources of mental development. Making the best use of a technological tool is a constant juggling act that requires a respect for the inherent values of all modes of communication. There is little question that intelligently opening up broader literary vistas necessitates striking an ecological balance among modes of communication. The electronic juggernaut cannot be avoided. If educators don't attend to the major communications technology of their era then they will be shaped by a vision they do not share.

We must all work to find the mutual fit needed so that the latest technology can work in an educational setting. Everyone is involved in the education of children. Some teach directly, others contribute by creating the environment in which that teaching takes place. Everyone interested in education shares a common cause: exploring the pedagogical possibilities and rejecting any model that cheapens thought or human dignity.

> *The future is always more peculiarly strange*
> *than any of our tidy imaginings.*
> Gregory Rawlings

REFERENCES

America's Children and the Information Superhighway. (1996). Santa Monica, CA: The Children's Partnership, 1996.

Brockman, John. (1996). *Digerati: Encounters with the cyber elite.* San Francisco: HardWired.

Burstein, D., & Kline, D. (1996). *Road warriors.* New York: Plume.

Caine, R.N., & Caine, G. *Education and the edge of possibility.* Alexandria, VA: ASCD, 1997.

Coles, R. (1997). *The moral intelligence of children.* New York: Random House.

DeGaetano, G., & Bander, K. (1996). *Screen smarts.* Boston: Houghton Mifflin.

Dertouzos, M.L. (1997). *What will be: How the new world of information will change our lives.* San Francisco: Harper San Francisco.

Garbarino, J. (1995). *Raising children in a socially toxic environment.* San Francisco: Jossey-Bass.

Gates, B. (1995). *The road ahead.* New York: Penguin.

Goetzee, J.M. (1996). *Giving offense: Essays on censorship.* Chicago: University of Chicago Press.

Gooden, A.R. (1996). *Computers in the classroom.* New York: Jossey-Bass and Apple Press.

Graber, D.A. (1997). *Mass media and american politics.* Washington, D.C.: CQ Press.

Gershenfeld, N. (1998) *When things start to think.* New York: Henry Holt & Company.

Greenawalt, K. (1995). *Fighting words: Individuals, communities, and liberties of speech.* Princeton, NJ: Princeton University Press.

Greenfield, P.M. & Cocking, R.R. (1996). *Interacting with video.* Norwood, NJ: Ablex.

Hamilton, J.T (1998). *Channeling violence: The economic market for violent television programming.* Princeton, NJ: Princeton University Press.

Haughland, S.W., & Wright, J.L. (1997). *Young children and technology.* Allyn & Bacon (A Viacom Company).

Hunt, E. (1995). *Will we be smart enough?* New York: Russell Sage Foundation.

Kafai, Y. (1995). *Minds in play.* Hillsdale, NJ: LEA.

Kagan, J. (1998). *Three pleasant ideas.* Cambridge, MA: Harvard University Press.

Kurzweil, R. (1998). *The age of spiritual machines: When computers exceed human intelligence.* New York: Viking.

Leonard, J. (1997). *Smoke and mirrors: Violence, television, and other american cultures.* New York: Free Press.

Levine, M. (1996). *Viewing violence.* New York: Doubleday.

Minow, N.N. & Craig C.L. (1995). *Abandoned in the wasteland: Children, television, and the first amendment.* New York: Hill and Wang.

Moravec, H. (1998). *Robot: Mere machine to transcendent mind.* New York: Oxford University Press.

Negroponte, N. (1995). *Being digital.* New York: Vintage Books.

Rawlings, G.J.E. (1996). *Moths to the flame.* Cambridge, MA: MIT Press.

Pappert, S. (1996). *The connected family.* Marietta, GA: Longstreet Press.

Perkins, D.N., et al. (1995). *Software goes to school.* New York: Oxford University Press.

Plunkett, J. & Rossetto, L. (Eds.) (1996). *Mind grenades: Manifestos from the future.* San Francisco: HardWired.

Reeves, B., & Nass, C. (1996). *The media equation.* Stanford, CA: Stanford University: CSLI Publications.

Rich, D. (1997). *MegaSkills: Building children's achievement for the information age.* New York: Houghton Mifflin.

Rushkoff, D. (1996). *Playing the future: How kids' culture can teach us to thrive in an age of chaos.* New York: HarperCollins.

Saunders, K.W. (1996). *Violence as obscenity: Limiting the media's first Amendment protection.* Durham, N.C.: Duke University Press.

Seligman, M.E.P. (1997). *The optimistic child.* New York: HarperCollin.

Stoll, C. (1995). *Silican snake oil.* New York: Anchor Books.

Strossen, N. (1996). *Defending pornography.* New York: Doubleday.

Turkle, S. (1995). *Life on the screen: Identity in the age of the internet.* New York: Simon & Schuster.

Walsh, D. (1995). *Selling out america's children: How america puts profits before values— And what parents can do.* Minneapolis: Fairview Press.

Zimring, F.E. & Hawkins, G. (1997). *Crime is not the problem: Lethal violence in america.* New York: Oxford University Press.

Chapter 2

MEDIA PRODUCTION IN A DIGITAL WORLD
Creating Meaning with Video, Film, and Computers

All media as extensions of ourselves serve to provide
new transforming vision and awareness.
—Marshall McLuhan

Media is the physical means though which information may be communicated or aesthetic forms created. Other chapters will deal with newspapers, books, mathematical notation, scientific inquiry, and painting. Here we pay special attention to understanding and constructing visual environments with relatively new technology. The use of such technologies for teaching and learning raises questions about the nature and purposes of literacy in a global, networked environment. Within this context, it is our belief that all students must be media literate so that they can turn the newer languages of wider communication to their own purposes.

Although this chapter focuses on the manipulation of media tools, we fully recognize the importance of both the production and the analysis components of media education. Educators must make sure that the process of learning by doing doesn't cause them to fall into the technical trap of marginalizing analysis. Students need to understand that all media are constructed and manufactured products with a wide range of commercial, social, and political implications. Usually eager to get on with production, they must be encouraged to reflect upon the complex interactions between technology, society, and culture.

The educational use of information and communications technology is spreading faster than any other form of curricular change. There is no longer any question about whether or not these tools will be integrated into the life of the school. The only question is when and how such new energies will be focused on literacy and learning. Clearly, the human dimension is critical. As educators incorporate the latest media into the schools, they must do everything possible to make sure that their use builds upon the bonds between human beings and enhances the human spirit.

CREATING PERSONAL MEANING

From a high-tech viewpoint, media literacy may be thought of as the ability to create personal meaning from the visual and verbal symbols we take in every day from television, advertising, film, and digital media. It is more than inviting students to simply decode information. They must be critical thinkers who can understand and produce in the media culture swirling around them. Being able to identify the capabilities, limitations, and possible combinations of contemporary media is important in approaching the potential of these systems to address personal, lifelong learning, and workplace needs.

From video cameras to editing machines, computer chips seem to be in everything today. Video recordings, like motion pictures and some computer programs, can portray subjects with motion and sound. When this is coupled with pacing and a sense of continuity, the medium is a great way to present information, clarify a complex concept, and tell a powerful story. Visual texts can come in many forms, but all involve a complex dynamic of power and pleasure. Although the emphasis here is on video production techniques, the basic concepts apply across visually-intensive media. For example, video can be mixed with sound and text and put out on the Internet or used in a computer-based multimedia report.

The Internet is proving to be a strange hybrid of print and broadcast media. However, the differences among media are becoming less clear as the Internet is viewed through appliances like WebTV and formats like streaming audio and video. The convergence of media will continue as high-speed methods of Internet access like cable modems become more widespread. The Internet changes the cartography of knowledge by making important discoveries—or nonsense—known all over the world in days. Anyone can play. Editors need not apply. Like all media, the Internet is a unique two-edged sword. It can help create constructive communities—or it can feed sick fantasies. Lonely isolation or vigorous learning ? It's up to us.

You can mix media up in many ways—shoot a video, digitize it, and put it on the Web. It is now possible to transcend physical boundaries by shooting a short video and sharing it online with students around the world. Yes, Netcams and full-motion (online) videos are bit choppy now, but they are improving. Over the last few years, there has been the increasing possibility of merging electronic media. Sometimes we do, and sometimes we don't.

Children can master the video production process and affect attitudes in ways not possible with other media. Some have camcorders at home—combining camera, microphone, and recorder in a single compact unit. It is common for today's schools to have VCRs and similar video equipment. There is no obligation to go digital. Even professional video producers often start and finish with the video medium. Schools often choose to do the same. Teachers and students may keep the medium pure or connect with other media.

Student video producers can take advantage of computers to add sound and motion to digital images. Some schools have digital video camcorders to make full motion video stories. These small, relatively inexpensive cameras can load their digitalized images onto computer hard drives. Editing software and easy-to-use animation programs can breathe life into a wide range of imaginative possibilities. Of course, there are many ways to edit video without computers; even some professionals still do. But digital or analog, the goal remains the same: to help students learn the essentials of media production so that they can control the interpretation of what they see and hear.

Figure 2.1. The Internet: A convergence of media.

Standard videotape is a relatively unstable medium to edit and rapidly degrades with each edit. Digitalized video can be transferred around and copied as many times as you like and the quality remains the same. Off-the-shelf software and a good school computer can create images that rival professional movie makers of the early '90s. To get their ideas "published," students can send their digital video productions out over the Internet. Even if you prefer the analog approach, it is usually fairly easy have the local cable company play a student constructed VHS tape on their public access channel.

Whether we move down one, two, three, or more media paths, the basic principles of video production remain the same. The goal of this chapter is to help readers design video production experiences for children and young adults. The basic idea is by constructing visual communications with the television medium, students can develop an understanding of media conventions by creating with the tools of the trade. The understandings that accompany video production can also help children become intelligent video consumers with analytical skills for assessing the content and influences.

Media literacy extends across the curriculum and across technologies. It is more important than ever. But for technology to make a difference in student achievement then school systems have to make a substantial commitment to helping teachers use it effectively.

VIDEO: YESTERDAY, TODAY, AND TOMORROW

What the epic poem did for ancient cultures–and the novel for modern literate societies – is now done for most Americans by television. As literature and the arts moved away from our common culture, the mass media moved in. Led by TV, the electronic media now permeates almost every facet of our lives. From its mass beginnings in the late 1940s to the mid 1960s television (with the exception of sports events) was produced in an expensive studio. It was a bit like the early days of specialized mainframe computing. Overhead costs went up and stayed up. Wide format cameras used two-inch tape, weighed hundreds of pounds, and took highly trained specialists to make them work. Then, as now, less than 10 percent of network budgets went into the actual production of television programming. Nonbroadcast use of videotape for instructional or personal purposes was rare.

In 1967, Sony changed video production by introducing small-format (1/2-inch) portable equipment. By 1970, 1/2-inch editing equipment was also in use but the quality wasn't quite up to broadcast standards. By the mid '70s, portable 3/4-inch (broadcast quality) VCR cassettes and editing equipment became available. This made possible remote TV news, personal production, and inexpensive training tapes for a narrow audience. It also allowed independent producers and cable companies to bypass large broadcasting structures.

Improvements in portable video recording-camera equipment has resulted in higher quality 1/2-inch cameras (under 5 pounds in weight) and lightweight 8 mm camcorders. The 1/2-inch video cassette system (primarily in the VHS format) has improved to the extent that it has become a standard format for industrial training, education, and classroom use. In entertainment, the 1/2-inch prerecorded video cassette format is bringing back family viewing–much of it displacing the broadcast networks' "prime time." Eight mm has been here for awhile and recording on CDs is now possible. Both formats are coming up to instructional quality and trying to establish an industry standard (avoiding a Beta/VHS type of incompatibility). For a few hundred dollars you can now buy a camcorder with a 3-inch LCD color monitor that makes it easy to take high- or low-angle shots (seeing exactly what you are getting) without going through contortions. In addition, inexpensive camcorders now come with a built-in auto-light that turns on and off as needed. It also gives auto-focus, auto-exposure control, flicker reduction, and digital white balance. A recommended feature is digital image stabilization. This makes everything look more professional because it smooths out unintentional camera movement (the mark of an amateur). These picture stabilizers compensate for hand-held camera shaking without affecting deliberate pans and tilts. Digital hyper-zoom features now let you get extra close and control the speed of the zoom with one finger. Digital wipes and fades add to the quality. We use a compact VHS camcorder (with all of these features) so that students can play it back on common VCRs.

As the technological dust is settling (it will probably never be completely settled), we have a wide range of portable equipment that opens up new (less expensive) production possibilities for classroom use and lifelong learning. Like using computers, video production is being demystified. Specific techniques that were formally the province of studio professionals are being harnessed for a host of instructional and home purposes. Now one will find as many camcorders as computers around the American household.

CONSULTING VISUAL ENVIRONMENTS

Utter acceptance and adulation of technology has always been an American hubris. Such an overweening arrogance, in life as in myth, courts disaster. To understand this will require far more than what we plan here. To get at such broad issues would require a perspective deeply informed by history, philosophy, psychology, and literature. This is best left to others. However, before peering into the construction site of the medium, a few reference points are in order.

In the fifties and sixties, children grew up being socialized and entertained by television. Although TV's impact was hidden from view, it was already quietly shaping public beliefs and policy. By the late seventies, television was being used as an electronic teacher and it was becoming clear that children and young adults needed a greater understanding of how video images shape ideas. Now the technology has advanced to the point where children can actually create–using camcorders to "write" with it. Like writing in any format, students need adult assistance in thinking independently and expressing themselves in what has become our dominant medium.

Television viewing and television production are parallel processes. The omnipresent technology (VCRs and camcorders seem to be everywhere) is allowing a large cross-section of Americans to pick up a video camera and explore the conventions of the medium. This new technology increasingly allows the user to shape what happens on the TV screen. In addition, learning the processes involved in producing video programming seems to help students become more intelligent video consumers at home while helping them visually express their thoughts and experiences at school. Teachers have always taught students how to interpret and use media message systems. Since television messages have become the most common mass communications in today's world, it would seem to be a natural part of the school curriculum.

When students learn to use the technology as an extension of themselves they take a measure control over the medium and their video-intensive environment. As with any human artistic or learning endeavor, there is an inescapable arraignment by experience and background. Creating in today's dominant medium does require some knowledge and skill in basic video production techniques. To do it well requires some understanding of visual composition and enough technical knowledge to properly use sound, music, lighting, editing, and camera angles to make the point.

PUTTING SIMPLE PRODUCTION TECHNIQUES INTO THE HANDS OF STUDENTS

Even younger students can use light video cameras. We suggest either a VHS, 8mm, or one of the new digital camcorders. Most are as easy to use as any "Instamatic" still camera. If the teacher isn't familiar with the equipment, it is helpful to assign four or five interested students with camcorders at home to become familiar enough with them to teach a few basic techniques to a small group. One teacher took a different approach. She gave the two school camcorders to special education students who were in her science/ language arts class. They learned how to use the equipment and then taught the others. In this way they were seen in a positive light by the other students. Whomever you choose to do the explanation, peer teaching and discovery learning are the best approaches regardless of teacher expertise.

Before anything is recorded, have students think, plan, and visualize what they will shoot. Writing an outline helps students figure how long they will spend on each scene. Winging it simply doesn't work. You need a storyboard or some kind of support structure. Groups can put together coherent themes for scenes developed by individuals or partnerships. We have found that a good starting point is to simply ask students to write a short scene about some situation that makes them laugh, cry, or get angry. Encourage thoroughness. Scenes that are well thought through are much easier to film.

Students can figure out how to get what they have written onto a storyboard. A storyboard is a visual sketch of precisely what will take place. It might be thought of as a cartoon-like scene sequence depicting what will be shot. Students can sketch out their productions on paper and place them in a looseleaf notebook for reference. Pages can be revised and decisions made about how to move the concepts (advanced students might do a script) into video and sound. (Remember that it takes time to learn to function as a group.)

Start with a Storyboard

Storyboards are used to illustrate individual frames or sequences in everything from TV commercials to feature films. Alfred Hitchcock, for example, is said to have personally laid out (on a storyboard) every frame of his films and TV productions. Walt Disney often covered a large wall with storyboard frames for an animated films. Steven Speilberg, Francis Ford Coppola, and just about everyone else uses storyboards of one kind or another. On occasion, we use a computer program called *Storyboard.* More often, it is a quick and simple sketch.

Although the focus here is on television, it is clear that this valuable visual tool (storyboarding) can be part of preproduction process in television, film, and computer media.

Figure 2.2. A storyboard is a visual outline for the creation of animation sequences.

We suggest starting with six frames per page to delineate the placement of characters, camera angles, light, sound, and sequence of scenes. Using two pages, it is possible to get the 10 to 15 frame minimum that we prefer. You can use simple stick figures–at least to start with. More thoroughly developed renderings of live-action images can come when needed. Keep in mind the fact that story concept and the narrative flow of the production are more important than artistic drawings. The goal is to inform the production team.

To devise a good storyboard you have to know the answer to the following questions:

- What is the story about and what is the sequence of action?
- Who are the characters and where are they placed in the scene?
- With whom are the characters in conflict?
- What is the problem and what is the solution?
- What is the setting–and what should be in the foreground, middle ground, and background?
- How should the lighting and sound (including music) be arranged?
- What camera angles and color should be in each frame?
- What types of sets, costumes, and makeup are required?

Captions can be placed under the pictures and notes can be made on the sides. It handy to keep sketch book or looseleaf notebook at your side as the production develops. We often meet everyday before the shoot to visualize the day's activities and rearrange a few things on the storyboard.

The storyboard can illustrate a series of shots (frames, images) in a logical, structured rhythm that is reminiscent of action comic strips. Thus the storyboard supports the visual language of video and cinema–providing an initial story structure and visual narrative. *Try it yourself. First watch a commercial on TV and count the number of shots employed. Then storyboard a 15 or 30 second commercial. Do the same for a selected sequence from a current film.*

TEACHING SIMPLE CAMERA TECHNIQUES

To begin with, students can examine quality TV programs, films, photographs, and paintings to understand how visual artists heighten the intensity of an image with light. A tour of a local museum would probably be more useful than a TV studio. Efforts must be made to help students understand some of the philosophy behind frame composition.

Holding the camera steady is one of the most difficult things for beginners. It is important to use a tripod, and learn how to brace the camera to get a steady shot—lean against a tree, fence, on someone's shoulder, anything to prevent the camera from jumping around.

Figuring zones of coverage and how cameras and people should move is another common difficulty for students new to video production. Usually the video camera is moved up or down, right or left, but not both in the same shot. It is important that students realize the camera not be moved without a reason. Learning how to figure zones of coverage and how both cameras and people will move is also important. Although video allows you to go back and forth, you usually move up or down with cameras—and usually you move right or left, but not both in the same shot.

Natural or artificial lighting can be a powerful tool for controlling mood and understanding. As students learn to control how light falls on a subject they shorten the distance between ideas and the video screen. Have students experiment with several light sources to see differences. It's a good idea to show several professional productions and identify lighting sources, changes, and how these techniques convey messages. The ability of light and shadow to shape objects affects the composition of the frame.

Teach students how to pan, tilt, and zoom. A panoramic or "pan" shot is a horizontal move of the camera. A "tilt" shot goes up or down. Students can practice tilting up, pausing, changing camera angle, and tilting down. To "zoom," start with a long shot (to establish where the action is taking place), and then zoom in. More advanced students can try to cover the zoom with movement of the subject or the camera.

There are other production techniques which students need to develop an awareness of and spend time experimenting with. Some of these include learning how to:

1. stop and start action
2. bridge sharp changes between scenes
3. allow visual action to carry the scene
4. use sound as a motivator
5. pace the production (on a video tape, information can usually get through to people at a faster pace than we think).

Conceptually students can be encouraged to:

1. treat one concept at a time
2. introduce their topic immediately
3. break subjects into clearly defined sections
4. plan how to involve the viewer

Assign each student a specific responsibility as part of the crew, hold them responsible for their area, and make sure they get full credit (on the video) for what they do. With all of these techniques it is important that the camera isn't moved without a reason. Remember that the very amateurishness of student productions can be refreshing. Enthusiasm and heart can communicate to people. With just a few of the basics, students' experimentation and common sense will take them further than some mechanical processes. Advanced video producers must also contend with the exhaustion and fatigue that accompanies the frantic pace of more professional producers.

LIGHTING

Using lighting is like a painter using brush strokes. When combined with good composition, good lighting can help the video makers guide the eyes to certain actions and objects.

Lights are nothing more than a source of illumination—it's what you do with them that counts. While a diffuse light can make a subject look dull, too much shadow can add too much mystery. Lighting from below (underlighting) has a sinister effect—back lighting can define depth and distinguish something from the background.

Most video producers tend to overlight—because the cameras of yesteryear needed it. New cameras and camcorders allow you to cut the light intensity. Leaving some dark places can build suspense, add interest, help tell the story, and articulate texture. Reflector boards can pick up natural light and illuminate faces.

"Soft" lighting creates a diffused illumination, whereas "hard" lighting creates clearly defined shadows. Many lighting arrangements fall between these two extremes. A typical set will have a key light facing the main figure, a fill light coming in from one side, and a back light behind the main figure. There are also ways of using transparent colored fillers to change the color of light. In Ivan the Terrible, for example, Einstein suddenly casts a blue light on the actor to suggest the character's terror as he realizes that an assassin is waiting to kill him.

A simple rule of thumb for beginners is: if it looks bad to the naked eye (which is more forgiving) then it is bound to look bad on camera, and throwing almost any kind of light on the subject can help a little. If you can get some kind of natural light—from the window or whatever—it helps a lot. Reflector boards, tinfoil, or a mirror can bounce light around the room—or off the ceiling or wall. Even a white tablecloth can reflect light up into someone's face. Light quality, direction, source, and color can control the look and function of a scene. Each of these can be manipulated on its own or combined to enhance the impact of a video image.

SOUND IN SINGLE CAMERA VIDEO PRODUCTION

Sound without pictures is radio. And pictures without sound are "technical difficulties." Sound can be used to set the mood of a scene, to aid in transitions, and to restore a certain dramatic equilibrium. Most of the time, sound is added in the post production phase. A simple cassette recorder can be plugged into a VCR or video editor to add new sounds.

More advanced video producers don't just use the automatic unidimensional mike in the video camera or camcorder. They usually use a shotgun or lapel (tie pin) microphone. Placing a shotgun mike a foot and a half in front of and above the subject gives excellent sound for on-location work. Varying the sound levels can add drama; "sound bridges" can create transitions when the sound from scene two (for example) starts at the end of the imagery of scene one.

A lapel (tie pin) mike also produces good sound. It is placed on the outside of clothing and worn 12 to 14 inches below the neck. Noise can come from necklaces or silk ties and any metal on metal sound is problematical. Even a hum in the lighting or an air conditioner can sound much louder on a videotape.

If more than one person is involved in speaking, you can have them hand the mike back and forth. Professionals leave multiple mikes going into a sound mixer. This allows them to emphasize the one they want, when they want it. A recording mixer simply takes sound from several audio channels and puts them together on a tape. Some advanced production classes even use dialogue replacement when they do the live audio portion in a loud situation. Some producers find that they can do the sound better after the video is done and they have a quiet room to work in. Many children believe that the actors make up what is said as they go along. They don't. Writing a full video treatment of any fictional or nonfictional subject involves the basic idea, the characterizations, the story structure, the creation of scenes, and assembly of scene elements to tell the story. The specific structure of each scene should be listed in terms of visual and aural details.

To sharpen students' skill in using sound in their own productions we suggest having them review professional videos and practice answering the following questions:

1. What sounds are present—street noise? music? How loud is it? and How does it change?
2. Does the sound come from its visually perceived source?
3. Is the sound happening before, after, or with the story action?
4. Is the sound related rhythmically to the image—like a music video?

5. How do the types of sounds identified function in the video? The interplay of sounds and images can concentrate our attention, set limits,
guide our expectations, and foreshadow what's coming next.

EDITING

Students can learn to approach video production as an artist approaches a
painting. What colors do they end up putting on canvas, and why? Using the
powerful images that they (or others) create can encourage novice producers
to challenge ideas that are taken for granted about how both the technology
and the world works. The key to helping student video producers is encouraging them to trust their own thinking so that they can validate their ideas
and visions.

Editing is the coordination of one shot with the next. It is the key to a
video's form, construction, and effect. Despite reluctance on the part of many
beginners, it is best for local producers to do their own editing rather than
taking it to Photo-Mat or a small production house. Hands-on editing is
essential to ensure the footage has been used to best advantage, proper pictorial continuity has been achieved, and the goals of the project have been
met. The cost of editing equipment for beginners using 8mm camcorders is
not expensive—whether it is rented or purchased. Operating some editing
equipment is no more difficult than loading the camera, setting the exposure,
and counting the frames. Like writing, one gets good at it by doing it—and
doing it again.

Editorial judgment is exercised before shooting by means of advance planning. Conscious, unconscious, or accidental editorial judgment during shooting stamps the camera person's individuality on each scene. Pictorial continuity also has a strong influence on the form and the internal structure of the
finished work. Amateur or professional camera operators must visualize the
footage before (and while) shooting to give the editors everything they need.
Complete footage is absolutely necessary for doing a good job of editing.
This means shooting all important secondary shots, especially cutaways.

The final expression of editorial judgments is in the editing process. All
superfluous footage should be eliminated. Even well-shot photogenic scenes
can have a negative effect if they complicate or throw the tempo off. Placing
cut-ins, cutaways, and other shots in their proper order, matching action,
eliminating bad footage, and adjusting tempo are crucial editing decisions.

It is almost impossible to edit video cassettes like film, by cutting and splicing. Audio cassette tapes can be cut and stuck back together again, but video
is not a series of linear frames. Video images go across the width of the tape

at an angle that makes cutting and splicing very difficult—even if you pull the tape out of its plastic container. Digital video cameras make all of this easier.

Most nonprofessional electronic editing of videotape is still done by hooking up the camera recorder (camcorder) to a VCR. Nearly all camcorders have connection terminals and the necessary cables. By plugging into the "line input" selector on the VCR to the "line" position, you can start transferring scenes from the camcorder (or another VCR) to the VCR. With a little practice, the playback and recording machines can be started and stopped simultaneously at the beginning and end of each tape segment you want.

As editing styles change, so does camera style—so it is important for students to understand both—even if they are only held responsible for one on a particular piece. It is essential to plan how the editing will be done before shooting. Multiple cameras make it easier—if less interesting—to get coverage and do "live" editing. Single camera work facilitates mobility and is usually more interesting. Film production is almost always single camera work whereas TV studios have traditionally used these cameras and steady (even) lighting that allows for quicker work.

Many of the new inexpensive camcorders allow for smooth transfer of scenes to a VCR. Less desirable is simply hooking two VCRs together and transferring the scenes you want. It is better to use an editor—whether it is of the cheap or expensive variety.

Classical Hollywood editing is the most familiar editing style. This is commonly thought of as shot 1, shot 2, shot 3, etc. The classical Hollywood style is the medium shot, long shot, and closeup shot. Close-ups position us where we could never be and slow motion allows us insight into the mechanics of motion. Music can add emotion and drama. Montage editing can be described as a visual language of conflict between images that crash together. Many commercials use this technique originally developed by Sergei Einstein (Potemkin, Battleship, etc.).

Mise-en-scene is an editing technique involving camera movement. Here you move the camera rather than making a cut. This style of editing involves long takes where the actors develop scenes. You can take one director (Woody Allen) and examine how the classical Hollywood style was used in one production (Annie Hall); the Montage style of cut, cut, cut (Sleeper); and Mise en scene (Hannah and Her Sisters). Doing this involves stepping back from the action and looking at it from a technical point of view.

The simplest (amateur) electronic editing of videotape can be done by hooking up the camera recorder (camcorder) to a VCR. Nearly all camcorders have connection terminals and the necessary cables. By plugging into the "line input" selector on the VCR to the "line" position, you can start transferring scenes from the camcorder (or another VCR) to the VCR. With a little practice—and use of the pause function—you can get the tape segments you want on one tape. The transitions can be irritating, but you can get the sequences the way you want them.

If you want to do some home editing you can get simple editing controllers for less than $200. Easy to use video editing tools make for smooth transitions. It is also easy to review and preview your work with these editing controllers, because data can be called up from a computer-type memory. Small format video producers of "industrial" or "educational" tapes prefer the more expensive JVC editing deck for VHS cassettes. Getting "broadcast quality," however, is still beyond the budget of many school districts and small companies.

SMALL FORMAT INSTRUCTIONAL TELEVISION PRODUCTION: AROUND THE WORLD AND IN THE CLASSROOM

Emerging technologies are continuing to change the video production environment. For example, small lightweight equipment can now transmit staff training information from a national teachers' association meeting to school districts thousands of miles away. New camcorders and briefcase size satellite uplinks allow the viewer to watch live events from halfway around the world. For a stiff fee, anyone can now gain access to satellites that supply visual information about everything from forest fires in British Columbia to troop movements in Iraq.

It doesn't take cutting edge equipment to generate a fresh experimental spirit. Professional video producers know that you can have a technological tour-de-force that is welded to a conceptual dessert; just look at some made-for-TV specials. The best way to reach an audience, saturated with glitzy authority figures, may surprise you.

The out-of-focus closeups, grainy shots, and shaky drifting cameras of student beginners drive professionals up a wall. But truth is stranger than fiction. Odd as it may seem, this "home movie" look is sometimes used by film makers and for television commercials. The idea is that ads that are rough-edged shots on home video equipment "sell reality." From the AT&T ads to Sprite-to-Surf (detergent), high school students are producing, directing, and acting in slice-of-life ads for the major networks. There is usually some professional supervision—particularly in the final edit—but amateurs can get a "look" that is so different from super-slick productions that there is stronger reality appeal.

A MODEL FOR "SERIOUS" VIDEO PRODUCTION

Many schools now see advantages in producing their own "quality" video tapes. They tape guest speakers and let people in the community know what is going on. Schools are no longer limited to off-the-shelf materials but can, with reasonable ease, prepare their own customized video materials to fit local needs. Do-it-yourself television can be locally produced by classroom instructors. The classroom teacher's attitude towards the handling of video materials has a major impact on student receptivity. Single video camera field recording systems open up new possibilities and applications—from student documentation of community activities to teacher self-development through recording their own lessons (micro-teaching). A well-designed, classroom-produced video can significantly affect both learning about the medium and the subject matter.

The district instructional media specialist can go beyond single camera field recording informal structures to a more elaborate set of concerns. These range from three-camera closed circuit TV studios to professional editing and special effects. For these semiprofessionals, interaction between instructional design and production is a growing concern. Implementing a marriage of complex media and instructional concerns is not easy.

Instructional media systems need context. A broad-based, interdisciplinary approach can help video imagery become a universal language breathing life into abstract equations and redefining learning possibilities. Many instructional TV products suffer from poor collaboration between production and instructional development. Much is lost in the transition when both work independently—or when instructional designers feel their task is over when production begins. It is most effective when the entire team is involved from beginning to end.

The somewhat advanced production procedures presented here are not just for "experts." Interested teachers and secondary students can follow some of the guidelines. Many media specialists find that they need to staff their video crews with students from the high school video club or students in advanced communications classes. These semiprofessional video design teams usually include a writer, message/visual designer, instructional designer, lighting specialist, sound person, camera person, director, and editor. It is important to remember that these are roles not people. As few as two people can cover them all on a small production. No one's job is complete until the audience is reached.

Production Steps for Media Specialists

1. Project Entry Phase

This phase brings the project manager and the client together to arrive at an understanding of the scope of the project—what they want to do and what they envision the final product will be. The manager is responsible for explaining the potential capabilities of the system to match the client expectations. The client assesses the appropriateness for his/her needs.

2. Analysis Phase

This is an essential step in which the major instructional design team analyzes the learner, the setting, the content, and motivation. The basic rule here is to know your audience. The team develops instructional goals based on the client's objectives and the instructional setting. This includes a job task analysis and means getting your hands dirty with subject matter specialists. The outcome is a written REPORT which can be communicated effectively to the production team and the client with implications for production.

3. Treatment Development Phase

The analysis phase outcomes are next taken to a meeting with the instructional design and production people in an attempt to come up with a treatment acceptable to both. This is a brainstorming creative phase. The intent is to develop a common concept of what the product will be which meets the concerns of both production and instructional design teams. The outcome is a set of very general alternative treatments addressing how this is to be approached. Many images are floating around in this phase of mental processing. The task is to describe what individuals are thinking and lock it into continuity.

4. Treatment Development

The function writer then drafts a written copy of the treatments discussed in the brainstorming session. At the same time, the production team works on the budget to determine the cost of producing individual treatments.

5. Match Between Treatment and Resources

The writer and the production team then meet with the instructional design team to find the best match between treatment and resources. If a match is not found, it is necessary to go back and start again until a match can be found. The outcome expected is a common image clarification of the project.

6. Script Development and Video Design

When all parties have arrived at a common vision, the script and content of the audio portion can be written. It is a good idea to get approval of the audio content before turning it over to the video design team.

The visual designer and message designer then work together to come up with a storyboard.

7. Early Formative Evaluation

In this very early evaluation stage, the first script, storyboard, and audio are presented to the whole group, including the client and content specialists. Depending on the production, it is often beneficial to get peer, student, or administrative evaluation of this initial stage. Often the plan is tested with students and experts in content design. It is important to have an inexpensive medium to test the audio, visual, and pacing of the project.

8. Recycle or Proceed to Prototype Development

It may be necessary to do extensive revision after the early formative evaluation. If the production meets with approval, it is finally time to begin the actual shooting and recording.

9. Major Formative Evaluation of Prototype

The revised visual product is ready to try with a sample audience.

10. Approved Audio and Video

At this stage, the polished audio is added and the finished images are captured on the medium. A set of common visual images and shared goals make management more effective and efficient.

The Instructional Design Process

1. Initial Meeting

In the initial contact between the "client" and video project coordinator, it is important to determine the real need of the client and provide the client with an overview of the process. The client is often overwhelmed, bewildered, or anxious. To meet the expectations for both parties it is helpful to formalize situations on paper. Needs assessment is on-going–listening, note taking, assessing. A task analysis does not need to be presented in a formal way with the client at first. It often is confusing and overwhelming.

2. Clarification of Content

Once the problem is identified it is helpful to get a 1 to 3 page content outline from the client or content specialist. This gives the manager a better grasp of what the overall content is, helps the client clarify the idea, and provides background information for goals and objectives of the project. Meeting formally at least once a week, even for a few minutes, keeps the project on track and keeps both sides up on their homework.

3. Goals and Objectives

Goals and objectives provide a rationale and purpose. These provide a reference throughout the project and are helpful to refer back to when writing storyboard and script. Goals and objectives should be specific and written in behavioral terms. Encourage the client to come up with his or her own list of goals and objectives before interacting together. Emphasize trying to think visually.

4. Media Selection

The environment, utilization, content, audience, and equipment resources are all determinants in the selection of media. It makes little sense to produce a good videotape if there is no good playback unit, for example.

5. Select Planning Team

Once medium is selected, put together production and instructional design teams to work on the production process–including the storyboard and script.

Production: The Planning Phase: Documentation, Accountability and Tracing the Process

Before any shooting, it is important to plan, visualize, and develop a written framework based on a thorough knowledge of the intended audience. An organized approach to even very simple video productions includes a clearly stated problem, or objective. Problem posing and formulation have been shown to be crucial links to problem solving and solution. It requires an analysis of the situation or message to be presented, including resources and goals.

Use of a log, flowchart, storyboard, or a computer program like *Storyboard* (or *Filevision*) can provide a visual reference as well as a written commitment to time and resource allocations. This kind of visual planner is important at the outset. Without it, intelligent decisions, scheduling facilities, handing out assignments, and time management are all made more difficult.

Writing an outline or overall framework for video production project helps determine how much time will be spent on each part of the production, including the actual filming. Scenes that are well thought through are much easier to film. It is helpful to use a storyboard as a visual sketch of what will take place. Pages can be revised and decisions made about how to move what was in the script into video and sound.

Small Format Video Gives Us a Lifelong Learning System

The 21st century is full of challenges whose resolution depends largely upon the unrelenting quality and quantity of lifelong learning. Fifty years ago, just about anybody could take the professional knowledge they learned in school (or skill knowledge they learned on the job) and with apply it throughout their professional careers. Now workers have to be constantly updated. "Narrowcasting" is made possible by cable and prerecorded video cassettes. Both, by their nature, can be so specialized in focus that you can have 24 hours a day of weather on the Weather Channel or hour after hour of exercise with fitness instructors. With teaching, in many parts of the country, becoming a "graying" profession–and many teachers having to teach an hour or more a day of physical education and health, videotapes can be a godsend. Ubiquitous VCRs, camcorders, and digital possibilities make it possible to zero in on even narrower training targets.

Tapping a mix of electronic learning resources is important for citizenship and improving human capital. A nation's advancement–or decline–is increasingly determined by the quality and number of educated people. Companies are finding they must get involved with literacy training.

Economic projections indicate that in the next ten years, twice as many jobs will require postsecondary education (some of it at the community college level). TV is an excellent medium for reaching diverse populations–some of whom have limited English language skills. Video is also effective in reaching geographically diverse groups of postgraduates with individually tailored lessons.

Changes in television technology are changing the way TV is produced and distributed. The process and products of video technology can now rely on equipment that is relatively inexpensive and easier to operate. Now is the time to make sure that money goes directly to what appears on the screen. Whether it is industrial, educational, personal, or professional network broadcasting, small-format portable equipment can change the nature of television. To communicate to a target audience requires an understanding of visual esthetics, message design, video technology, and the characteristics of effective instruction. It doesn't require hordes of middlemen or a bureaucratic structure. The electronic instruments can be refined by a wider range of professionals–or even amateurs. There is no substitute for thorough planning and continued follow-up. The nature and needs of the audience should shape the programming all through the process.

Smaller companies and public agencies are finding that they can keep their workers up to date with effective, small-format video productions. In the search for deeper and more coherent learning systems, smaller shops may even have an advantage in tailoring instructional material for a very specific clientele that they know intimately. By avoiding a bureaucratic structure with huge overhead costs, low cost instructional TV production can help cut the disparity between large/small companies, rich/poor citizens, and urban/rural areas.

FUTURE DO-IT-YOURSELF VIDEO PRODUCTIONS

As world culture becomes saturated by video imagery, visual literacy has been added to the list of new literacies. The rapid diffusion of VCRs, camcorders, and related home "entertainment" technologies means that children may already be familiar with the specifics of how to use the technology. But it is the rare student who systematically approaches the subject with some degree of depth. Yet it is how the mental processing is activated that determines the quality of video message, production, and reception.

As computers add video processing to their list of functions, the use of interactive electronic visualization tools will expand into new domains for learning and knowledge creation. Every era of instructional technology has its own combinations of interesting ideas, issues, and possibilities. When other new media were introduced—whether writing, books, or whatever—the combinations were rearranged. And within a short time, users became participants in the construction.

Children seem more comfortable than adults in adopting new uses of video. As television production technology evolves, we have cheaper and easier to operate equipment. This gives students the freedom and opportunity to create aesthetically pleasing visuals. Learning the conventions of electronic imagery can help students look for creative meaning while becoming more intelligent video consumers.

Neither children nor adults can afford to view the world through a myopic prism. Video can be used to help children and young adults come to terms with themselves, current communications media, and the world.

> *Actually, of course, our specific vivid experiences make up the foundation upon which our usable concepts are constructed. They provide us with the rich material from which we shape our relationship between experience and idea will therefore strike an appropriate balance in the classroom between the tangible and the intangible—between what we observe through our senses and what we understand through our ideas.*
> —Edgar Dale

MUSIC VIDEOS AND STUDENT PRODUCTIONS

Critical viewing and production can help students engage in a dialogue out of which they can construct their own definitions and priorities. Students can intelligently construct their own creations of visual music. The first step to learning is successful imitation of the best to be found in a medium. After watching music video, students can explore some of the structures and procedures. They can then produce their own videos based on poetry written by students and backed by their own favorite songs.

Music videos work well as a starting point with students, because they gain and maintain attention, use imaginative visuals, and choreography, and employ exciting music. The techniques used in music video involve storylines and themes, film/video conventions (rack focus, trucking shots), symbolism, humor/fun, jump cuts, and computer animation. By designing student music videos, students can gain skills in visualizing, creating storyboards, and writing a treatment. Producing student music videos involves camera work/VCR operation, recording music and sound effects, audio transfer, lighting and editing.

In watching music videos done on the regular networks, students can also ask basic social questions. Some examples of questions that can be explored include: What is the range of positions and social identities offered to the adolescent viewer by MTV? What is gained or lost if you accept TV viewing conventions or the values of MTV?

Using music video can help students work together to collectively accept, reject, and critically sort out how television offers students a place to stand in relation to other individuals or groups. Music videos can be used to teach specific production skills such as editing, storylines, computer graphics, lighting, visual imagery, symbolism, camera angles, and photographic styles. Intensive scrutinizing of the production values of these musical advertisements (CD's) can also help students identify the function of sound in other video productions.

Ideas for Student Video Production

1. Create Original Music Videos

Have students create their own music videos based on a favorite song or recording.

2. Design a Poetry Video

Assign students to write, record, and shoot a poetry video based on their own original writing.

3. View and Produce Scenes from Different Perspectives

To understand how music adds texture to a film or video story, view a scene–like the airplane segment from *Out of Africa*–with the sound off. Then view it a second time with the sound on. Using camcorders, encourage students to use closeup shots, panning, tilting, and zooming techniques. Then have them add music to the track.

4. Create a Short Video Segment

Have students design a video segment from a movie video. Students build their own story or TV ad from selected video segments and add their own soundtrack taking selected parts from the dialogue.

RECORDER
Writes down how the group members figure out a problem and then reports the answer

ANIMATOR
Takes an extra special level of responsibility for keeping the work interesting, lively and on task

CHECKER
Checks to make sure that all group members understand the problem

READER
Reads the problem to the group

Figure 2.3. Assigning roles for group work.

5. *Jigsaw Editing*

Give students 10 or 12 short segments of video and have them arrange each clip under the following headings:

Setting:
Characters:
Motivation:
Time:
Plot:
Cause and Effect:

Based on their classifications, have them design a coherent film.

6. *Practice Video Techniques*

Create a TV advertisement using video techniques such as flashbacks, cuts, and dissolves. Have students demonstrate how these techniques convey messages to consumers.

7. *Photography Guessing Game*

Encourage students to take part in the adventure of acquiring and viewing just about anything in the environment. Start by encouraging students to view objects from a different perspective. Zoom in on an object, hold, tape, and have students guess what it is from the closeup. Then have students shoot their own closeups for discussion.

8. *Shooting a Single Scene*

Using a single scene, see how many different ways you can view that scene. Discuss the effects of camera angle, panning, and zooming techniques.

9. *Using a Video Camera for Storytelling*

After critically viewing popular programming, such as music videos, students can construct their own set of electronic images to go with the music. Indeed, the very act of using a video camera for storytelling can become a personal tool, seeing through the electronic void–helping to open doors to visual and technological literacy.

10. Video Time Line

Videotape a short but telling scene from a common theme in the life of the group. Have the students imagine where their life fits on the continuum. Describe visually the major elements of the past and what will happen in the future. Use a computer graphics program to print out a long time line.

11. Two-Minute "Bites"

Have students work together as a crew with one responsible for sound, one for lighting, one for camera work, and one for direction. Tape a community event. Boil it down to a two-minute "bite." Discuss how the evening news boils-down information to do to a story.

12. Disseminating Your Production

If several student groups are doing a similar short project, hook up two VCRs and record one tape with all the material on it. Take that tape to the cable company and have them show it on the public access channel. (All cable companies are required to provide free public access—and most of them are more than willing to play a VHS video cassette.) As with writing in the language arts, it is important that students share their work with a real audience—sometimes it is the class and other times it may be the whole community. With digital cameras, it is even possible to put things out over the Internet.

The practical video production suggestions in this chapter are designed for different skill and experience levels. Whether it is elementary school children with camcorders—or adult educators with Super VHS video cameras—we have tried to reflect the possibilities for the nonbroadcast use of video. In analyzing a student video, it is helpful to compare the beginning with the ending. How does the ending bring closure on the narrative, unity of plot, and specific devices of motivation? When two shots are joined, we can ask: Are the shots graphically continuous and what rhythmic relations have been created?

By doing their own video productions, students can go a long way toward answering the question of how TV programs are made. Students will discover, among other things, that television programming is made by people working with technology. They will also find that a video segment or program is not just a collection of elements but a series of aesthetic judgments that are made to suggest a system of relationships between the parts. Whether or not the video is in a narrative form, it usually tries to tell a story in a manner that captures interest.

Students learn that if they fill their work with strong visual images (at their energizing best) their video productions can draw private energy from the viewer. At an advanced stage, they can even go beyond dealing with rational subject matter to creating radical systems for their videos. The result might suggest not only new things to think about but new ways to think about them.

CROSS MEDIA STRATEGIES: COMPARING VIDEO TO PRINT

> *Our brethren in television are light-years behind (print). They are dealing in a still vastly more complicated medium and they're dealing in time frames that I don't think they've even begun to master. They have turned loose an incredible number of people...to stand around on lawns and mountaintops with microphones thrust in front of them, with no responsible editors between them and what they're uttering into the microphones. ...They're still struggling to assert themselves as a serious information medium, and the literacy level, the expertise level, even the sense of what is news in relation to the camera, all this is still very raw...*
>
> – Frankel

Television's Attributes

• *Attention demand*–the continuous movement of the screen evokes first an "orienting response" and then, as movements become rapid and music louder, a general activation of the nervous system.

• *Brevity of sequences* –this property refers to the brief interactions among people, brief portrayals of events, and brief commercials (from 15 to 60 seconds long).

• *Interference effects* –the rapid succession of materials that possibly interfere with the child's rehearsal and assimilation of new material.

• *Complexity of presentation* –the presentation of material to several senses at once–sight, sound, and printed words, especially in the commercial.

• *Visual orientation*–television is by its very nature concrete, oriented toward visual imagery, minimizing detailed attention to other sources of input information.

• *Emotional range*–the vividness of the action presented is greater than other media.

Activities to Connect Video to Print Material

1. Compare Television-Based Books with the Print Version

Look in advance for a TV special or movie that is of good quality—and appropriate for the age group. The teacher can read excerpts from the book or the class can read it as homework. Discuss how TV treated certain characters—as compared with the book. How did the two media differ in ways characters were added or left out? How were certain characteristics changed? How was the plot, setting, ethics, or language changed?

2. Compare Newspapers and TV News

Compare a front page news story in the daily a.m. newspapers with a two minute videotaped excerpt from the evening news. *The New York Times* and *The Washington Post* are prime examples of story sources. Make a point of discussing how TV uses condensed quick headlines and special effects (sometimes computer graphics) to increase their "market share" (ratings).

Creating the On-Screen Image

Many of the visual ideas that work with video also work with digital media. To achieve a powerful visual impact, you need a clear vision about the way each sequence should be viewed. Like a real movie director, students who wish to create in the medium need to decide on the lighting, sound, and editing patterns to make their work come alive. Television, film, and multimedia computer programs are often more effective than stage plays (or print) in directly involving the the viewer with the actions and the emotions being expressed. Visually-intensive media can connect the viewer directly with the action on the screen.

Rhythm and pacing are important. We view rhythm as the visual gradation—the series of steps that form successive stages. Pacing is usually taken to be human interaction or emotional gradation. A work's overall rhythm is decided by changing the intensity patterns of scenes. Intensity levels do not have to flow from low to medium to high. Action could, for example, go from low to high and back to low again.

Viewpoint is the position you want the viewer to take in relation to what is going on. This might include everything from stepping into a character's shoes (subjective viewpoint) to putting the viewer into a godlike (omnipotent viewpoint) position.

Every scene must move the story forward. Need, conflict, and suspense are part of this movement. Keep in mind the fact that questions are usually raised or answered at the conclusion of most scenes.

Framing usually refers to the balance and symmetry. The subject of a frame should rarely be placed directly in the middle of a frame. Take the time to study lighting and pictorial elements in painting and good illustrations. When using a close up have the subject positioned in varying degrees to the right or to the left. Sometimes its just a little off center. Sometimes the key subject just occupies a third of either side.

Lighting can be both expressive and functional. Every image needs lighting to convey meaning. Good lighting can clarify the setting and project a certain atmosphere. When combined with color, it plays a vital part in the relation building the image that appears on the screen. Striking a balance between light and dark provides the illusion of a three-dimensional space. A hard or soft keylight can be set up in front, over, or even under a subject. A backlight is used to separate a character from the background. So-called fill lights can be used to soften a scene or in long shots, to pick up background details. When shooting outdoors, remember that light changes as the day progresses. So be ready for rapidly changing light conditions. Shoot all the long shots as quickly as possible. Rain usually means trying again later.

The best dialogue usually consists of short exchanges. Remember, sometimes thought or physical action can reveal the character or situation more clearly than the spoken word. Ambient sound, sound effects, and music can give the audience some of the information necessary for comprehension. Music can, for example, advance action in a scene, link dialogue, and explain what is happening. Sound can also express emotion, mood, and draw attention to detail in a way that influences viewer response.

Editing is just as important in film or video as it is in print. Whatever the medium, editing is the foundation that everything rests on. The editing process can change the viewpoint and meaning. It also influences the rhythm, mood, and visual presentation. The smooth and logical sequence of your production is most important. If it is well done, it is not noticeable. Let the viewer participate, but never call attention to the editing or any other technique you employ. The idea is to amplify the narrative in a way that enables the viewer to relate what is happening on the screen to events, dialogue, or situations previously viewed.

Video recording and film share a close relationship; they both can portray a subject in motion, with sound. New digital media often builds on the same basic principles. As new media forms emerge and overlap, intelligent consumption and creative production can go hand-in-hand. Working to understand a medium leads to questions about how to produce your own material and asking what tools will allow you to do it. Poems, paintings, and some musical compositions are an expression of an individual mind. Video productions and their visual associates are usually collaborative. One person may be held responsible for the overall effect, but it takes a team effort to tell a story and make things come alive.

MASS MEDIA AND THE MODERN CLASSROOM

There is general agreement that media culture is an important part of student life today. It is also clear that electronic media can be a vehicle for classroom learning. New subject matter standards recognize the deep and varied connections between students' learning experience and the mass media. Active, participatory learning and student control are central to making good use of the technology. Creating media messages provides opportunities for hands-on problem solving. It also encourages a deeper understanding of the medium being created. The basic idea is to use the skills of critical analysis, reasoning, and communication in a world where media and technology play a major role. Media comprehension and production can inform a broad range of literacies. Are classroom teachers well equipped to guide their students to think critically about the information presented to them by the media ? Do teachers have the technological resources and skills to teach the basics of media production ?

A recent survey by the U.S. Department of Education suggests that only one-fifth of the teachers across the country feel that they are well qualified to teach in a modern classroom (*New York Times*). It is clear that we need to upgrade standards for prospective teachers, enhance the skills of inservice teachers, and change how we recruit, prepare, retain, and reward America's teachers. Contradictions? At a time when there is general agreement about higher standards for teachers, the states are actually lowering standards just to get warm bodies into the classroom.

For better schools and better teachers, America needs a change in public thinking about the value of teaching. And we need to do something about the number of good teachers leaving the profession because of low pay, poor working conditions, weak school leadership, and the lack of professional development. The whole package is important, but rich professional development opportunities are key to improving and updating what's happening in our schools. Even new subject matter standards and great technological tools don't mean much if teachers don't understand how to make use of them.

Teachers well versed in teaching reading and writing can apply many of the same principles to electronic media. If you're not sure that schools should attend to electronic media, consider how much influence each medium exerts in students' day-to-day lives. From television to the Internet viewers are exposed to the banal, the extreme, the violent, the useful, and the pastoral, all within seconds. It is a mix of the throw away and the indispensable. Learning to sort it out is crucial. By the time a student finishes high school, she will have spent an average of 11,000 hours in school but over 15,000 hours watching television and an average of 7,000 hours on the Internet. Fortunately, as time on the Internet goes up, television viewing often goes down.

In addition to TV, the average American student has seen hundreds of feature films, many thousands of commercials, and logged countless hours working or playing with computers. It is little wonder that visually intensive media has shaped their perceptions of the world and of themselves. But possibilities are opening things up.

In the last few years, children's television has grown to include a spectrum of possibilities almost as wide as adult television. From *Nickelodeon* to *Sports Illustrated for Kids*, children are spending less time watching adult programming and more time watching their own shows. Some of the changes are the result of a federal rule requiring three hours a week of educational programming. Some changes reflect the marketplace. For example, there are programs for very young children that are linked to toys and other products. Even PBS, which is still the leader in educational programming, is selling merchandise based on characters in its shows. Everything may be more commercial, but at least it is more diverse *and* more benign. They may be reaching for camcorder sales, but some programs even let children look behind the scenes and explore the production process.

ENRICHING TEACHING AND LEARNING IN AN INFORMATION AGE

Although teachers have long had a love-hate relationship with mass media, they are increasingly integrating video and media production techniques into the context of their classrooms. Many states now expect students to be able to access, analyze, evaluate, create, and communicate with electronic media. National subject matter standards also support teaching students how to create media messages using today's technology. New technology standards for different grade levels point to the importance of studying film, video, television news, and advertising. These skills are viewed as essential for learning and constructing meaning in a media-saturated society (Carnegie Council on Adolescent Development).

Figure 2.4. Mass media and the modern classroom.

The nature of mass media can provide a powerful entry point to meaningful experiences in the classroom for all students. Being able to create in a given visual medium is becoming almost as important as being able to write in a print culture. The primary goal is not just self-expression or vocational readiness. Hands-on production can lead to informed analysis and give students a degree of creative power as they approach the dominant media of our time. "Reading" and "writing" with electronic media is becoming as important to literacy in today's world as traditional reading and writing.

Technological misconceptions and misunderstandings must be dealt with if deeper understanding is to emerge. Negative possibilities abound. Artificial intelligence and virtual reality are just two examples of computer-controlled technologies that could cast a shadow or illuminate education in the future. Choice and control are key to the intelligent use of any media. Although it is far from certain, our new technology could powerfully amplify learning about the nature of truth, beauty, and morality.

Teaching and learning are taking on new meaning in a digital world. Computers and their associates may well become the next great medium for storytelling. The interactive cinematic narrative made possible by new media give us multiple possibilities for a new genre of literature. Multimedia computers and online communication also have an immense capacity for helping us dynamically explore the physical, biological, social, and cultural world. No medium provides ultimate answers. But at its best electronic media enhances understanding and opens the mind's eye to a sense of mystery and wonder.

REFERENCES

Bazalgette, C., & Buckingham, D. (eds.) (1995). *In front of the children: Screen education and young audiences.* London: British Film Institute.

Bertelsmann Foundation. (Ed.) (1995). *School improvement through media in education.* Gutersloh, Germany: Bertelsmann Foundation Publishers.

Birkerts, S. (1994). *The gutenberg elegies: The fate of reading in an electronic age.* New York: Fawcett Columbine.

Brook, J., & Boal, I. (Eds.) (1995). *Resisting the virtual life: The culture and politics of information.* San Francisco: City Lights Books.

Buckingham, D., (1994). *Children talking television: The making of television literacy.* Basingstoke, Hampshire: Falmer Press.

Buckingham, D., & Sefton-Green, J. (1996). *Cultural studies goes to school: Reading and teaching popular media.* Basingstoke, Hampshire: Taylor & Francis.

Carnegie Council on Adolescent Development. (1996). *Great transitions: Preparing adolescents for a new century.* New York: Carnegie Corporation of New York.

Coley, R.J., Cradler, J., & Engel, P.K. (1997, May). *Computers and classrooms: The status of technology in U.S. schools.* Princeton, NJ: Educational Testing Service, Policy Information Center.

Cradler, J. (1995). *Summary of current research and evaluation findings on technology in education.* San Francisco: WestEd.

Davies, J. (1996). *Educating students in a media-saturated culture.* Lancaster, PA: Technomic.

Duncan, B., D'Ippolito, J., Mcpherson, C., & Wilson, C. (1996). *Mass media and popular culture (version 2).* Toronto, Canada: Harcourt Brace.

Gee, J.P. (1996). *Social linguistics and literacies: Ideology in discourses.* Cambridge, MA: Harvard University Press.

Godwin, M. (1998). *Defending free speech in the digital age.* New York: Times Books/ Random House.

Greenfield, P.M., & Cocking, R. R. (1996). *Interacting with video.* Norwood: Ablex.

Hoffman, D.D. (1999). *Visual intelligence: How we create what we see.* New York: W. W. Norton.

Lynch, A. (1996). *Thought contagion.* New York: Basic Books.

Meyrowitz, J. (1985). *No sense of place: The impact of electronic media on social behavior.* New York: Oxford University Press.

Murry, B. (1997). *Is the Internet feeding junk to students?* APA Monitor (American Psychological Association) p. 50.

Natale, J. A. Making smart cool. *Executive Edycator, 17,*10: 20-24.

Negroponte, N. (1995). *Being digital.* New York: Random House.

Rawlings, G.J.E. (1996). *Moths to the flame.* Cambridge, MA: MIT Press.

Silverblatt, A. (1995). *Media literacy: Keys to interpreting media messages.* Westport, CT: Praeger.

Sornson, R., & J. Scott. (1997). *Teaching and joy.* Alexandria, VA: Association for Supervision and Curriculum Development.

Tufte, E.R. (1997). *Visual Explanations.* Cheshire, CT: Graphics Press.

Turkle, S. (1995). *Life on the screen: Identity in the age of the Internet.* New York: Simon & Schuster.

Tyner, K. (1998). *Literacy in a digital world.* Mahwah, NJ: Erlbaum.

Wallach, L., Dorfman, L., Jernigan, D., & Themba, M. (1993). *Media advocacy and public health: Power for prevention.* Newbury Park, CA: Sage.

Wexelblat, A. (Ed.) (1995). *Virtual reality: Applications and explorations.* New York: Academic Press.

Zettl, H. (1990). *Sight, sound, motion: Applied media aesthetics* (2nd ed.). Belmont, CA: Wadsworth.

Chapter 3

COMMUNICATING IN THE FUTURE
THE LANGUAGE ARTS AND
LITERACY BUILDING TECHNOLOGIES

The future is not a result of choices among alternative paths
offered by the present, but a place that is created—created
first in the mind and will, created next in activity.
    – John Schaar

The future is not just some place we are going to, it is an environment that we are creating. The paths to it are made, not found. The experience of arranging the future changes both the maker and the destination.

As the new language arts standards make clear, we live in a historical moment when the media on which the word relies is changing its nature to an extent not seen since the invention of movable type. At its best, learning the language arts has been—and will continue to be—an active constructive process that focuses on the discovery of meaning. Another constant: children need rich social experiences with whatever medium they are using.

Reading and writing are rooted in oral language. Children learn how to construct meaning when they talk to adults at home and to peers at school. Exploring environmental print (signs, logos, etc.) and experiencing new language forms helps children form an oral language base that supports their literacy development. Reading and writing are just the tip of today's language arts iceberg. Speaking, listening, thinking, and communications technology are important parts of the equation.

Literacy growth begins before children enter school and continues as they experiment with literacy activities. Schools build on the child's experiential background as they teach children how to apply a wide range of decoding strategies to comprehend, interpret, and appreciate print and nonprint texts. Personal experiences and electronic resources are often incorporated into the design of today's language and literacy lessons.

All students must have the opportunity to develop the communication skills they need to participate fully as informed and productive members of our democratic society. When children have a language rich home and school environment they more capable of meeting high standards. While content standards are emphasized here, we recognize the fact that education should be more about the development of self than worrying about outcomes. Quality teaching, good assessment, and equity in resources are key to preparing students for the future.

SUBJECT MATTER STANDARDS

Content standards can help teachers by articulating professionally defensible ideas about how a field might be framed for purposes of instruction. The English Language Arts Standards Project is one of several efforts to suggest goals for various school subjects. The language arts standards grew out of current research and theory about how students learn language. Teachers played a major role in their development.

The literacy umbrella has been extended. Today literacy includes visual literacy, computer literacy, networking literacy, and media literacy. Things are changing fast at the classroom level. Many teachers now help their students go beyond more traditional literacy skills to create with video "pencils" and computers. They often share the results on the Internet. New standards, changing definitions and new technological implications have not changed the goal of the language arts curriculum. Achieving literacy for all children remains the destination.

The power of the literacy experience still guides educators, who believe that it's important for students to experience the world through stories found in fiction and nonfiction, poetry and plays. It is important as it has ever been to involve children in literacy activities through a literature-based language arts. The difference is that these days, literature, communication, and thought are bound together with meaningful interaction and electronic media. We are getting to the point where children can become active virtual characters in a computer-based children's story. No matter how interactive it gets, electronic tales won't replace print. But interactive cyberstories will become an increasingly interesting literary genre.

Each generation of technological advances adds to the possibilities and makes the interplay between different media more complicated. Verbal storytelling has not been pushed aside by the written or the printed word. All are part of today's literacy equation, including the thinking that must be done to use and interpret how each medium uses symbols to represent knowledge.

At the moment, the prime example of electronic media is television. It has been around for over fifty years and may well be the most important communications machine of the twentieth century. It has cut into everything from reading to regional differences. But it never replaced the need for reading and writing. It just soaked up a lot of time and added another medium that needed to be understood. Electronic media is changing again. TV networks are down and hundreds of specialty channels are up. In the last few years the explosive growth of computers and the Internet shows how quickly the rug can be pulled out from under any medium. Using the Internet, for example, cuts into time for television viewing.

Print, video, and digital networking increasingly overlap as they open new and transformative environments for language and literacy. Who knows what technological hybrids will grow up in the twenty-first century. Fortunately, we do have some powerful guides. Philosophy and theories of learning change less rapidly than technology. Dewey, Piaget, Vygotsky, and Freire reach across the decades to inform us. Still, teachers need to develop their own philosophy, connect to the most recent research, and go about creatively involving students in a full range of literacy activities.

As we drift into the twenty-first century, technology is changing the way people use language and communicate with one another. Technologies like the Internet have opened up information searches and person-to-person communication. The World Wide Web and its associates have created a space for language that often runs and slips over the boundary of public and private language. The result is that people find themselves using language in public in ways they never would have before. Networking literacy may be next. In spite of a multitude of overlapping literacies, language remains a tool with which we bring things together to create meaning in our lives. It's just that many of the means and tools have changed. Besides methods and media it is important to debate questions of what we should teach, who should teach it, and how it should be organized.

Determining how things should change means defining what qualities of knowledge should be associated with schooling. The results of the decisions or nondecisions that we make today will determine the curriculum that will be in place tomorrow. Writing and reading print will continue to serve as the axle around which the school-based wheel of language and literacy revolves. Concurrently, electronic and digital literacies will become increasingly important and serve as a primary means of mass communications.

Whether communications technology is relatively old (books) or new (computer workstations), it is bound together by perceptual style and a shared media culture. The fact that less than one out of six words is now delivered by print is presenting teachers with a different set of instructional challenges. Forward looking educators are coming to view good communication skills as including an understanding of traditional, recent, and future literacies.

Since very ancient times men have been interested in their languages.

As one of the most remarkable, complex, and familiar attainments, language has excited their curiosity. It is so much a part of their human existence that to understand themselves they have seen that they must first understand language.
– H. A. Gleason

Concerns that Cut Across Communications Media

Certain common concerns seem to cut across training in all literacy areas. The various reports have pointed out that poor reading, writing, and computer skills, were related to a pervasive lack of instructional emphasis on developing higher order skills in all areas of the curriculum. The ability to think clearly is an objective that fits in neatly with any conceivable language and literacy future. Another example of a consistent teaching goal is that of imaginative interaction with the text (print or nonprint). This helps students become engaged in learning about a medium—from reading print to interpreting visual imagery.

To manipulate a medium students must be exposed to good models over which they can exercise some control. Good writing, for example, often begins with imitating a master's style. Reading high quality literature, for example, has a positive influence on students' writing. Likewise, becoming a more intelligent video consumer or student video producer (camcorders, Web sites, and the like) requires exposure to good examples. As students construct their own interpretations, they can revise their work based on the best that a medium has to offer.

Revision and editing are essential, yet difficult concepts to get across to students. "Writers" in any medium must refine their ideas in the revising stage. The task is not complete until things are added, subtracted, deleted, rearranged and "polished." Editing comes next. Collaborative revision and peer editing can rearrange the work so that it is put in the best possible form. Finally, it is presented to a real audience; in the classroom or on the Web. When teachers are trained in the medium they can act as editors who revise rather than correctors who red-pencil errors.

All communication skills depend on intellectual tools that cut across disciplines. Whether it is metaphor from English or analogue from history, these mental tools can serve as a kind of glue that connects thinking to learning. Preparing students to meet the literacy demands of today and tomorrow requires a firm base in basic arts and sciences disciplines. It also requires learning how to use technological and informational resources to gather and synthesize information so that knowledge can be created and communicated. Caution is required, but there is no need for either the video screen or the textbook to pockmark a child's intellectual development.

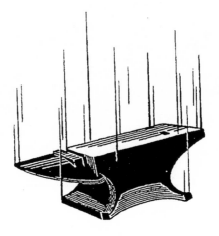

Figure 3.1. Coming to grips with communications technology.

Traditional tools of analysis from the language arts (like book reviews) can be used to assess new media. New media, in turn, can be used to teach traditional basics and help students manipulate new symbol systems. In this way, both old and new literacy elements can enrich a student's emotional and intellectual development.

> *Books are not absolutely dead things,*
> *but do contain potency of life in them*
> *as active as that soul whose progeny they are.*
> —Milton

Media Convergence, Learning Style, and Change

We live in a visual age where both print and video media are being mixed by computers. A convergence of electronic communications media is self-accelerating. Now that computers are print and video processors, video, graphics, and print database can be mixed so that students can interact with realistic images and sound. A newspaper article, for example, can be made to appear in one window on the video screen and broadcast news (about the same topic) on another. Carefully selected elements of print and imagery can also be viewed in a sequence that is different for each viewer/reader.

Print publishers, video (film) producers, and computer manufacturers are collaborating more than ever. Some of the results can be downloaded from the Internet. A model of future communications can be found in the recent collaborative ties between Apple Computer, Lucas Film (Star Wars, etc.), and National Geographic—widening the media horizons of all three. Such joint ventures serve up a menu of visually intensive information by mixing text, video images, and graphic art. This can open up the possibility of having individuals choose alternative paths to knowledge acquisition.

A majority of teachers and school administrators prefer print and auditory learning that flows along in an orderly sequence. The traditional reading and writing mode doesn't work as well with the majority of today's students. Many of those placed in charge of school reform sincerely call for more of the same—done more efficiently. When the adults who are organizing the schooling process try to improve education, it is only natural that they fall back on what worked for them. Thus, some of today's school reform effort is simply a recycling of itself. This is a bit like looking at learning from the point of view of an intelligent but narrowly focused Cyclops. It is time to consider technology and develop our peripheral vision.

No matter how good the equipment, knowledgeable adults are needed to facilitate tapping into these new resources—while making sure that young people also master traditional skills. Technology can help, but the human touch is needed to make learning real. Good advice for any teacher: teach in a variety of ways and keep an open attitude toward children you don't understand well. Remember, it is not necessary to choose between categorizing students by their home environment and ignoring their culture altogether. If students are respected and taught, they will learn.

New instructional tools are starting to emerge that can help teachers build on a student's background and preferred learning style. This can expand the teacher's repertoire of methods in a way that fits the learning of all students. Helping students internalize symbol systems from a variety of multimedia sources can personalize learning without lowering academic standards.

Electronic tools are bound to affect thinking, behavior, and the development of self-guidance skills. Such nonhuman surrogate peers can assist in a range of cognitive processes and prepare students in the socially shared world of work outside the school setting. This means using information and communications technology to solve shifting problems—while preparing students for continued learning on the job.

Education is no longer just for children and adolescents. Rapid technological advance has changed that. From the office to the factory, workers now spend more time in instructional situations on the job than they ever did in a public school classroom. There is only one scientific-industrial-technological revolution, and it is making the modern world. Continuous training is needed just to keep up. Sooner or later all peoples will either connect to it or they will languish.

Teachers as Change Agents

Frontline teachers are turning from being scapegoats for society's neglect to collaborators in institutional change. Working conditions and opportunities for influence can only get better. If teachers are going to play a central role in creating enabling environments for young people, they must come to grips with a plurality of literacies, and it requires teachers and students who can participate as knowledgeable, reflective, creative, and critical members of a variety of literacy communities.

Simply improving the genetic pool of teachers won't get us very far without institutional restructuring and making schools more pleasant. Many top candidates who are recruited into teaching leave within five years to take jobs in industry that pay twice as much and provide more stimulating working conditions. Present institutional arrangements can do much to dampen a spirit of change and renewal. Some school bureaucracies are worthy of Franz Kafka. In other districts are so large that they don't have the sense of community—or the personal bonds between teacher and student that is so necessary if teachers are to take professional responsibility for student progress.

Once on the job, teachers need the time, energy, and resources to attend conferences, classes, and other intellectually invigorating activities. They also need more control over their working environment and the resources to explore ways of reaching youngsters with new information and communications technology. The benefit to students will be an enhancement of communication skills a renewed love of learning. The process will require cooperative work between school districts, universities, the community, and individual educators to prepare and reinvigorate teaching professionals.

Teachers look forward to incentives for exploring the multiliteracies that will be essential for the twenty-first century. They also want to be involved in developing more effective ways to engage students in the best that has been thought, said, and written in the world. Everyone realizes that the search for the proper mix of "old" and "new" literacies will not end with a simple "that's it!" We are now living in a changing multiliterate society that needs to blend instruction in the usable communications past with the uncertain communications elements that are converging on the future.

What's missed most isn't something that's gone,
but possibilities that will never happen.
– Margaret Atwood

Changes in Language Learning

Understanding language requires an understanding of the media symbol systems that represent reality. The process of communication depends upon the ability to comprehend these symbols. Whether it is residence is paper, electronic databases, or video imagery, communication tools have the potential of making the tasks at hand easier. They also define the whole relationship to the task, from the nature of learning to a culture's metaphorical references. A new medium usually takes on the characteristics of a unique cognitive tool, requiring new approaches to understanding.

Developing literate minds means creating communities of literate people who enter into an intellectual partnership with the full range of technologies that amplify communication. It also means helping students perform well outside school settings where decision-making must take place in a variety of contextualized situations.

There is a natural reciprocity between a multitude of literacies and the human mind. Constructing a curriculum that incorporates new electronic literacies is like building a house out of blocks. The fact that many of these building blocks have already been fashioned increases the potential for conveying ideas, reaching people, and preparing them for dealing with the unexpected situations found in life and at work. In any environment, students must take risks, occasionally fail, pick themselves up, and keep on trying.

Taking advantage of enabling communication possibilities means considering how powerful tools can optimize language learning modalities. It also means taking into account how new literacies redefine our relationship with the world. As these new opportunities unfold, the function and conventions of schooling must face similar transformations.

Language interferes directly with common outward reality,
the everyday reality and, therefore,
with the common prose of life.
–Hegel

THE ROLE OF LISTENING IN THE LANGUAGE ARTS

It is often assumed that listening was a communication skill that primarily developed outside of school. Schools were traditionally responsible for this reading and writing aspect of language learning. We now know that both home and school environments have a major influence on all aspects of language and literacy. As the media changes, students seem to be spending less time reading and writing and more time listening and viewing.

Comprehensive listening is an interactive process by which spoken language is converted into meaning. It is much more than hearing or paying attention. Some strategies require instruction and all require practice. Instruction must involve students with specific strategies that involve comprehensive listening (to understand a message), critical listening (to detect manipulative or persuasive language), and appreciative listening (conversation or literature read out loud for enjoyment). Instructional materials need to pay some attention to discriminative listening (distinguishing sounds and interpreting nonverbal communication) and therapeutic listening (listening to a speaker talk through a problem).

Active listening is a particularly important skill. It is a little like what used to be called interruption. But we now realize that it is important and polite to say something after a complete thought has been spoken. You should not wait out a series of disconnected thoughts.

Whether or not students comprehend or remember a message is determined by what happens before, during, and after the message. A background of prior knowledge about the content helps them relate to what they hear to what they already know. Louise Rosenblatt used the term *efferent* to describe the practical listening used to understand a message. It is the most common type of listening students do in school. Students use efferent listening to identify important pieces of what they hear and remember. Whatever the medium, after listening children need the chance to apply what they have heard so that there is a good reason for remembering the information heard.

How much a student learns from listening to any one medium has a lot to do with how that medium is used. When it comes to remembering, drill and practice activities are weak substitutes for active inquiry. Neither paper nor electronic workbooks do much to break the surface of the listening-learning process. For learning to occur, the student must be actively engaged in listening, thinking, conversing, writing, seeing, and doing. Receiving, attending, assigning, forming mental imagery, and applying meaning are the essences of listening. And yes, we can teach students to become active listeners and learners

It still makes sense to plan for activities where children view and listen to media presentations, each other, and the teacher. To balance this out, the teacher listens to children. A balanced program that combines readiness for listening, with active participation, evaluation, and discussion of the listening activity is most effective.

An Applied Approach to Active Listening

1. A Student Listening Checklist

- A purpose set for listening?
- Do I look at the speaker or video screen and think about what is being said?
- Are the main ideas clear to me?
- Can I predict what idea is going to be presented next?
- Can I summarize what I heard every few minutes?
- Can I fit in the new ideas with what I already know?
- Can I evaluate the accuracy and completeness of the information?
- Can I do a good job of explaining what I've heard to someone else?

Students need to be conscious of the listening strategies they use and be able to make plans for improvement. The following checklist may be used to involve students in the identification of individual strengths and needs. Through this kind of self evaluation, discussion, and individual conferences they can become aware of desirable listening behaviors and develop ways of becoming better listeners.

2. Sharing Literature with Children

Literature listening time can be one of the most useful thirty minutes of the day. When teachers or parents share literature with children (by reading to them), interest and comprehension go up. There are also a number of videotapes of authors reading selections of their work (Judy Bloom, for example).

Whether it is the author on videotape, the teacher, or parent, children will listen to poetry or stories that they might not search out on their own. And once their interest is piqued in a topic—by even a short excerpt—they are much more likely to read the whole story—or search out books by the same author.

For the teacher:
Prepare for story time by:

- Becoming familiar with the vocabulary, mood, and concepts of the book.
- Setting the mood. Some teachers use music—others use an artifact that could serve as a symbol for the story.
- Introducing the story. A question to be shared can be written on the board. After a brief discussion, students can predict what might happen.
- Reading expressively and clearly.

Remember too many activities and discussion can kill interest. Sometimes it is better to simply let impressions sink in from the reading. This way each child can take something important to them from the experience.

"Would you please tell me which way I ought to go from here?"

"That depends a good deal on where you want to get to." said the Cat.

"I don't much care where," said Alice.

"Then it doesn't matter which way you go," said the Cat.

"So long as I get somewhere," Alice added.

"Oh, you're sure sure to do that," said the Cat, "if you only walk long enough."

Alice in Wonderland

Figure 3.2. Sharing literature with children.

3. Categorizing Information

Information can be organized and categorized in groups when the speaker's message or the book that the teacher is reading aloud contains many comparisons or pieces of information. Webs, semantic maps, or cluster diagrams can also be used. Put the main idea in a circle in the middle and have the major points going out on spokes. Subdetails can come off the spokes.

4. Note-taking

Beginning in the early grades, children become aware of the fact that note-taking can help you remember what you are listening to. This can be combined with webs, outlines, or listings to structure information in an oral presentations.

5. Asking Questions

Students should be able to ask questions to clarify information. As they are listening, children must sometimes ask questions to eliminate confusion, to increase their understanding of the message, or to connect what is being said to their world.

6. Brainstorming

Brainstorming is a device to help students think of a multiple of listening possibilities. After showing just the beginning of a videotape, stop the tape and brainstorm possible directions the video may take.

In our example, we used the French version (for English-speaking students) of Daniel Defoe's classic Robinson Crusoe. We stopped the video after the introduction and asked, "If you were stuck on a desert island with only a leather belt and a metal buckle, what would you do to survive?"

Students were divided into small groups and for ten minutes were encouraged to brainstorm responses. In the initial stage, our purpose is to present any and all ideas. We put a ban on criticism—the goal was to generate ideas.

In stage two, students evaluated the items generated by the group and decided which had the most merit, which were the most ridiculous, and which were the most realistic. (It is best if someone is appointed to record the ideas.) All groups presented their most realistic and most ridiculous ideas to finish the brainstorming session. This activity helps students feel connected to the video before much listening and viewing takes place.

7. Action Alphabet and Word Formation

The first goal of this activity is to teach the sounds of a second language alphabet and actual word formation. Additional goals include improving first level listening skills, phonics, and spelling, and facilitating group participation and cooperation.

These activities are to be done before or after viewing an elementary spelling or reading video which concentrates on sound letter relationships.

Students individually form a letter of the second language alphabet using their bodies to represent the letter. This can be done in either a standing or lying position. The class then guesses the letter and pronounces it. Video segments can be used to reinforce and embellish the responses. After viewing, the students can also work in groups of five, six, or more to form words or phrases taken directly from the video segments. One student can be chosen as leader of the group that will direct the others to form the letter or word.

Selected concepts from the video can be translated to word cards and placed in an envelope. One envelope is given to each group. Each student selects a letter at random and the teacher tells the group the word to be spelled. The group works together to figure out the spelling of the word. The teacher is only to intervenes if the group as a whole cannot figure out the spelling. Groups can take turns forming words in front of the whole class while students listen and spell the words on paper. Action alphabet activities can easily go from letters to words to sentences.

8. Connecting the Newspaper to TV News:
The Newspaper Treasure Hunt

The daily newspaper, particularly if it is in a second language, can be an intimidating document for students to tackle. It is imposing in format and vocabulary for early readers who are accustomed to materials geared toward their competency levels. By preparing imaginative exercises using a newspaper and a taped news broadcast, a teacher can provide an introduction and demystify those pages filled with newsprint and connect to a second language video segment.

It is important that the newspaper and video segment cover some of the same ground. The TV news items or conversations should be shown first so that what students have listened to (and seen) is then applied to print. This means using print and video material from the same day.

The Newspaper Treasure Hunt is an exercise that can be applied to a variety of reading levels. A list is drawn up with columns of words and phrases extracted from a sample paper. This list of cartoons, pictures, words, concepts, and short phrases (to be found in the newspaper) is handed out to the students along with the paper. Students are divided into pairs and each partnership is given the same newspaper. They are then asked to begin the treasure hunt: Students put the page number which the item is located on the answer sheet and then circle the item in the newspaper. A time limit is set for the search to take place. When time is up, the students can compare their "success" rates. This exercise can be modified for a range of ability levels.

The teacher can go over the newspaper with them as the class collaboratively searches for connections with the news program. An additional application could involve making up a creative story composed almost entirely of headlines and subheadings. If two VCRs are available, students could even re-edit the evening news.

9. Critical Listening: Using TV Advertisements

Students can analyze television advertisements that they have viewed looking for techniques like:

- the testimonial–movie or sports star
- transfer–moving the prestige of one thing to another
- bandwagon–"Physicians recommend Anacin over any other product..."
- snob appeal–an elite or exclusive group uses it
- plain folks–"a regular country boy like me..."
- reward–"10 million dollar prize from Advertising Clearinghouse..."
- glittering generality–motherhood, truth, justice, "the American way"
- name calling–putting a bad name on something
- card stacking–choosing any fact that supports one side of the issue

After listening to TV ads and identifying the persuasive or manipulative technique used, students can practice and present a 60-second skit incorporating some of these "propaganda" devices.

10. Performing and Listening to Poetry Reading

Put students in groups of two and assign each partnership a poem (or let them choose one). Give them time to practice alternate line readings of the poem chosen. Take turns presenting each partnership poem to the class. Here is a sample poem for a junior or senior high school audience:

Student 1
    Warring thoughts try to split my skull
Student 2
    This writing moves through streets of birds

Student 1
    My hand thinks out loud
    a word calls to another
Student 2
    On this page where I write
    I see beings that come and go
Student 1
    The book and the notebook
    unfold their wings and rest
                            – Octavio Paz

Although many of the video/listening strategies described here were developed for second language training, they work equally well for students learning their native language. It is estimated that students spend at least half their communication time in the listening language mode (Adams, et. al, 1980). The other half of the time is split between talking, reading, and writing.

Listening may be the most important mode because it is the first one that students acquire and it directly influences efforts in both old and new literacies. Inner listening, for example, is crucial as students internally dialogue with themselves as they create and revise. Deciding what to listen for, when to listen, and how to listen are acquired skills.

Five levels of listening have been clearly identified. Passive listening tends to be a solitary process without much mental activity. Listening to the radio while you are writing–and some television viewing–falls into this category. Listening to gain information means associating concepts, recalling details, forming sensory impressions, and paraphrasing information. Listening to understand involves linking ideas together and relating those ideas to past knowledge and information. Critical listening requires listeners to analyze what they hear, detect bias and emotional appeal, see implications, and make recommendations. Appreciative listening cuts across all cognitive and affective levels. It involves a personal response to what is heard that is built on background knowledge and a wide range of cognitive skills. Real world connections count. As the language arts standards point out, students must be motivated to willingly, effectively, and joyfully integrate their knowledge into their lives outside the classroom.

Listening instruction is becoming ever more comprehensive. It is beginning to focus on predicting, creating imagery, critical listening, organizing, categorizing, attention directing, reflective discussions, and the asking of higher level questions. By taking an active applications approach that combines video and collaborative activities, teachers have found that they can break through the crust of mystery and neglect that surrounds learning listening skills.

THE LANGUAGE ARTS IN A MESMERIZING AGE OF GADGETS

From television to the Internet, commercial programming does little to get you to think critically about what you are hearing and seeing. Students can view commercials to critically examine persuasive language and propaganda devices. Children can learn to critically analyze the structure, style, and strategies of commercials and news—making comparisons to expository and persuasive forms of writing. They can employ the following questions: What are the speakers' credentials? Purpose? Bias? Do they use deceptive language? Unsupported inferences? Do opinions dominate the talk? Propaganda devices? *Do you believe the message?*

Students can also construct visual parallels, written examples, or a brief dramatized commercial to open things up for analysis. You might consider videotaping a 30- or 60-second student commercial.

Electronic media can supplement learning by reflecting (visually) the wholeness of language, math, physical science, social sciences, and the humanities. To sense the infinite potential of our dominant electronic media requires fresh influences that reflect new sensibilities and challenge the viewer. Using electronic media as a kind of "Hamburger Helper" that makes a paltry dish appear appetizing is a temptation. It takes an extra effort at every level to strive against an intellectually barren environment—particularly when that environment is made powerful by technology.

When faced with the impact of the image, we often get the sense of having undeniable evidence. Whether it is TV or the Internet, viewers maybe incapable of watching critically or distancing themselves from what they are watching. This can prevent them from trying to find out who is right and and it can get in the way of understanding the total context in which something takes place. The effect is to block some information because what viewers retain cannot be contradicted or canceled out by any subsequent inquiry.

When good teachers are allowed to follow their hunches, the technology can become a tool for creating successful learning environments. Some teachers, for example, take a five- or six-minute piece of the the video action and use it to illustrate a particular point. Watching a one- or two-hour movie or TV show on the VCR just doesn't work. Short video excerpts can even be run twice to reinforce a concept. Connecting these short viewing segments to classroom activities can amplify both.

Children can learn to construct ideas from a range of activities—conversations, the printed word, actual experience, film, or electronic imagery. Whether it is print or the video screen, what we perceive falls within the framework of concept formation. Like print, the television or Internet medium can be mentally processed at differing levels of complexity. Relating back to a powerful visual experience that the children have had may help them apply their ideas and experiences to new video-visual landscapes.

How certain aspects of language and literacy are categorized and organized influences how meaning is attached to any concept. The process is an individual act strongly influenced by the video screen. By the time they are five years old, American children are accustomed to life with a machine (television) that continuously tells them things they know to be untrue. Many get more of the same with the Internet. Relying upon a host of cognitive inputs, they use the raw data of experience to produce a personal understanding of what they see and hear. Sometimes they can sort out fact from fiction; sometimes they can't. One thing is sure: Providing guided practice with persuasion, propaganda devices, and deceptive language can at least provide an element of informed control over loaded words and doublespeak.

Figure 3.3. Teaching cats to bark.

Amplifying Video: Collaborative Learning Activities for Increasing Comprehension

Increasingly, teachers are using video, computers, and the Internet to enrich their lessons and motivate students. By developing their roles within various literacy communities, students can see how language usage communication skills vary across different contexts and audiences. When it comes to visually-intensive media, sometimes teachers need to allow two or more viewings of a brief segment for students to gain the intellectual and visual tools necessary for students' comprehension, retention, and application of what is presented. Despite the time spent with television or the Internet, few viewers or users seem to have a clear idea of how the process works. Teachers and students need good instruction about the media to help them take responsibility for their own viewing.

I. Techniques for Using Instructional Video

    a. Provide a mental set for what the students' will see.
    b. Help students figure out what topics in the video are relevant.
    c. Provide some kind of outline of the video's major points.
    d. Explain how the information in the video fits in with the course subject matter and how students are expected to use it.
    e. Integrate with other instructional techniques to make the video interesting.
    f. Relate the new information gained from the video to concepts that students are already familiar with.
    g. Ask students to select pictures or draw illustrations that could represent the video's major points.
    h. Have students collaborate (in pairs or small groups) to organize the concepts they have viewed into a creative summary.

2. Analyze Television Characters

Examining a group of characters in television programs can give students insight into TV's portrayal of various groups of people. Have students select categories they wish to study: children, women, teens, blacks, older people, teachers, etc. Split the class into four groups and instruct each group to pick a category from the list.

Each group must set up criteria for collecting data on their topic. Some examples of criteria include: appearance, age, behavior, job/responsibilities, how others responded to the character. The group must decide on ways to gather information and be ready to share their findings and conclusions with the class. Encourage discussion of the results. What effect does this have on viewers? How did you feel about the characters you were viewing?

3. Map a TV Program

This method for increasing comprehension allows students to participate in video presentations by graphically organizing, summarizing, and predicting. These concrete word drawings can serve as mental models and tools. Once you learn how to use them, you will find them useful in graphically organizing concepts.

<blockquote>
supporting idea   supporting idea
Main Idea
supporting idea   supporting idea
</blockquote>

Here is an example of predicting what you might learn from a video segment about dinosaurs:

[student generated map before viewing]

<blockquote>
What did they look like? What did they eat?
Dinosaurs
Where did they live? What happened to them?
</blockquote>

After viewing or reading, attach the details to a summary map:

<blockquote>
What did they look like?   What did they eat?
reptile like, some very large   Many ate plants
How Dinosaurs Lived and Died
Where did they live?   What happened to them?
many lived in warm swamps   Drastic climate changes killed them
</blockquote>

4. Develop Probable Scenes Before Viewing

Before introducing a video story to the class, select about 20 key words from the segment and write them on the board. Working in groups of two or three, have students arrange the words under the following headings:

SETTING | CHARACTERS | PROBLEM | SOLUTION | ENDING

All the words must be placed in some category and each word used only once. Once the the students have finished the task, they must construct a story based on where they placed the words. Different groups will come up with very different settings, problems, and solutions, as well as endings. Encourage students to read their stories aloud before viewing and making comparisons.

5. Expose Students to the Video Content (Before Viewing)

The see-say-write method of teaching is designed to help students remember information through cognitive associations. The opportunity to read, speak, organize information, and write about the topic to be studied before viewing can help with vocabulary development, comprehension, and critical thinking about the video content.

Preparing the Lesson
1. Select important words from the video segment which students may be unfamiliar with. (Include names of people, places, dates, activities, etc.)
2. Write these words on an overhead transparency.
   (Note: Do not let the students see the words just yet.)

Performing the Lesson
3. Pair off students in working partnerships.
4. One student faces the area where the words will be projected. (These students will be called the see-sayers.) The other students should have their backs to the words. (These students will be called the writers.)
5. The "writers" should divide four sheets of paper in eighths (32 boxes).
6. Tell the students that you will show the "see-sayers" a list of words for 60 seconds. They will read one word at a time to their partners (the "writers"), who will write each word in a square on one side of the folded papers. Students must work quickly and try to get as many words as possible.
7. Present the words to the "see-sayers."
8. After a minute or so, remove the words. As you do so, reassure the students they were not expected to finish the list.
9. Have students tear their sheets of paper on the folds leaving them with eight squares of paper for each larger sheet.
10. When each group has a stack of words, tell them to arrange their words in some sort of order, in categories.
11. Ask each group to present their arrangement to the rest of the class. Point out different methods students used or could have used.
12. Show the video segment.

6. Ask Effective Questions (After Viewing)

Discussion following viewing is an important instructional technique. If the purpose was made clear before watching, good follow-up questions can lead to productive discussions. A few questioning levels and techniques follow which may make viewing more productive.

Literal questions involve direct factual answers. What characters said, how they acted, where the story took place, what happened are literal questions which usually involve skills of recall.

Inference questions require students to read into the story and use knowledge to solve a problem not answered directly in the video. Inference questions after viewing a nature show might include: Are these animals used to having people around them? Why do you think so? Why do (or don't) the people carry weapons?

Extrapolation questions ask students to come up with possible future scenarios based on hunches surrounding the facts of the program. Questions such as: What would happen if there were no laws to protect these animals? What do you predict will happen if the laws remain unchanged?

7. Use a Storyboard to Increase Student Comprehension

The construction of a simple storyboard can help students become more intelligent video consumers and understand the content of a production. Students can take the basic concepts contained in a video segment and construct their own storyboard. To ensure that students participate actively (and collectively plan), have them make a storyboard which they will explain to the class. The teacher could give them part of a story, show part of the tape, or show the whole segment and ask them to change it. The storyboard of a five-minute video segment might include a dozen or so simple sketches that show the sequence of action. These can be in small numbered boxes of a full-page diagram for each illustration. The storyboard allows students to see the component parts as well as the sweep of the action. Pictorial frames can be rearranged, added, or deleted. Using a storyboard, students can predict the action, visually represent it, or creatively rearrange it. If you have access to a camcorder, students can create an original storyboard, film their own explanation of the action sequences, and then go on to actually videotape what they have presented.

SHARED LEARNING: MESHING INDIVIDUAL AND GROUP PERFORMANCE

The view of teaching as the transmission of content has been expanded to include the management of a vast range of knowledge acquisition tools accessed by a multitude of literacy-intensive technologies. Helping young people strike a balance between high-tech and high-touch learning requires active group activities along with more passive viewing of short video segments.

As the schools try to greet the future, "back to basics" should not be read as "back to not thinking." The curriculum must shift to help students critically perceive, analyze, interpret, and discover the range of meanings in the electronic media. By combining high quality segments of instructional television and dynamic collaborative activities, learning can be enriched. Being literate today means more than traditional subject matter; it means understanding how technology and good pedagogy can change the way we think, learn, and try to achieve democratic goals.

Whether the video screen connects to an antenna, cable TV, satellite dish, computer, or the Internet, technological change can be a bit poisonous for some people. The trick is to turn socio-technical problems into opportunities. Coupled with human interaction and control, technological forces can become positive energies of change. Educators can harness the technology to reach more people with greater depth and permanence. Electronic media doesn't have to confine us. It can extend the possibility of using our communicative skills collectively.

Story Starters for Getting to Know You

Answer most of the questions and discuss the answers with the person sitting next to you. At the end, share a few answers with the whole class. Anyone who finishes early can draw a picture of an answer on the back. This activity is designed to help you think about yourself, your peers, and help you practice communication skills. Everyone gets a copy and completes each sentence.

[To vary this activity, have students make up some sentence stems, trade papers, and complete the sentences started by another student.]

How I See Things

Name_____

My two favorite movies_____

My favorite TV program_____

I like to read about_____

My two favorite books_____

I like stories about_____

I'd read more but_____

I would rather use the Internet than_____

My two favorite musical groups_____

I get angry when_____

My idea of a good time is _____

Today I feel_____

School is_____

My favorite learning experience was_____

I wish teachers would_____

If I were a teacher, I would_____
My best teaching experience was_____
I can't understand why_____
On weekends I_____
If I had three wishes, they would be_____
I don't know how_____
I wish people wouldn't_____
My greatest disappointment was_____
I feel proud when_____
I would like to be_____
I wish I could_____
I look forward to_____
I wish someone would help me_____
The changes that I'd like to see in our classroom are_____

AN INTEGRATED APPROACH TO LANGUAGE AND LITERACY

As they learn the language arts, children need opportunities to use all of their senses as they explore the world around them. New communications and information technologies are part of that world. They can provide important foundations for integrating an expanded sense of literacy in the classroom. Critical analysis is important, but teachers can still welcome new technologies into the classroom fold. Electronic technologies have heightened our sense of the need for change and have raised our expectations of what students must know to be competent in the language arts. Teaching and learning in the Age of Information require building a new vision of multiple literacies that reaches across the curriculum.

Reading, writing, speaking, listening, visualizing, observing, and disciplined thinking are all part of the standards for the English Language Arts. The standards also suggest honoring students' responses to literature by accepting a wider range of interpretations and allowing students to discuss their perspectives with one another. Virtual book clubs, the Internet, and interactive childrens' literature are all part of language and literacy today. Information and communications technology is integrated into many of the curriculum suggestions.

Interactive electronic teaching tools are now rich enough to let students seek out resources and work with them at their own pace. Students can use the technology to reach out to distant databases, visual resources, and other students around the world. Such resource-based learning is immensely powerful for individual classrooms and distance learning of all kinds. Student inquiry, problem solving, and research of all kinds are different today. Electronic media will continue to impinge upon the familiar and educators will continue to struggle to keep up with the tumultuous changes in communication technology.

Media literacy is part of today's language arts. It may be thought of as the ability to comprehend, use, and control systems of print and nonprint media. Understanding various symbol systems and the relationship between each medium are other elements that are as important to media literacy as they are to the traditional language arts. Electronic and print media can work together to enhance reading, writing, speaking, and listening. Electronic media is especially powerful when it comes to shaping perceptions of the world and changing values. Children spend so much time with television, film, computers, and the Internet that teachers must draw on this shared culture to reach every student. A new medium rarely erases the need for the old. To be fully literate in today's world requires understanding and using overlapping media. As the language arts standards suggest, there are many opportunities to teach about, through, and with all media in an integrated language arts program. Clearly, information and communications technology can reinforce and accelerate learning.

As the traditional boundaries of literacy give way to multiliteracies, the road to maximal literacy will increasingly be mediated by the texture and rhythm of electronic resources. Achieving some level of control over distance, time, and the integration of text, image, and sound has profound implications. If done wrong, electronic media can be dehumanizing and distancing. If done right, it can help spread the power of education deeper and farther than ever before. As with any area or method of inquiry, high quality, technology-based learning depends on teacher-generated motivation, direction, and instruction.

Creating and Communicating Today and Tomorrow

Literacy is much broader and more demanding than it used to be. Today, it includes the capacity to accomplish a wide range of language and communication tasks associated with everyday life at the beginning of the twenty-first century.

When it comes to school, it is the job of the teacher to figure out how the individual students in their classrooms will best develop as readers, writers, and communicators. Teachers are key to successfully integrating new media possibilities into the educational process. To do it right, they need pleasant and sustained professional development opportunities that help them explore the relationship between literacy, technology, and learning.

A good integrated language arts program can still be literature based. It is just that this has become much more than print on paper. Print has many advantages, but even some literature is visually intensive, online, and interactive. Entire books, with interactive possibilities, are now available on CD-ROM or DVD disks. When working in this new digital environment, authors have to learn new ways of creating rich and powerful stories. In this new genre of literature writers have to anticipate the "reader" making all sorts of twists and turns in the story. The more freedom the participant feels, the more powerful the plot. Combining a directed plot with interactivity requires close collaboration between writers and computer scientists. When the procedural power of the computer is matched to the conscious selection of elements by an author, the result is what might be called "cyberliterature."

In the last few years, the use of technology has emerged as important for everything from participatory literature to information searches to person-to-person communication. Computers, television productions, and the Internet are now part of how children experience literature and share their findings by dramatizing, telling, and showing. Whatever the medium being used, children must continue to think critically about what they are doing as they compose, revise, edit, and share what they have done in a language-learning community.

Children bring their knowledge of the world to the process. They learn best when they have the personal opportunities and reason to use language skills. The goal of language arts instruction is to make meaning with words and images—helping youngsters become masters of the process. Doing this involves engaging children with authentic language, communications, and literacy activities. Students need the opportunity to brainstorm, think creatively, and work collaboratively.

Language is more than a tool; it is a medium of communication that permeates human thought and life. It offers countless possibilities for representation, expression, and thought. The goal of language learning is making sure that all students develop the literacy skills they need to succeed in school and in life. At its best, learning the language arts is an active, constructive process in which the learner focuses on the discovery of meaning. Learning language and using language to learn help students make full use of communication possibilities across the curriculum. Language arts is more than a subject, it is part of everything that happens in the classroom and in various areas of life.

Figure 3.4 How I see things. Image adapted from elements of a Roy Lichtenstein painting.

RESOURCES AND REFERENCES

IRA/NCTE Standards for the English Language Arts Students:

- read a wide range of print and nonprint texts
- read a wide range of literature from many periods
- apply a wide range of strategies to comprehend texts
- adjust their use of spoken, written, and visual language
- employ a wide range of writing (process) strategies
- apply knowledge of language structures and conventions
- conduct research on issues, interests, and questions
- use a variety of technological and information resources
- develop an understanding of diversity in language use
- make use of their first language to gain skills in English
- participate in a reflective and critical literacy community
- use spoken, written, and visual language for a purpose

These are brief selections. For a full description see the document.
[National Council of Teachers of English / International Reading Association]

Adams, M. J., & Anderson, V. (1995). *Reading/writing connection.* Chicago: Open Court.

Allington, R.L., & Cunningham, P. M. (1996). *Schools that work: Where children read and write.* New York: HarperCollins College Publishers.

Cafolla, R., Kauffman, D., & Knee, R. (1997). *World Wide Web for teachers: An interactive guide.* Boston: Allyn & Bacon.

Cooper, J. D., & Pikulski, J. J. (1996). *Hello/share literacy activity book.* Boston: Houghton Mifflin.

Fosnot, C. T. (Ed.). *Constructivism: Theory, perspectives, and practice.* New York: Teachers College Press.

Graves, M. F. (Ed.). *The first R: Every child's right to read.* New York: Teachers College Press.

Guthrie, J. T., & McCann, A. D. (1997). *Reading engagement: Motivating readers through integrated instruction.* Newark, DE: International Reading Association.

Leu. D. J., Jr., & Leu. D.D. (1997). *Teaching with the Internet: Lessons from the classroom.* Norwood, MA: Christopher-Gordon.

Merrill, P. F. (1996) *Computers in education.* Boston: Allyn & Bacon.

National Commission on Teaching & America's Future. (1996). *What matters most: Teaching for America's future.* New York: Teachers College Press.

Osborn, J., & Lerehr, F. (Eds.), (1999). *Finding a balance: Reading instruction in the 21st century.* Hillsdale, NJ : Erlbaum.

Vaughn, S., Bos, C. S., & Schumm, J. S. (1997). *Teaching mainstreamed, diverse, and at-risk students in the general education classroom.* Boston: Allyn & Bacon.

Chapter 4

NUMERACY
Literacy, Mathematics, and Technology

A mathematician, like a painter or a poet, is a maker of patterns.
If his patterns are more permanent than theirs, it is because they
are made with ideas. – Godfrey Hardy

Numeracy is tied to mathematics the way literacy was traditionally tied to reading. Innumeracy...equals mathematical illiteracy...equals social consequences.

At the very time physicists are probing cosmic spaces and mathematics is fueling the foundation of science and technology, we have created a general public proudly admitting ignorance in performing simple mathematical tasks. These same people would never admit shortcomings in their ability to read and write. The attitude of many American students toward mathematics could be summed up by singer Joan Jett: "Bad Attitude, How To Get It and How To Keep It." It is little wonder that developing positive feelings towards mathematics is a major goal of the standards developed by the National Council of Teachers of Mathematics (NCTM).

Besides negative attitudes, two major areas of concern have surfaced in recent studies of American mathematics education. The first is how poorly our youth stacks up against students in other countries in comprehending modern mathematical thought. The second is how the emphasis on computation and arithmetic has diminished the ability to deal with the various levels of mathematical reality. The Standards suggest that genuine mathematical power is the the ability to explore, think clearly, conjecture, and use a variety of mathematical methods to solve authentic problems. Problem solving, reasoning, technological tools, communications skills, and connections between math topics and other disciplines are all part of what it takes to develop logical thinkers who can apply mathematical skills in the real world.

INTERNATIONAL COMPARISONS

Americans were surprised by the poor performance of high school students on the most recent International Mathematics and Science Study (TIMSS). While elementary students showed some improvement, American high school students were in competition with South Africa and Cyprus for the lowest scores (U.S. TIMSS, National Research Center). Little has changed since these surveys. The good news is that when you are near the bottom of the international barrel, it should be relatively easy to show positive growth.

The United States is in the midst of a great economic boom. Unfortunately, neither our teachers nor our schools have shared in the vast expansion of wealth. In spite of more Internet connections, our schools have not changed much. Many still house students in inadequate "temporary" classrooms with few up-to-date textbooks, computers, or supplies. In some cases, the working conditions and teachers' salaries are as bad as the facilities. It is little wonder that so many new teachers quit after a few years.

Teachers are near the top of the professional income ladder in countries like Japan. In Germany, the status of teachers is equally high. In the U.S., the opposite is true. American teachers need enough money to live on, and their pay should reflect the respect they deserve. Despite low prestige and pay, more graduates from some of the top colleges are answering the call to teach. They say that they want to make a significant social contribution right out of college. This social idealism will help a little if we can make the working conditions attractive enough to keep teachers on the job, but we need at least two million new teachers. How many of our best and brightest college students will sign on for long-term missionary work? Until teachers' working conditions and pay improve, students, parents, college faculty, and our society will continue to devalue teaching; the losers will inevitably be the children.

International surveys (TIMSS) suggest that American students at all grade levels have gained a shallow familiarity with hundreds of facts, concepts, and equations, but they do not probe understandings in depth. Mathematics and science education in this country is a little like the Great Salt Lake: 70 miles long, 30 miles wide, and 12 feet deep. Doing less better—and at greater depth —would certainly help.

Another part of the problem in the United States is the way mathematics has been taught in American schools. Most traditional instruction consisted of teacher talk and testing. It is not a question of "new" verses "old" math, but mathematics verses arithmetic. Of course, addition, subtraction, multiplication, and division are as important to mathematics as spelling and grammar are to writing. It is just that arithmetic concepts shouldn't be the only concern.

Figure 4.1. Child fleeing school. Computer-generated image including elements of a painting by Steve Gianakos.

Memorizing rules and performing routine practice problems in preparation for chapter tests won't generate much excitement. Neither will viewing mathematics as an inaccessible mix of involved calculations, difficult algorithms, and right answers. In reality, equations and formulas are rarely more expressive than ordinary words and experiences. Math doesn't have to be dull or boring when compared to other things going on in life. The ideal math program would have students graduating with the same positive attitudes towards mathematics that they had when they entered elementary school.

Among other things, the Standards have helped us redefine what we want our students to know and what we want our schools to do. Schools should, for example, be able to produce citizens who are able to manage their personal finances, balance a checkbook, arrange mortgages, avoid the lottery, and invest shrewdly for old age. But it will take higher levels of mathematical literacy to avoid the more complicated kind of social follies that grow out of a lack of mathematical understanding.

CHANGING MATHEMATICAL REALITY: NCTM STANDARDS

The mathematics standards have helped schools adjust to recent techno-logically-intensive changes in how mathematics is taught. The last decade has been an extraordinary time of accelerating change in mathematics. One example is the way students now have access to the World Wide Web, via computers. Even the availability of handheld graphing calculators was uncommon in 1990 (NCTM, 1998).

The recently revised Standards elaborate on a wide range of mathematical and technological issues. More emphasis is placed on math processes, including the ways students should acquire and use mathematical knowledge in authentic situations. The Standards recognize the fact that the presence of electronic media shifts the approach to mathematics content and changes the way students think about the subject. They also point out that technology works best when it supports clear curriculum goals.

There is general agreement that students should understand how to use mathematics in an increasingly technological world. Technological tools such as calculators, computers, digital laboratories, and web browsers are all part of math these days. Multimedia computers and the Internet allow for the collection and analysis of data in a way that can make meaningful applications of mathematics more visual, relevant, interactive, and interesting. All of these tools and their associates can help students engage mathematical ideas in meaningful ways.

MATHEMATICAL LITERACY

Mathematics is the language of nature.
– Galileo

The power of the universal language of mathematics can come alive in electronic images. Graphic images are enabling mathematicians to mimic the geometry of nature, solve complex networking problems, and explore visually hitherto unseen boundaries between chaos and the ordered world. Once only abstract equations, graphic visualizations of mathematics are now attracting people from other disciplines who see descriptions of phenomena in their own fields (artists and scientists, for example). The mathematical application of technology can be felt in all aspects of modern life from predicting weather to bringing TV to a global audience.

Mathematics is not merely a set of rules waiting to be imparted to eager (or not so willing) young minds. Mathematics, like any language, is a form of communication, a symbolic language, invented rather than discovered, evolving as the need arises. If school reading programs were to take the same stance as mathematics, students would never read prose or poetry but spend all of their time with phonics, grammar, and spelling. Language is the common basis of mathematics. Many adults remember using rhythm and poetry to help memorize their times tables. Skills in the arts such as drawing, painting, singing, reading, rhyming, and measuring can serve mathematics instruction. Most of us know that patterns of language are acquired early on. But too many parents and teachers don't realize the importance of laying the foundation for mathematical thinking when children are very young.

Children enjoy sorting, matching, grouping, questioning, explaining, and discussing their math work. Puzzles, beads, blocks, cards, and see-through boxes of seashells and buttons can all help with concepts like estimation and measurement. Manipulating natural and created materials can lead to exploration, discovery, and problem solving. Good stories help. So does art work that visually express mathematical concepts like *under*, *half*, and *bigger than*. Children can put captions under their artwork and hang them around the room. Across all grade levels, low-tech media can be coupled with problem solving to illustrate concepts from geometry, fractions, and visual-spatial reasoning. On the high-tech plane, digital technology and today's children can both grow to the point where they will seamlessly benefit one another. As students use mixed media tools to develop and articulate their mathematical understandings, they are able to delve more deeply into content.

INCLUDING ELECTRONIC TECHNOLOGY

Students are preparing to work in a society where computers and the application of math concepts are increasingly important. Electronic technologies such as calculators, computers, micro-based laboratories, and web browsers are part of the math standards discussion because they can all help teachers with mathematics instruction. These technological tools can make mathematics and its real world applications accessible in ways that were impossible in yesterday's classroom (Rojano, 1996).

Technology helps teachers make interdisciplinary connections by providing access to important information with visually-intensive tools. This helps facilitate an in-depth exploration of mathematical and scientific topics that used to be too complex for the typical elementary classrooms. Simplifying data gathering allows more time for analysis and interpretation. For example, students can access information about a country's agricultural production, physical landscape, economy, transportation capabilities, and energy resources. They can do this for today, 1945, or they can project forward (with less accuracy) to 2020. With such information in hand, students can compare ratios, percentages and proportions with something they found in newspapers or in real-life experience.

Once students gather their data they then can use technological tools such as graphing calculators and spreadsheets to gather real-world information quickly. Data can be easily transported from the Internet into spreadsheets, word processing programs, and multimedia presentations. As technology is becoming more a part of classroom life, teachers can look to their students, "the Net Generation," to help make the transition to more student-centered learning. According to Teenage Research Unlimited (1997) many children and teens feel comfortable on-line. When students were asked what they do on the Net, many replied they manage their finances, check facts, find out the scores of their favorite teams, or chat on-line with friends. But when parents, teachers, or librarians aren't around it can become a great goof-off machine.

MATHEMATICS AND THE VISUAL

In today's world, visual considerations are more important than ever. Mathematicians, scientists, philosophers, artists, and mystics have long debated the nature of color. Aristotle believed that all colors are created by mixing black and white. Even Leonardo da Vinci could not figure it out. He declared at one time that their were six primary colors ... at another time it was eight. Seventeenth century Jesuit mathematicians suggested three primary colors–red, yellow, and blue–that together with black and white could be combined to make any color. Sir Isaac Newton solved the problem by intercepting a beam of sunlight with a prism. He proved that white light was composed of all visible colors of the spectrum and could be recombined back into white light. It was Newton's mathematics and his scientific method that got the era of modern optics off the ground.

Our world abounds with color and motion, feeling, and thought. Yet the average individual rarely equates mathematics with such worldly realities. One forgets that mathematics is the study of pure pattern. The patterns of mathematics (number, space, logic, infinity, and information) are directly linked to the psychological activities of perception, emotion, thought, intuition, and communication. Making these mathematical patterns visual is one way to move the average individual into a closer understanding of applied mathematics and his or her own thinking process.

The eye has always been one of our basic senses. But until recently, the eye was all but banished from mathematics instruction. Einstein said he preferred visual thinking as a mode of thought for creative work. He explained that the axiomatic structure of a theory is built psychologically on the experiences of the world of perceptions. In spite of his influence, those who thought in formulas have dominated the study of mathematics until very recently. Now computer-generated graphics in areas like fractal geometry have brought graphic representation to the forefront of mathematical research–moving mathematics back into the realm of an experimental science.

Students can profit from the opportunity to visualize and internalize mathematics in ways that make sense and have personal meaning. Complex mathematical formulas simply do not have the same accessibility. A mix of media can give students a less anxious time with difficult material. Curiosity can be aroused through the visual senses. A teaching approach focused on the visual and the analytical can turn around attitudes, improve basic skills, and focus on important problem solving applications (Hamm, 1998). In addition, empowering students with the ability to visualize abstract concepts helps them relate to the real physical meaning. This is a great help in transferring school-based instruction to real-world applications.

Causing students to question and take a second look at their visual world is an eye opening mathematical experience. Investigations into such questions as "Why are circular holes punched into the ceiling tiles in our classroom?" or "Why are rooms usually built in a rectangular shape?" involve students in a personal way with familiar surroundings. Mathematics takes on significance outside the classroom when students explore why manhole covers are round, or fire hydrant bolts five-sided. The student responses, whether accurate or not, call into play creative mental constructs. It can also help with the manipulation of ideas and spatial reasoning.

Teachers in the early elementary grades often do a good job in using concrete materials to teach concepts of addition, subtraction, multiplication, and division, but higher level concepts taught in the later elementary grades often fail to be introduced with visuals. Square root or finding a square of a number is one example. Rules are presented and memorized: multiplying the number by itself equals the square of that number. What is the point in finding a square number, or worse yet, the root of that square? Is there a difference between 5 x 5 and 25? Introducing such a concept by having students build a square with blocks or draw a square on graph paper gives them a visual model of what square means and how 25 may have a different shape and different purpose than 5 x 5. The root of the square can then be easily seen (the sides, base, or root of the square) and applications discussed and used in constructing their own problems.

Figure 4.2. Apply mathematics to real life: Why are manhole covers round? A digitized image including elements of a painting by Mark Kostabi.

Shaping mathematical behavior and thought patterns is an important task. But concrete experience with math manipulatives is not the only good way to fathom the underlying structures of mathematics. Visually-intensive technological tools can take students beyond concrete reality to mental models of mathematical processes. This kind of modeling is particularly useful for building estimation skills and understanding abstractions. Electronic images that provoke thinking can, at least occasionally, be as effective as real-world experiences. When arithmetic lessons fail to generate interest, electronic imagery can move students beyond the boredom. By generating pictures in the mind, abstract concepts can be penetrated in ways previously impossible.

TV MATHEMATICS AND LEARNING

A primary objective of educational TV programs is to promote positive attitudes toward mathematics and technology. Online with "Doug" is a Saturday morning ABC TV program that demonstrates how to avoid pitfalls on the Internet. It provides students safe, fun, and informative links along with safety tips. Another interesting math and science program is "Bill Nye the Science Guy" on PBS television channels. In both shows, problem-solving and real-world mathematics are presented in a variety of ways intended to spark interest across a broad spectrum of mathematical concerns. It brings home the point that mathematics is related to many real-world situations and used as a bridge between science and the humanities.

Broadcast television represents one technological door to mathematics learning. Although many teachers are catching up with technology, the National Teacher Training Institute for Math, Science, and Technology, (NTTI), launched in 1990 by public broadcasting station Thirteen/WNET in New York, continues to lead teachers in how to use video and the Internet in boosting student learning. Sponsored by the Corporation for Public Broadcasting, NTTI now involves 26 broadcasting stations, providing teachers with specific strategies, resources, and interactive lesson plans that help them effectively integrate technologies into classroom instruction. NTTI provides an interactive teaching methodology where technologies such as video and the Internet are combined with hands-on activities. The wealth of educational programming on public television presents students with vivid demonstrations of science and math phenomena. Connected to real-world contexts, video and Internet resources help tie math and science to students' lives.

FROM THE CONCRETE–TO THE ABSTRACT
–AND BACK AGAIN

Children learn mathematics more effectively when they can concretely experience the principles they are studying. Video and computer-based learning is an ally in moving math along a path from concrete experiences to abstract manipulations. Using animated electronic imagery, for example, can bring students closer to abstract mathematical understandings and real-world applications.

Using electronic tools requires an increased ability to think, learn, and express ourselves in terms of imagery. The most powerful way to use technology is in combination with concrete experimentation. The following activity gets students involved either as part of a video crew or as active participants.

How Airplane Design Affects Flight Performance

Students will work together to create a video teaching tape. Assign a group of students to a video crew. They will use camcorders to film the session. The remainder of the students will actively participate in teaching about airplane design and flight.

Objectives:
Introduce students to the concepts of lift, gravity, thrust, and drag in relation to paper airplane design and flight. Provide practice in measurement and graphing skills.

Materials:
Scratch paper, three sheets of 8 1/2 x 11 white paper per student, group recording sheet with each student's name and columns to record distances for two types of planes, meter sticks, chart paper video camera, and recorder.

Background Information
Lift and gravity concepts: Gravity–pulls the paper down, lift– is air pressing up, this keeps the paper from falling immediately. Air presses back on flat paper more because there is more surface area.

Thrust and drag concepts: Thrust is forward movement. Your hand movement provides thrust for a paper airplane; fuel provides thrust for a real plane. Thrust provides some lift. Drag, or friction, caused by air pushing against the plane, slows it down.

Procedures:
1. Introduce, discuss, and demonstrate concepts of lift, gravity, thrust, and drag.
2. Crush scratch paper in a ball, then drop the ball and a flat piece of paper at the same time. Ask students to predict what will happen and why. Which will hit the ground first? why?

3. Next, instruct students to hold the crushed ball, turn your hand over and push down quickly. What happened? What will happen when you do the same thing with the flat paper? (Students should feel the air push against their hand as they move their hand down).

4. To investigate the effects of thrust on lift, have students move a piece of paper forward and note how the back lifts up. To investigate the effects of drag, have students move a piece of paper through the air horizontally, then vertically. Compare the resistance (a thinner surface pointing forward produces less drag.)

5. Encourage students to make two types of planes (dart or sharp-nosed, and blunt-nosed) See directions.

6. Ask students to predict on their recording sheets which model will fly farthest and why. Next, the video crew will film the demonstrations.

7. Have students go outside or to a clear space, take planes, meter sticks, group recording sheets, and a pencil. Instruct students to lay out meter sticks end to end; you may wish to mark off meters with chalk or paper.

8. Have one student stand on the starting line and call out when to throw, have two students ready to help throwers measure their throws, each student throws both planes. Record each student's distances. When finished graph the results.

9. Discuss the results with the students. Instruct students to explain their findings. What factors affected the results (ways planes were thrown, wind, etc.)?

Evaluation:

Have the video crew show the recorded tape to the class. Review the aerodynamic concepts of lift, gravity, thrust, and drag in relation to airplane design and flight. Have students reflect on the measurement and graphing skills involved. What math standards were used? Explain.

COMPUTERS IN THE MATH CLASSROOM

The computer is one of the most important tools of modern mathematics. The powerful visualizing capabilities permit us to create, manipulate, and communicate ideas. They also enable us to solve problems visually. As teachers learn to use computers to achieve their instructional purposes, concrete experiences can be amplified. What better way to help students become rich in mathematical knowledge and creativity?

The latest computer and video tools can be harnessed for problem solving and mathematical learning. New computer software, video technology, and various combinations of the two can be utilized to involve students more directly in the learning process. When students are able to see relationships more graphically and witness theory in electronic representation of practice, a deeper understanding of underlying principles emerges.

Empowering students with the ability to visualize abstract concepts helps them relate to the real physical meaning and make applications. Visualization can help students understand and see things they can't in a lecture (helps combine visualization with instruction). Whether used in class, after class, or in a class demonstration, the computer makes abstractions more concrete. The animated graphing of functions, working simulated problem sets, demonstrating constructions, adding color, movement, and manipulation help bring concepts to an interactive visual level. We now have the technology to make math truly come alive.

New learner-centered software gives students control of the goal and strategies to reach the goal. Feedback is informational, not judgmental, and encourages students to make estimates or approximations. Problem-solving goals for computer use include teaching students to take intellectual risks and chances as well as using computers to communicate about intellectual content. Content objectives must include curricular integration and empower the user. Goals for computer use are embodied in adaptability and control of the subject and allow for ease of use plus positive cues and reinforcement. We now have good computer programs that allow students to pose a mathematical hypothesis and visually test its accuracy.

Computers can help students develop algebraic thinking by acting as dynamic "function machines." They form a bridge between concrete examples and algebraic representations. Digital technology and networks exist for exploring variables and relationships among variables. In addition, they are an effective way to reveal mathematical patterns and relationships (Clements & Sarama, 1997).

Examples of Three Kinds of Interactive Software

• Teasers by Tobbs (O'Brien, 1996), students solve puzzles with missing entries by applying an operation at the easier level. The program becomes more difficult on another level, students work with open sentences and linear relationships. For example: Find as many ways as possible to complete _____ + _____ = 57. This program leads students to form a pattern, becoming more aware of linear relationships, developing rules, and setting the stage for symbolic representations when they encounter formal algebra studies.

• Spreadsheets are electronic tables where students can enter a formula that performs calculations on a number or series of numbers. Students can ask "what if..." and answer questions with many numbers. Spreadsheets extend beyond simple numerical mathematics. Students can use a spreadsheet program to explore how long it would take to travel to a planet in our solar system, calculating speed, distance from earth, and time of arrival.

• LOGO is a computer programming language designed to explore communicate mathematical ideas. LOGO provides another concrete way of introducing children to algorithms, routines, subroutines, and variables. Children must tell the computer exactly what to do. The computer specifically creates concrete algorithms in a way that would otherwise be inaccessible to young students. For example, students form a square 8 units on a side by typing a command such as [repeat 4: forward 8, turn right 90]. The square can then be labeled "Box 8." This introduces students to the idea of subroutines. It also reinforces the idea of mathematical functions, so when students replace "8" with "n," they create a different picture for each value of n. These mathematical ideas are visual and meaningful to children who create them. Prior to the existence of this technology, these ideas were not easily introduced, nor as important for young students (Turtle Math LCSI 1994, a version of LOGO).

Computer programs affect student's minds for the better when they are used correctly. In a recent examination of how computers affect mathematics learning, the 1996 National Assessment of Educational Progress Survey showed significant academic gains when students used computers for more complex mathematics (National Assessment Governing Board, 1996).

SHAPING MATHEMATICAL BEHAVIOR

We are just beginning to examine some of the factors that shape mathematical behavior. It is becoming increasingly clear that being able to think mathematically requires more than large amounts of exposure to math content. Teaching and learning mathematics involves more than a knowledge of content and process. Students need direct decision-making experiences. Applying mathematics to real world problems widens young minds. Mathematical problem solving requires flexibility and resourcefulness. It also requires using knowledge efficiently and understanding the rules which underlie domains of knowledge. The best mathematics instruction also leaves space for a child's mind to play with applications.

Research suggests that students' foundations (cognitive resources) for problem solving are far weaker than their performance on tests would indicate. Shoenfeld's studies suggest that even mathematically talented high school and college students (who experienced success in upper division math courses) had little or no awareness of how to use math heuristics (rules of thumb). When nonstandard problems were not put in a textbook context (oriented toward solutions), students experienced failures and ended up doing distracting calculations and trivia instead of applying the basic concepts at their disposal. Even students who received good grades frequently had serious misconceptions about mathematics (Shoenfeld, 1992). Mechanical procedures in domains where little is understood is one thing. Learning is quite another.

These difficulties with transferring knowledge from the classroom to the real world point to a major issue in the teaching of mathematics. They indicate that the substance of the subject matter we teach—the focus of nearly all of our attention in the classroom—determines only part of what our students learn. The ways that we teach mathematics and the lessons that students abstract from their experiences in doing mathematics are most important in shaping mathematical behavior.

When instruction focuses almost entirely on mastery of facts and mechanical procedures, students are not likely to develop some of the higher order skills necessary for actually using mathematics. If we want students to learn problem-solving skills, then we must focus on the development of these skills. An effective problem solver brings his or her own substantive knowledge and experience to facilitate the solution, and retrieves and applies features of situations to which the information is relevant. The Standards point out that mathematics taught in isolation leads to isolated thinking and infrequent use in real world situations. Connections between subjects and peers are central to helping children to talk and think mathematically.

CREATING MATERIALS THAT ARE ENGAGING

The math curriculum still revolves around textbooks. There is a movement underway to revise textbooks, bringing them closer to the NCTM standards. New textbooks or commercially developed CD-ROMS hold promise for engaging students, but they are only part of the answer.

Problem solving is a part of everyday experience. It starts with problem identification, proceeds to problem resolution, and involves the student in decision making. Whether it's with concrete materials or visually-intensive electronic tools, problem solving must involve students in experiences which transcend the classroom and the school. Whether it's on or off-line, the best approaches allow for productive probing of authentic situations.

There is a natural human tendency to do things that have some utility. Many students don't see the point in mastering material that is detached from the world outside of school. In school students usually do math alone–without tools (like calculators). In the world of work, they usually work together in agenda setting groups using any tools they can get their hands on. (In school, that's often called cheating.) Some on-the-job work requires solving rapidly changing problems. Specific skill training can be very limiting. Forging ahead without examining the future needs of citizens can be short-sighted and self defeating.

FACILITATING MATHEMATICAL UNDERSTANDING

Teaching is a blend of subject matter knowledge, pedagogical skill, practice, and energetic enthusiasm. When these elements come together, teaching for mathematical understanding widens young minds.

The best mathematics instruction builds on resourcefulness and creativity while leaving space for a child's mind to play. One of the best ways to remind students that mathematics deals with real world situations is to focus on problems that deal with real world applications. Most students are fascinated with the mathematical unknown, genuine problems, and complex dilemmas. Yet few recognize that decision-making, probing, debating, and conflict have anything to do with mathematics problem solving.

In solving problems it is usually not clear just what information is needed to solve a given problem–nor is it usually clear where needed information can be found. Everyday problems tend to be ill structured; even the criteria for what constitutes the "right" solution are unknown. Using current issues and practical real world examples as a focus for mathematics problems has multidisciplinary implications for all subjects. There are problems of energy depletion, population growth, food supplies, disease, warfare, agricultural production, transportation, space exploration, and trade, to name a few. It is not difficult to find newsworthy events which make use of mathematical applications.

Issues drawn from our daily existence provide avenues for getting at other curricular areas and using mathematics in a way that has real meaning. Students will soon realize that mathematics is more than a piece of information to be memorized in a textbook or captured in a procedure. The Standards, real world problems, and digital technology provide some fresh avenues for instruction.

MIXED MEDIA ACTIVITIES

Learning is enhanced by lessons that present information in multiple formats and include multisensory activities and experimental opportunities. Some of these include concrete manipulatives like geopieces, cuisinaire rods, blocks, fraction pieces, base ten blocks, popsickle sticks, chips, etc. High-tech possibilities can amplify any approach to understanding. Video, CD-ROMS, the Internet, and integrated information systems are high-tech possibilities for teaching concepts and providing practice.

1. Using Video Segments in Math Class (K-6)

Tape selected segments from a television program which deal with concepts you will teach throughout the year. Show five minute segments on specific topics—from music video on basic facts, to game show quizzes on fractions, to problem solving soap opera drama. Build on the short TV episode by adding activities, manipulatives, props, etc. Show a short video segment during your math lesson and support it with relevant activities.

2. Acting Out Word Problems (K-8)

Have students draw pictures of what the problem is about, act out the problem, or have one student read the problem leaving out the numbers. Once students begin to visualize what the problem is about, they have much less difficulty solving it.

3. Graphing with Young Children

Instruct students to bring their favorite stuffed bear to school. As a class, sort the bears in various ways: size, color, type, etc. Graph the results with the class. Have students sort the bears in another way and paste paper counters or stickers on paper to make their own personalized graph.

4. Estimating and Comparing (K-1)

Place a similar group of objects in a container for each child which are color coded. Pass out recording sheets divided into partitions with the color of the container in each box. Have young students examine the container on their desks, estimate how many objects are present, and write their guess next to the color on the sheet. Next have the child count the objects and write the number she counted next to the first number. Instruct the child to circle the greater amount. Then write a number sentence using the greater sign(>). Switch cans or move to the next station and repeat the process. A variety of objects (small plastic cats, marbles, paper clips, colored shells, etc.) add interest and are real motivaters.

5. *Performing Simple Adding and Subtracting Computations*

Use manipulatives and have students paste counters beside the numbers. Some students need to see the whole pattern, so have them place counters where the answer will go.

6. *Using Logo Programming With Young Children*

Seymour Papert developed the Logo language to teach children geometric concepts. He believes children can learn mathematical relationships more efficiently if they can project themselves into the world of mathematics. Children who can program a computer to draw a square or circle must understand the nature of a square or circle well enough to "teach" the computer. Young children are just becoming familiar with geometric shapes and the vocabulary. Using a logo program, such as "LogoWriter," the teacher can develop short procedures and program the computer so young students can see the shape immediately when they punch in the word. Here are a few sample procedures using "LogoWriter."

```
To Red Square
setc 3
repeat 4[fd 40 rt 90]
end
```

The young child simply types in the words red square and the figure appears. Because children delight in watching the figure drawn on the screen at their command, a wait command can be added so that the shape remains on the screen for a certain amount of time and then disappears so the next child can try it or they can try it again. Simple procedures like these can be modified by changing the color number (setc) to blue, yellow, green, etc. and the shape: rectangle, circle, triangle, star, or any mix of geometric ideas. Here's another procedure with a wait command added.

```
To yellow rectangle:
setc 4
```

repeat 2[fd 40 rt 90 fd 80 rt 90]
wait 60

...*g Counting Using Simple Arithmetic*

...ively simple technological tools, like calculators, allow even
...udents to "count" by pressing +1 and repeatedly pressing the
...Students quickly master the challenge by counting to 100 this
...ents may wish to count by 2's to 100 and continue the process.
...ntinue counting by 3's, it leads to the discovery that it impos-
...exactly at 100. An important question arises "which counting
...be programmed in the calculator to arrive exactly at 100?"

...*dents Generate Problems*

...ts construct their own problems on a topic of their choice.
...to use survey data, newspaper stories, or current informa-
...s one source). Encourage calculator use.

...*g Statistical Surveys and Graphing*

...ss into small groups of four or five. Have them brainstorm
...vould like to find out from the other class members (favorite
...ws, kinds of pets, etc.). Once a topic is agreed upon and
...cher, have them organize and take a survey of all of the
...emember several groups will be doing this at once so allow
...d movement.

...tics are gathered and compiled, each group must make a
...cal descriptive graph which can be posted in the classroom. Encourage
originality and creativity.

10. *Applying Column Addition*

Help students look for patterns within the addition problem such as finding a ten, grouping numbers together, multiplying numbers, or rounding up
or down. Ask students for other helpful ways to solve the problem.

11. *Learning the Nine Tables*

Use a touch approach when presenting the 9's multiplication tables. For example: 4 x 9 can be done on your fingers. Have children hold up both hands. Tell them to count 4 fingers on their left hand and fold the fourth finger down. They will have 3 fingers a space and 6 fingers, or an answer of 36. The fingers to the left side of the space are tens, the fingers to the right ones. Practise showing students a fact by using your hands and having them write the problem. Discuss why this works for 9's and find other properties of magic 9's.

12. *Dealing with Global Problem Statistics (middle school)*

Charts and graphs are visual communication forms that reveal statistical data at a glance. These visual models can help lead to a better understanding of global problems and real-world situations. Using world population statistics and calculators have students make comparisons between land size and population. Some sample activities:

1. Graph the regions by size according to population, and land size
2. Calculate how many people per square kilometer in each continent. Chart your answer.
3. Describe what you can infer about each continent by looking at these statistics.
4. Look up annual food production for a region of your choice. Write a description of how this compares to its land size and population.

13. *Collecting TV Data*

Have students survey their families' viewing habits. The survey questions could follow the same format as the Nielsen survey data. This kind of survey includes what programs are watched, what time the TV is on, how many people are watching at a time, etc. Compose the survey instrument with the class based on information they would like to find out. (A note to parents outlining the intent of the activity and the assignment is helpful.) After the students have gathered the data for a week's time, have them summarize the information. Compare such items as the average time spent watching TV for the class, most popular times for watching, most popular shows, etc. These are excellent ways to integrate charts and graphs into the technology curriculum. This kind of activity can also lead into social education and values clarification activities. Questions such as how much TV viewing is good? What other things do you give up when you spend time watching television? How much talking goes on while the TV set is on? can be explored.

Ask for volunteers to spend one week not watching television. This group must keep a record of what they did instead of watch television. Encourage volunteers to share their reactions to the experiment with the class.

14. Exploring Mathematics in the World of Work

Have students gather information about mathematics in the workplace and careers that spark their interest. Draw up a simple survey form listing occupations that students are interested in, and spaces to gather data about ways mathematics is used on the job. Have students interview workers, parents, community professionals, and friends to find out how they use mathematics, and mathematical tools in their work.

Assemble and display the data in visual form (charts, graphs, etc.). Look for patterns and comparisons. Are there generalizations that can be made? Conclusions that can be drawn?

15. Creating a Video Display of Fractal Geometry (art)

Computer Art Resource has released two videotapes of art that can be generated using fractal mathematics. This can lead to some interesting math discussions and lessons in modern geometry applications. (Computer Art Resource, P.O. Box 2069, Mill Valley, CA 94942, 415-381-4224)

16. Investigating with Raisins

Description: Students use science and mathematical data they have collected about raisins to decide the mean, median, mode, and range of each group's raisins. Statistics are used in the research to arrive at their judgment of which group has the greatest amount. Students then use this information to create a recipe book and write a brief report describing their research and making recommendations about the best raisin recipe. This investigation involves the science and mathematics concepts and skills of problem solving, communication, reasoning, making connections, number sense, computation and estimation, and statistics.

Materials: calculators, graph paper, notebook, class recording sheet
Background Information:
  Students will need to be familiar with the following statistics terms:
  mean – the average of a set of data.
  median – the middle number or the average of the middle 2 numbers
    when the set of numbers are arranged in order.
  mode – the number occurring most often in a set of data.

range – the difference between the largest and smallest number in a set of data.

sample – a segment of a population selected for study to predict characteristics of the whole.

tally – a way of recording information

Objectives:
1. Student groups of four or five will be assigned a chart to record their group's statistics and collect the statistics from every other group.
2. Groups will collect data from the class.
3. Groups will systematically collect, organize, and describe their data on a class data sheet.

Class Raisin Data Sheet:
name of group:_____
1. Estimate the number of raisins in your individual box:_____
2. Find the group estimate:
   Mean_____
   Median_____
   Mode_____
   Range_____
3. When all groups have entered their data, then the class is faced with the following statistical challenges:
   – Find the average number of raisins in the sample.
   – Determine the mode, range, median and mean for the class
4. Student groups are to explain their strategies and reasoning.
5. Last groups are to create a local newspaper advertisement with the intent of making students use raisin recipes they have just researched. Have students use the facts they have discovered to help sell their raisin cook book.
6. Students will work as a team in a powerful, organized and purposeful manner.

Evaluation:
As a group, write a report about the investigation your class just finished. Include at least one graph. The report should describe how their group collected and compiled the data, explaining the information the group included in their graph or graphs. End the report by either recommending or rejecting one of the cookbooks as the place to go for good raisin recipes. Be sure the students back their recommendation with facts from their research.

17. *Planning an Internet Lesson*

Here are some guidelines for introducing the Internet in the classroom:

1. *Choose an interesting Internet topic.* Students should be involved in the choice of the topic. A mathematics topic could be brought up and discussed by the class.

2. *Give students a chance to explore the topic on the Web.* Encourage students to use several search engines to expand the search.

3. Have students come up with a meaningful activity that explores several Web sites.

4. *Encourage students to publish their work on the Web.* This provides them with the opportunity to show their work. It builds self-esteem, is highly motivating, and increases performance.

5. *Have students use the Web for circulating information.* The Internet and the World Wide Web have become major communication tools. Together with other digital possibilities, they are dominating technologies in modern life. Anyone can publish almost anything, play games with people overseas, or use multimedia e-mail with voice, graphics, and animation.

The Internet is a hybrid of print and broadcast media. Our ability to reach out on the Web provides an abundant amount of instant information. However, rapid and continuous change make it difficult to provide a lasting picture of specific technical details. There are, for example, hundreds of Web sites for exploring mathematics. They come and go like shifting sands on the beach. But their ephemeral nature is no reason to avoid today's possibility of communicating with experts, teachers, and other students around the world.

Information and communication technologies allow us to create visual mental constructs to interpret mathematical concepts, algorithms, rules, and applications. The process requires multiple meaning-making strategies. As part of an investigative approach—such as feeling, measuring, drawing diagrams, and graphing—students can use a multitude of media to acquire sensory data, internalize meaning, generalize, and demonstrate understanding. The wide range of visual hands-on possibilities for mathematical excursions can put real excitement and meaning into mathematical learning.

Whether it's multimedia computer programs or the Internet, the eye is being brought back after centuries of mathematical banishment. A specialized code (like formulas and equations) is no longer the only avenue to mathematical thinking. Powerful technologies are gathering their potential for breathing a new enthusiasm into mathematics instruction. Mathematicians can now deal directly with three-dimensional images that simulate concrete mathematical situations as they are found in the real world.

TEACHING AND LEARNING MATHEMATICS IN TOMORROW'S SCHOOL

Mathematics is something students should do, not have done to them. Large quantities of factual material and follow-the-recipe labs can get in the way of understanding real-world applications. Fortunately, the focus of the classroom is shifting toward an emphasis on mathematical reasoning and authentic problem solving. Critical thinking, problem solving, computing, communicating, and teamwork are more important than memorization. Even in the primary grades, students can learn to describe, compare, and communicate their multiple approaches to solving real problems. In fact, developing a concrete understanding of math in the early grades lays the best foundation. A good way to learn math is by doing–and then thinking about the results. The next step is for students to figure out how what they are learning relates to the everyday things in their lives.

Figure 4.3. Innumeracy: The results of mathematical illiteracy. Computer-generated image of a design by Murray Greenfield.

There are some great ideas and wonderful innovations out there. Some teachers and some schools around the country are making all the right moves. But little overall change is happening. Isolated successes in teaching mathematics can be informative. However, a numerate citizenry requires public school teachers with the resources, professional skill, and will to do a better job of educating all of our children.

Technology will make the teaching and learning of mathematics fundamentally different in tomorrow's school. One problem is making sure that our wiz-bang inventions are employed in a manner that serves deeper mathematical understanding. Another challenge is constructing the pedagogical and curricular interfaces in a way that builds on the best of high-tech wizardry and the natural curiosity of children.

Achieving mathematical literacy in a media-intensive era depends on putting clear curriculum goals in place. Then figure out how the technology can help you reach those goals. The next step requires the creation of engaging software, networks, and materials. Whatever the mix of media tools, the numeracy building process must allow for probing, synthesis, and many opportunities to perform emerging understandings. The ultimate goal is making sure that everyone can apply the power of mathematics to decisions affecting the quality of life.

RESOURCES AND REFERENCES

Selected Principles and Standards for School Mathematics

All students should:
- understand numbers and the meaning of operations while using computation tools effectively.
- understand various types of patterns and functional relationships and use them to represent and analyze mathematical situations.
- analyze geometric characteristics, use visualization and spatial reasoning to solve problems both within and outside mathematics.
- understand and use attributes, units, and systems of measurement and apply a variety of techniques and tools for determining measurements.
- pose questions, collect, organize, represent, and interpret data to evaluate arguments and apply basic notions of chance and probability.
- focus on solving problems as part of understanding and applying a variety of strategies to build new mathematical knowledge.
- recognize reasoning and proof as essential and powerful parts of mathematics.

- express mathematical ideas clearly to others by organizing and using mathematical thinking to communicate.
- recognize, understand, and use connections among different mathematical ideas.
- create and use representations to model, organize, record, and interpret mathematical phenomena.

These are brief selections. For a full description:
Standards 2000: Principles and Standards for School Mathematics
National Council of Teachers of Mathematics. Reston, VA

Clements, D., & Sarama, J. (1997). Computers support algebraic thinking. *Teaching children mathematics 3* :320-25.

Cole, K. C. (1997). *The universe and the teacup: The mathematics of truth and beauty.* San Diego, CA: Harcourt Brace.

Hardy, G. (1940). *A mathematician's apology.* Cambridge: Cambridge University Press, p.60.

National Assessment Governing Board. (1996). *Mathematics Framework for the 1996 National Assessment of Educational Progress.* Washington, DC: The College Board.

National Council of Teachers of Mathematics. (1998). *Principles and Standards for School Mathematics: Discussion Draft.* Reston, VA: National Council of Teachers of Mathematics (NCTM). Prepared by the Standards 2000 Writing Group.[This is the revised edition of Curriculum and Evaluation Standards for School Mathematics .]

National Council of Teachers of Mathematics. (1991) *Professional Standards for Teaching Mathematics.* Reston, VA: National Council of Teachers of Mathematics (NCTM).

National Council of Teachers of Mathematics. (1989), *Curriculum and Evaluation Standards for School Mathematics.* Reston, VA: National Council of Teachers of Mathematics (NCTM).

Rojano, T. (1996). Developing algebraic aspects of problem solving within a spreadsheet environment. In *Approaches to algebra: Perspectives for research and teaching.* Netherlands: Kluwer.

Schoenfeld, A. (1992). On paradigms and methods: What do you do when the ones you know don't do what you want them to? *Journal of the Learning Sciences 2*(2) 179-214.

TIMSS International Study Center. (1997). *Third International Mathematics and Science Study* (TIMSS). Boston: Boston College.

Chapter 5

SCIENTIFIC LITERACY

The world looks so different after learning science.
For example, trees are made of air, primarily.
When they are burned, they go back to air, and in the flaming heat
is released, heat of the sun which was bound in to convert the air into tree.
And in the ash is the small remnant of the part which did not
come from air, that came from solid earth instead.
These are beautiful things, and the content of science is wonderfully full
of them. They are very inspiring, and they can be used to inspire others.
— Richard Feynman

In a world filled with the products of scientific inquiry, an understanding of scientific concepts is a necessity for everyone. The habits of the mind fostered by computer interactions is but one example of how a product of science can change everything. Using such tools to become familiar with the natural world adds a new dimension to what it means to be scientifically literate in today's world. Goals like recognizing the diversity and unity of the natural world remain the same. It's just that nature—and the approach to the subject—are being altered by technology.

We must all be mindful of the world's scientific, technological, and social changes, and we must be ready to respond to them. Understanding the important ideas of science and recognizing some of the important ways in which science, technology, and communication depend on each other helps. So does having students use the tools of science to deeply probe a manageable set of ideas in a way that allows them to experience how one thinks and acts as a scientist.

Everyone needs to use scientific information to make choices that arise every day. As the National Science Education Standards make clear, scientific rules, processes, and ways of thinking are important competencies for all students. Excellence and equity are directly linked to the call for having all students engage in scientific inquiry—describing objects, observing events, asking questions, experimenting, and constructing explanations. The next step is to test the results against current scientific knowledge.

117

Understanding and learning about the natural world can be exciting and personally fulfilling. At its best, learning science is an active process that combines hands-on learning with reasoning, considering alternative explanations, and communicating emerging ideas to others. With the help of supportive educational programs, teachers and students can form interlocking communities that focus on learning and nurturing scientific achievement. The goal of science education is to ensure that all Americans are familiar enough with basic scientific concepts and methods to allow these processes to positively influence personal interactions and social-political decision-making.

> *For a successful technology, reality must take precedence*
> *over public relations, for Nature cannot be fooled.*
> – Richard Feynman

CONNECTING SCIENTIFIC LITERACY TO DAILY LIFE

All students should have the chance to learn about science through an inquiry-based process that reflects the intellectual traditions of contemporary science. Scientific literacy must begin in the early grades when students are naturally curious about their world and eager to explore it. Science education and accompanying notions of scientific literacy have gained a stature at par with reading, writing, and arithmetic. The Science Education Standards helped. But standards is one thing, practice quite another. Whether viewed from a cultural or a practical vantage point, science is seen as something that everyone agrees is important that hasn't succeeded in getting through to the majority of our citizens.

> *Knowing is not enough; we must apply.*
> *Willing is not enough; we must do.*
> – Goethe

Science is usually portrayed to the public as the most rational of human enterprises. Yet the reasoned approach that supposedly characterizes the practice of science has had little effect on the American public. In *The Myth of Scientific Literacy*, Morris Shamos points out that in spite of all the effort, *by any reasonable measure we remain a nation of scientific illiterates* (Shamos, 1995). Fortunately, there have been a few signs of improvement over the last few years.

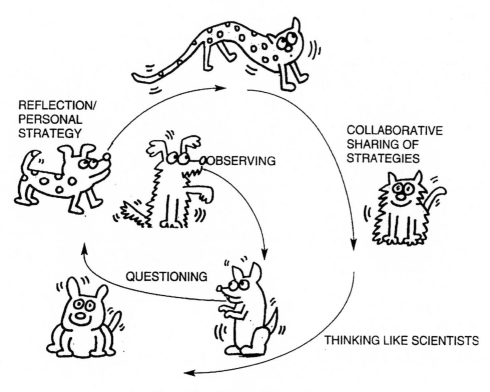

Figure 5.1. Thinking like scientists.

The new Standards have started us in the right direction. They stress the processes of science and emphasize inquiry and cognitive abilities like logic, evidence, and extending knowledge to construct explanations of natural phenomena. The Standards also reflect the principle that children can be introduced to the laws of nature through their understanding of how technological objects and systems work. This can be as low-tech as can openers or as high-tech as multimedia computers.

Ability in scientific problem-solving can be developed by firsthand experience with technological products and systems in their world. In addition, understanding the technological parallel to inquiry in science can lead to a deeper understanding of how people are involved with both. It can also lead to a more complete understanding of the role of science and technology in society and in personal life.

One of the important goals in elementary science is to provide a firm foundation for linking what students are learning in science to the activities normally pursued by children and adults outside of school. Scientific reasoning is most likely to become a lifelong skill if it is frequently applied to problems encountered in life. When early work in science offers models that are useful in future experiences then it is more likely to be taken seriously. Making what students learn in school relevant to their lives today and tomorrow has all kinds of positive consequences.

INQUIRY-BASED SCIENCE AND THOUGHTFUL QUESTIONS

The right question at the right time can move children to peaks in their thinking that result in significant steps forward and real intellectual excitement.
– Eleanor Duckworth

Scientific inquiry refers to the diverse ways in which scientists study the natural world and propose explanations based on the evidence derived from their work. Inquiry also refers to activities in which students develop knowledge and understanding of scientific ideas. This includes an understanding of how scientists study the natural world. Scientists make observations, ask questions, design investigations, gather evidence, formulate answers, and communicate the results. Inquiry at any level requires reasoning capabilities and skill in manipulating technological tools to answer the questions raised. Just as scientists do at a more advanced level, students need to base their work on knowing something about the concepts, principles, laws, and theories of the *physical, life,* and *earth* sciences.

Science can be viewed as a continuous process of trying to discover order in nature and looking for consistent patterns of the universe through systematic study. It is a way of thinking and asking questions about the workings of the universe and considering alternative explanations. *The question* is one of the cornerstones of scientific investigation. It guides the inquirer to a variety of sources revealing previously undetected patterns. These undiscovered openings can then become sources of new questions that can deepen and enhance inquiry.

Children are more likely to be open to new approaches and they have a natural curiosity when it comes to inquiring about the world. Even very young children learn by experiencing things for themselves, thinking uniquely, and communicating what they have done to others. Scientific inquiry can help children's curiosity to blossom. Questions such as "Where does wind come from?" or "Why is the kettle hot?" have been asked by children throughout history. Clearly some of their answers were wrong. But the important thing is that the children never stopped asking—they saw and wondered, and they sought an answer.

Asking Thoughtful Questions

Have you ever wondered about nature, about how things work? What questions do you want to know the answer to? One question leads to many more. Like scientists who search for knowledge, children are intrigued by the unknown and unexplained. Questioning is basic to societal and scientific progress. "Things scientists don't explain and the questions they don't raise" are usually their laments as they search for discrepancies in the work of other scientists (Martinello & Cook, 1994).

Science is still occupied with many of the questions from Aristotle's time. What makes up the universe? What constitutes matter? What and where is mind? We may now ask these questions in a more piercing way. And we may demand answers that have been rigorously tested through experiment or observation. As in the past, deeper understandings will provoke new questions we do not have yet have the knowledge to ask. In the final analysis, it is the human dimension that determines the limitations and miracles of science.

THE NATIONAL SCIENCE EDUCATION STANDARDS

Reforms in science education are coming about slowly despite recent dismal scores from the Third International Mathematics and Science Study (TIMSS, 1997) where U.S. students in eighth grade were behind at least half of the students in other developed countries. The TIMSS study unleashed an intense debate over the goals and methods of science teaching. The resulting frustration helped generate support for the science education standards. The National Science Standards were developed by the American Association for the Advancement of Sciences (AAAS) and the National Academy of Sciences. The Standards have shown to be an important point in this major reform effort. There is now general consensus on what concepts should be learned by students from kindergarten through twelveth grade. The challenge is translating these expectations into the classroom.

A broader dissemination of inquiry-based science materials and the training of teachers in how to use them is the task ahead. National reform documents are calling for more focused content and different methods of teaching than in the past. Too often, science curriculums attempt too much and are repetitive from year to year. Rodger Bybee, chair of the content working group that helped develop the National Science Standards, compares the usual school experience with science to a couch potato channel surfing on television. They don't stay tuned long enough to discover what the show is all about. Meaningful science often means that less really is more. It is usually better to focus on a few science topics and *explore them in depth* than to try to skim through the entire science curriculum. Studies have confirmed that when this approach is coupled with inquiry-based science, test scores go up. This is true even among groups that have not traditionally performed well in science (Kahle, 1997).

INTERDISCIPLINARY SCIENCE EDUCATION

When it is taught as an active hands-on subject, science can be an exciting experience for students and teachers. Science can provide many opportunities for integration with other subjects. Teachers need subject matter knowledge that is wide and deep enough to work with the current influx of second language learners and students who must face the grinding poverty found in many American cities. This often requires optimizing language and broad-based literacy development possibilities to get at content.

To use and understand science today require an awareness of how the scientific endeavor makes use of closely related domains (like language and technology) and how it relates to our culture and our lives. The best science teachers are usually those who have built up their science knowledge base *and* developed a repertoire of current pedagogical techniques. Many skilled science teachers now begin by making connections between science, communication skills, technology, and real-world concerns of the type that might be found at home or in a good newspaper. By stressing real investigations and participatory learning, teachers can move children from the concrete to the abstract to communicating with others.

Teaching strategies in standards-based science education includes plenty of participatory experiences and opportunities for students to explore science in their lives. The focus on thinking skills, work teams, and inquiry involves posing questions, making observations, reading, planning investigations, experimenting, providing explanations, and communicating the results. By working together, students can develop effective interpersonal skills as they set about critically examining data. This sometimes means designing and conducting real experiments that carry their thinking beyond the classroom. As science instruction becomes more connected to children's lives, enriching possibilities arise from inquiring about real-world concerns.

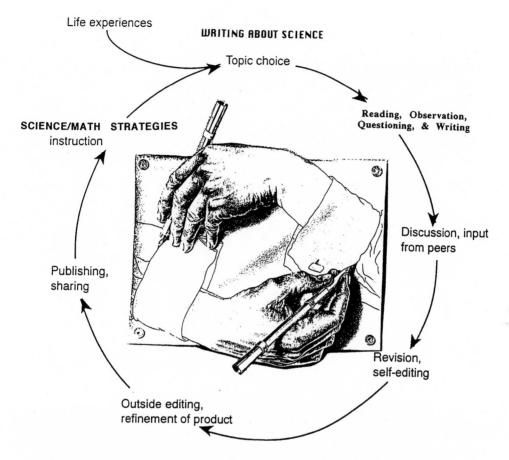

Figure 5.2. Computer composite image containing an element from M.C. Escher's Drawing Hands (1948) Michael Sachs Collection.

DEEPENING OUR UNDERSTANDING OF THE WORLD

Reports of the end of science are greatly exaggerated.
In my belief the scientific enterprise is still beginning.
— John Maddox

Science and technology have grown in importance and influence in the last fifty years. But as communications and information technology—and modern life in general—have become ever more dependent on this branch of knowledge, there is a surprisingly small number of Americans who receive significant training in the area. Even college students often fail to recognize the difference between astrology and astronomy. Scientific and technological illiteracy is a growing problem threatening the strength of the country–as well as its research capabilities, environmental quality, and the democratic process itself.

As science and technology continue to grow in significance and influence, ignorance of scientific and technological issues pushes citizens further and further from intelligent participation. Due to increased public concern about environmental problems, depleting natural resources, and the current technology explosion, the need to increase public awareness and sensitivity has become a major focus in science education. A scientifically literate public is essential to living intelligently in a society that is increasingly dependent on science and technology. Our society, our culture, and our lives are now intricately entwined and dependent upon scientific and technological knowledge. Science does its part by explaining the principles and laws that govern the natural world. Technology is the societal application of science.

To calculate the benefits and risks of modern technology–from biotechnology to future energy sources–requires at least some understanding of scientific and technological principles. Citizens must be prepared to think globally and act locally to improve the quality of life and the welfare of the world's population. Both are closely linked to science, technology, and the ability of societies to manage and use resources wisely. The world has witnessed more technological changes in the last the last 20 years than all previous recorded history. Within a single century, scientists have designed the first airplane, the first atomic bomb, the first satellite, the first space shuttle, and the first Pathfinder probe to mars. Robot spacecraft have beamed back computer-enhanced video pictures of distant planets, and genetic engineers have viewed the DNA structures on their video display terminals.

These changes are not without consequence. Medical science has helped triple the world's population since 1950. Technological tools have accelerated the depletion of natural resources and created the growth of synthetic products. Scientific laboratories have provided us with pesticides, hydrocarbons, and radioactive wastes. What happens in a lab affects each of us. The danger to a democracy, as Socrates pointed out, is "the mixture of unwise power and powerless wisdom."

Time present and time past
Are both perhaps present in time future
and time contained in time past.
–T. S. Eliot

THE CULTURAL, POLITICAL, AND ECONOMIC INFLUENCE OF SCIENCE

Scientific views of nature change over the years. For example, until this century, it was thought that time was absolute. Then it was discovered that the speed of light was the same for observers moving at different rates. This led to the theory of relativity and the dismissal of the unique absolute time concept. Surveys indicate that neither teachers, students, nor the citizenry in general were aware of this or other major scientific breakthroughs (National Assessment of Progress, 1995). Students exhibited high degrees of misunderstanding about science concepts and the application of those concepts. Many were aware of the technological offspring but not the science that fathered the whiz-bang, high-tech possibilities.

Science and technology have become increasingly important in the lives of ordinary citizens. For the average individual, awareness of the social, moral, and ethical implications of science are crucial to understanding the role of science and technology in a complex world society. The new science education standards suggest focusing more attention on the social impact of science and technology (Weld, 1999). Real progress in science is not measured by accumulating startling discoveries but by the progressive deepening of our understanding of the world and ourselves.

Today's approach to science teaching assumes that science and its products have meaning for everyone. The central belief is that science is understandable and useful for people when it is put in a meaningful and useful context. It helps if the context of scientific inquiry is a personal one that involves direct contact between learners and specific objects, events, and situations in life. Curiosity can be aroused by real-world issues, problems, and nonconformities. Approaching science with a broad awareness of the personal and social dimension of scientific understanding helps students connect abstract scientific knowledge to their own needs and concerns.

Knowledge arises from experience. This usually involves some combination of vicarious experience, collaborative inquiry, and hands-on experimentation, providing students with active involvement with science, and the application of science. Various technological tools can serve vehicles for viewing the organization, meaning, value, and beauty of science. Today's standards-based curriculum focuses on such issues and provides practice with decision making for daily living and the future of society.

Meaningful science often begins with events and objects that can be seen and studied locally. The application of scientific principles is a central focus. Technological implications are as easily understood—and misunderstood—as anything that might be labeled as "pure science." Once motivated and involved, students can be led to a consideration of deeper meaning and ideas. Deeper probing and curiosity usually follow, not meaningful personal involvement. The growth of a wider understanding of the world view of science and technology has implications for both abstract, science-based enterprises and the essence of democracy. We will all be diminished if the necessities of economics eventually enforce a social division by dividing us into islands of the trained, who understand enough to devise and operate an increasingly complex technology, within a sea of onlookers, bemused, indifferent, and even hostile.

CONSIDERING SCIENCE, TECHNOLOGY, AND SOCIETY

One of the reasons for focusing on cooperative work on real problems is to help students grow as cooperative citizens who are able to deal with the societal problems of our time. Many of the most important human changes have been brought about by the governance, practice, and foundations of science. This includes the creative, psychological, economic, and political dimensions of scientific discovery and technological innovation.

The information revolution is but one example of a significant change that was sparked by the products of science. One important result is a new type of globalization, an international system of technology and finance based on communications technology. Much of today's so-called globalization is Americanization, with mass media (from MTV to the Internet) spreading American popular culture and economic institutions. It is important to recognize the fact that some of the products of science made this all possible—and such overwhelming power is rarely benign.

Our success as modern society depends on having all citizens participate in the governance and practice of science and the control of resultant technology. Curiosity about the the products of science is stimulated by providing critical analysis, involvement, action, and the promise of improving performance in other domains. It also means having a reasonable social conscience informed by the principles of science. Increasingly, we are coming to recognize science as a discipline laden with moral and ethical dimensions that is concerned with a resolution of future societal problems.

According to the National Science Education Standards, the view that science content is simply a body of knowledge to be mastered is changing. Science teaching today means going beyond the classroom to focus on the broader impact of science and technology. Community resources (human and material) are finding their way into school science programs. Local museums, industries, hospitals, nature trails, parks, zoos, and the Internet are rapidly becoming part of the equation (National Science Education Standards, 1996).

LEARNING ABOUT SCIENCE WITH MEDIA

Teachers can capitalize on students' knowledge and experience as the structural bridges of learning. This standards-based model is influenced by a family of theories about knowledge and learning called constructivism. The basic idea is that all knowledge is not passively received. It is actively constructed by the learner as he or she comes to experience the world. Learning is a complex and recursive process of engaging in collaborative experiences, thinking about those experiences, seeing how they fit in with prior constructions, and formulating new constructions.

When technology is fully integrated into the experience of learning and teaching science the connection between the two becomes seamless. In our daily lives it has become so pervasive that we often don't notice it. Schools are next. When we think about making connections to our students we need to explore the ever changing role of technology in their lives. Still, it is children's need to use technology that really counts. For example, suppose a class was exploring the causes of different weather conditions. To research the effect of rain and snow on people, students might turn to the World Wide Web to gather weather reports. They might bring in some clips from the Weather Channel and discuss the visual imagery. In these simple examples, they are using the computer and television programming to collect data, part of the process of doing science.

Teachers are finding that there is more than one way to communicate ideas. Some students are not motivated by traditional textbook methods or lack the skills and interest necessary for content mastery in the print medium. One way to arouse curiosity is through the visual senses. Teaching that is focused on visual and concrete learning can turn attitudes around, improve basic skills, and get students involved and committed to application-oriented problem solving. Again, we suggest that it is best not to focus on technology for its own sake, rather set up a situation where it acts as a needed and useful resource.

The Internet may dominate the suburbs, but television is still the common ground of students of all backgrounds and abilities. The strength of the video message and its role in students' lives means that it must be taken seriously. Electronic media can provide visual experiences into a vast variety of scientific phenomena that are otherwise inaccessible. It has the ability to capture motion, and visually show how things work, and it can go everywhere, under the ocean, into outer space, inside a nuclear reactor, to the moon and Mars. Nothing will replace playing with a magnet, watching an egg hatch, or planting seeds, yet the ability of television and the internet to offer a wide variety of topics that intrigue a young viewer makes it an important aid in learning.

The experiences of today's students are different from those of students twenty years ago. Students have logged thousands of hours of vicarious TV and Internet explorations. They are more sophisticated, harder to amuse, and more easily bored with material less current than last night's TV news. They are less tied to books than those of previous generations. As teachers reach for ways to motivate today's science students, television and computers can be powerful allies. The TV science teacher is not new. In the 1950s, "Mr. Wizard" demonstrated the amazing facts of science to on-screen observers. Many scientists today credit their interest and curiosity about the study of science to that early video teacher "Star Trek." In the 1960s, it created a cult of viewers and sparked some interest in learning about science and technology. Students can still have a lot of fun finding out how the real world of physics stacks up against the world of any science fiction movie or TV show.

Today's science is expanding so rapidly that the time spent in science classrooms with textbooks from a few years ago seems grossly inadequate. Tomorrow's teacher will need many media to expand the learning process. With limited teaching materials, time, and teacher expertise, the Internet may be seen as an amplifier of science education as it multiplies time spent in the classroom many times over. Taping excerpts from television documentaries, NOVA, or even the evening news for inclusion in science classrooms, stimulates discussion, brings a view of science that sparks issues and debates.

An example of *some television programs* that have proven successful with teachers are:

NOVA	Wild Wild World of Animals
The Discovery Channel	Bill Nye the Science Guy
Disney Channel	On line with Doug
PBS, 60 minutes	The Weather Channel
3-2-1 Contact	Discover: The World of Science
Science & Technology Week	Wild America
Mr. Wizard's World	World of Animals
Science Documentaries	National Geographic Specials

A few Internet web sites:

Jason Project–The mission of the JASON Foundation is to excite and engage students in science and technology.
   http://www.jasonproject.org/

Amazing Insects Internet Project–Elementary school students from around the world share insect sightings. Site includes lesson plans, data collection sheets and classroom data summary forms. http:///www.minnetonka.k12mn.us/SCHOOLZ/grove/and/insect. proj/insects.html

Astronomy Village: Investigating the Universe–A multimedia curriculum resource aligned with national education reform efforts. htt://www.cotf.edu/AV/

EnviroNET: The Space Environment Information Service–Students sponsored by NASA provide a talking site with models and information on the space environment. http://envnet.gsfc.nasa.gov/

K-8 Science Teachers Networking Project–Projects, forums, labs and links from the University of Idaho. http:/radon.chem.uidaho.edu/~teachnet/

CAMCORDERS, PICTURES, AND SCIENCE EDUCATION

Another expression of visual media is having students use video cameras for visual presentations. Getting students involved in collaborative projects, researching, locating, shooting, and displaying their data in an audiovisual presentation promotes optimal learning. Involving students in projects which require visuals such as photographs, slides, or videos requires their focused attention on the subject and knowledge of the topic. Pictures must be taken for a specific purpose. This process calls for close attention to material under study. Visual literacy, the ability to comprehend nonverbal messages and create with visuals to communicate a message also comes into play. Putting on a visual presentation gets students involved with skills of classifying, ordering, personal problem solving, and collaboration.

Teachers' own slides or videos are often more interesting to students than professionally prepared ones. The thought that the teacher had the experience of being at the place where the slide was taken sharing a part of her life motivates and involves students in a personal way. Slides don't have to be shots of exotic places. Students respond positively to slides or videos taken of familiar areas. They can produce visual projects (a vacation trip, for example) and feel a sense of pride and ownership in these productions. Video, Internet, or pictorial storyboard creations require many of the same skills needed in scientific endeavors–researching, organizing, classifying, and communicating findings.

Drawing or painting pictures related to the subject of the science project is a simple but useful visual technique. Student illustrations can be reduced and copied onto acetate sheets. The sheets are then cut apart and set into slide mounts. Students have the option of creating their own designs, tracing a picture, adding color and deciding on the order and logic of the slide placement. Slide presentations offer a variety of benefits to the class and the presenter. Student interest is usually high; students stay involved and motivated. Students often experience less frustration than when using other media. Slide presentations are more flexible and easy to edit. We often use *Powerpoint* with a computer to get the same effect.

Digital is the most powerful adjective in consumer electronics today: digital television, digital camcorders, digital cameras, digital editors, digital cell phones, etc. The quality of digital photos now equals the quality of standard film camera snapshots. With digital video, you can copy over and over again without loss of signal or image fading. Editing video, text, and sound for a multimedia presentation or a multimedia report is easier than ever. But whatever technology you use, developing an understanding of nature is key to most science programs. Skills in observation, problem solving, researching, exploration, experimentation, synthesis and analysis, are all important. Given this list, it is not surprising that diverse resources and media are being harnessed to provide rich experiences in science education.

SCIENCE AND TECHNOLOGY ACTIVITIES THAT CONNECT TO THE STANDARDS

1. Using Community Resources

Museums are one way to link science and community resources. Students can play the role of curators. Working in pairs have students investigate objects such as bones, fossils, shells, etc. Have students find out all they can about the object using the full range of resources available at the museum or naturalist center.

To add an element of interest and adventure, each object can be accompanied by a fictitious but plausible scenario. In one fictional story students were told to imagine that the bone was brought to them by the FBI who expressed concern that it might be human. (The Smithsonian actually gets many such cases each year.) Students must try to determine the origin, then they are to find what animal the bone belonged to, what part of the skeleton, etc. (Chicken bones work just fine.) At the end of the activity, students return to the group and present their problem and the findings.

2. Interdisciplinary Activity: Bridge Building

This is an interdisciplinary activity which reinforces skills of communication, group process, social studies, language arts, mathematics, science, and technology.

Materials:

Lots of newspapers and masking tape, one large heavy rock, and one cardboard box. Have students bring in stacks of newspaper. You need approximately two feet of newspapers per group. Bridges are a tribute to technological efforts which employ community planning, engineering efficiency, mathematical precision, aesthetics, group effort, and construction expertise.

Procedures:
1. For the first part of this activity, divide students into three groups. Each group will be responsible for investigating one aspect of bridge building.

Group One: Research

This group is responsible for going to the library and looking up facts about bridges, collecting pictures of kinds of bridges, and bringing back information to be shared with the class.

Group Two: Aesthetics, Art, Literature

This group must discover songs, books about bridges, paintings, artwork, etc. which deals with bridges.

Group Three: Measurement, Engineering

This group must discover design techniques, blueprints, angles, and measurements, of actual bridge designs. If possible, visit a local bridge to look at the structural design, etc.

2. Each group presents their findings to the class.

The second part of this activity involves actual student bridge construction.
1. Assemble the collected stacks of newspapers, tape, the rock and the box at the front of the room. Divide the class into groups of four or five students.
2. Each group is instructed to take an even portion of newspapers to their group and two or three rolls of masking tape. Explain that the group will be responsible for building a stand-alone bridge using only the newspapers and tape. The bridge is to be constructed so that it will support the large rock and so that the box can pass underneath.

3. Each group is given three to five minutes of planning time in which they are allowed to talk and plan together. During the planning time they are not allowed to touch the newspapers and tape, but they are encouraged to pick up the rock and make estimates of how high the box is.

4. At the end of the planning time, students are given 10 to 12 minutes to build their bridge. During this time there is no talking among the group members. They may not handle the rock or the box. A few more minutes may be necessary to ensure that all groups have a chance of finishing their constructions.

Evaluation:

Stop all groups after the allotted time. Survey the bridges with the class and allow each group to try to pass the two tests for their bridge. Does the bridge support the rock and does the box fit underneath? Discuss the design of each bridge and how they compare to the bridges researched earlier.

Follow up/ Enrichment

As a follow up activity, have each group measure their bridge and design a blueprint (include angles, length and width of the bridge) so that another group could build the bridge by following this model.

3. Building Visual Models: Concept Circles

Science teachers can make use of a variety of diagrams to help students grasp important concepts, like mapping concept circles to demonstrate meaning and develop visual thinking. Have students represent their understanding of science concepts by constructing concept circles following these rules.

1. Let a circle represent any concept (plant, weather, bird, etc.).
2. Print the name of that concept inside the circle.
3. When you want to show that one concept is included within another concept, draw a smaller circle within a larger circle; for example, large circle planets, smaller circle earth.
4. To demonstrate that some elements of one concept are part of another concept, draw partially overlapping circles. Label each (water contains some minerals). The relative size of the circles can show the level of specificity for each concept. Bigger circles can be used for more general concepts, or used to represent relative amounts.
5. To show two concepts are not related, draw two separate circles and label each one (*bryophytes*–mosses, without true leaves *tracheophytes*–vascular plants with leaves, stems, and roots).

4. Active Learning: Involving Play in Art and Science

Play is important not only in the development of intelligence of children but emerges over and over as an important step in invention and discovery. Curiosity, play, following hunches is particularly important in developing one of the most valuable scientific tools—intuition.

1. Ask students to bring in materials which are cheap, durable, and safe (toys, household objects, etc.). With older students, you may want to include hammers, nails, bolts, lumber, etc.

Figure 5.3. Bicycling with science. Computer Composite image.

2. Divide students into groups of five or six. By playing with the assembled objects, have students make discoveries about the sound potential of the objects they have brought in. Using the objects available to their group, students are to design a device that makes sound. Encourage students to use a variety of objects in as many different ways as possible. When individual designs are complete, have students share their ideas with the group. The group must pick one design and work on its construction. The important thing during this noisy period of play is to explore the rich realm of possibilities before arriving at one solution.

5. Creating a Sound Garden

Ask students to imagine things they could hear in a garden, birds, the sound of the wind, leaves, human noises, etc. Discuss various ways sound could be generated in a garden, through wind, by walking, or sprinklers going, for example. Next, have students brainstorm ideas for a sound garden. Encourage creativity, fun ideas, and original inventions. Suggest inexpensive things that will hold up outdoors and will be safe for other children to play with. (Things that make sounds when walked on, when touched, etc.). Have students draw up a design for their planned construction. Then bring ideas and items from home to contribute to the project. As a group, plan and construct your sound garden based on the items. Designs may have to be altered as the class progresses on the project, enabling students to see the on-going development process as ideas progress and are adjusted to fit the materials and needs of construction. Students must determine the best way to display their sound structures so that they will be accessible to others, function well, and create the best visual display in the garden.

5. Exploring Earth's Pollution

Pollution is defined as an undesirable change in the properties of the lithosphere, hydrosphere, atmosphere, or ecosphere that can have deleterious effects on humans and other organisms. A part of the task for students is to decide what an undesirable change is, or what is undesirable to them.

Tell the students they are going to classify pollution in their neighborhood and city. The classification will be based on their senses and the different spheres of the earth–lithosphere (earth's crust), hydrosphere (earth's water), atmosphere (earth's gas), and ecosphere (the spheres in which life is formed). Give each student an observation sheet or have them design one that shows examples of pollution for a week

6. Using Video Segments to Teach

Tape short segments from science and technology programs which deal with issues and concepts in your curriculum. Excerpts from science programs like NOVA, Wild Kingdom, Science and Technology Week, 3-2-1 Contact, or even the Weather Channel and the evening news offer a wealth of material. Design short projects based on these segments. An endangered species mural, a chart of weather patterns for the country, a computer newsletter, an audiotaped radio news release, etc. Students are great at coming up with their own projects, especially once you have sparked their interest on a topic.

7. Using the Newspaper to Teach About Science and Technology

Major newspapers, like *The New York Times* and *The Washington Post* have weekly science and technology sections. Select a list of significant terms from the lead stories, pass out the papers or photocopies of the articles, and have students construct science fiction stories with the words and ideas from the feature science news page.

8. Experimenting With the Unintended Consequences of Technology:

SOAP DROPS DERBY: Students will develop an understanding that technological solutions to problems, such as phosphate-containing detergents, have intended benefits and may have unintended consequences.

Objective: Students apply their knowledge of surface tension. This experiment shows how water acts like it has a stretchy skin because water molecules are strongly attracted to each other. Students will also be able to watch how soap molecules squeeze between the water molecules, pushing them apart and reducing the water's surface tension.

Background information: Milk, which is mostly water has surface tension. When the surface of milk is touched with a drop of soap, the surface tension of the milk is reduced at that spot. Since the surface tension of the milk at the soapy spot is much weaker than it is in the rest of the milk, the water molecules elsewhere in the bowl pull water molecules away from the soapy spot. The movement of the food coloring reveals these currents in the milk.

Grouping: Divide class into groups of four or five students.

Materials: milk (only whole or 2 percent will work), newspapers, a shallow container, food coloring, dish washing soap, a saucer or a plastic lid, toothpicks.

Procedures:
1. Take the milk out of the refrigerator 1/2 hour before the experiment starts.
2. Place the dish on the newspaper and pour about 1/2 inch of milk into the dish.
3. Let the milk sit for a minute or two.
4. Near the side of the dish, put one drop of food coloring in the milk. Place a few colored drops in a pattern around the dish. What happened?
5. Pour some dish washing soap into the plastic lid. Dip the end of the toothpick into the soap, and touch it to the center of the milk. What happened?
6. Dip the toothpick into the soap again, and touch it to a blob of color. What happened?
7. Rub soap over the bottom half of a food coloring bottle. Stand the bottle in the middle of the dish. What happened?
8. The colors can move for about 20 minutes when students keep dipping the toothpick into the soap and touching the colored drops.

Follow-up Evaluation: Students will discuss their findings and share their outcomes with other groups.

9. Leaving Room for Serendipity

Science activities often have surprising results. For example: try a simple activity that uses a ping-pong ball and a funnel to demonstrate pressure. Show the class a ping-pong ball inside a funnel. Set up the problem. Ask how far students think the ping-pong ball will go when they blow into the funnel. What happens? Students will soon discover as they blow into the funnel, the ball doesn't move. They are proving Bernoulli's principle that when air moves faster across the top surface of a material, the pressure of the air pushing down on the top surface is smaller than the pressure of the air pushing up on the bottom surface. Here there are many variations of the "right answer."

MIXING METAPHORS AND DISCIPLINES

Science is focusing more on science as a human endeavor with aesthetic and social implications Precision and search for truth may not mean much online, but it has always been central to science and the arts. Science and its technological associates are building on a broad base of the humanities. In fact, many of the liberal arts disciplines have always built on the technology of their time. The same trend is evident today.

In the future, digital technologies will allow for a wider range of sensory input and output, with virtual reality going hand-in-hand with our humanness. The fact that there is a renaissance in art, music, and dance at the same time as high technology becomes the dominant force in our economy is not simply coincidence. Advances in technology have resulted in a high-touch cycle of reactions that push our machines to take on more of our human characteristics.

Today's technology is changing the way we think about ourselves. Computational interpretations of the mind could conceivably encourage us to think more clearly about the process of cognitive functioning. More often than not, it reaches to the ridiculous. Input and output a problem? How much downtime do you have? Are you off line today? The computer metaphor is even used for describing dreams. And "clearing the program" is what happens during sleep.

Even human illness has become a metaphor for some of the products of scientific inquiry. Biological illusions are a reminder that the explosive growth of computers and the Internet has certain parallels to natural systems. Recently we received an E-mail message from the university computer center. It read: "A worm hit our computers last week. We managed to hunt it down and kill it. But be on the lookout for a new macro-spamming microvirus—remember, computational ecosystems that are globally cross-linked are vulnerable because there is an ominous trend towards programs that mimic pestilence in the physical world." Perhaps cybernetic plagues are just the price we have to pay for having the adaptable technological tools we need to function in this new networked world.

Beyond new centers for disease control, future communication technologies will require a wide range of thinking and emotional skills, going well beyond the narrow range of linguistic and mathematical skills we are now teaching. The imaginative processing of visual, artistic, musical, movement and interpersonal skills will create interesting technological synergies. The rich media mix that will come from the synthesis of human and machine interaction will add an interesting set of possibilities.

THE SOCIAL IMPLICATIONS OF SCIENCE, ART, AND TECHNOLOGY

Creative expression is a basic human need that each culture expresses through its available technology. Some cultures see the visual arts as a form of meditation that brings out the vitality and beauty of the universe. Others see it as a precious heritage—a way that reveals to ourselves (and others) the inner vision that guides the whole enterprise. Art in all cultures uses gestures and symbols to help people take part in a universal search for meaning and expression. In America, the mass audience has made several brands of visual art (particularly video) a part of everyday life. The potential that new technology holds for producing and assisting in both visual and print literacy is partly understood. However, the relationship of computer-controlled visual images to the traditional visual arts and print literacy has yet to be explored.

Artists are using technology to explore new ways of relating to images and print. Nancy Burson, for example, has used computer controlled technology to combine the faces of five models into one "ideal" face and a computer-based image warping system to produce a single androgynous image of two nudes, one male, one female. The same artist has fed models of the aging process into the computer system—making it possible to project how a person or place might look a decade earlier or later. The most ubiquitous presenter of information, the video screen, is influencing how people see even the most human of artistic images. The way we see the human image is changing, as it did in the nineteenth century. As artists are trained via the video image, it changes how people are drawn and painted. Artists see the way they are trained to see and people look different on the video screen.

Just as technology is being used to teach art, art is being used to teach technology and science—whether through three-dimensional graphics, problem solving, or whatever. There are a number of ways to access print, art, and science through laser videodisc computer interface. Whole art museums can be toured in the classroom or students can interact with real astronauts on the moon. The technology allows us to amplify both art and science. Various computer controlled interfaces allow for different degrees of image interaction. Computer generated text and graphics can be overlaid onto the videodisc output. This allows print and graphics to be keyed over realistic video images of art and science. These round interactive picture books allow students access to hundreds of thousands of realistic images, from a universe many of them might not ever see or experience. Demonstrating the tie between art and science, a computer enhanced video image of the rings of Saturn recently won the American photography award as best art/picture of the year. Taking this computer controlled technology and matching it to the child's learning style makes learning about the outside world more efficient. Media literacy requires the linking of technology and the humanities to produce meaning.

*Science and art let us get outside ourselves;
instead of seeing only one world, our own, we see it under multiple forms,
and as many as there are original scientists and artists,
just so many worlds do we have at our disposal.*
—Marcel Proust

THE FUTURE OF SCIENCE AND ITS TECHNOLOGICAL PRODUCTS

Knowledge of science can nurture creativity and deepen our understanding of the world. Science teaches us to ask ourselves: *Is there a better way to do it.* Few scientific or technical problems exist without their aesthetic, moral, economic, or social components. The combination of powerful intellectual tools are the most valuable things to be learned, whether coming from the humanities or science. Digital technology can help because it enables us to visually take possession of scientific abstractions. Aesthetics, analog, and metaphor, the scientific method and media literacy are all intellectual tools that will be essential to the sharpening of analytical and perceptual skills in the future.

Science and its technological offspring can be viewed as socially significant adventures inspired by curiosity about the universe. You never know what might turn up. The Internet started as a communication tool for scientists. The much more effective Internet II will put science and educational institutions back in the drivers seat. For most Americans, the garden variety first version will continue to change how people learn, work, shop, invest, and communicate. As this tool of science becomes the nervous system of our our society, it is important to recognize the fact that we are dealing with a new medium. The Internet is only one example of how multimedia literacies will influence the transmission of values, the modeling of roles, and the mastery of scientific disciplines. Like many scientific creations that sneak up on us, it would be myopic to ignore any of the enormous technological changes that will affect science education and schooling in the years to come.

Science is a way to figure out how something gets known and the extent to which things are known. Becoming scientifically literate means understanding rules of evidence, handling uncertainty, using technological tools, and thinking about things so that judgments can be made. In learning science you learn to handle trial and error and you develop a spirit of invention and free inquiry. All of this is of tremendous value far beyond science.

Will science and technology, as Descartes suggested, "make man the master and possessor of nature"? Or is Bacon closer to the mark when he wrote that "the goal of scientific tools should be to ease man's estate"?

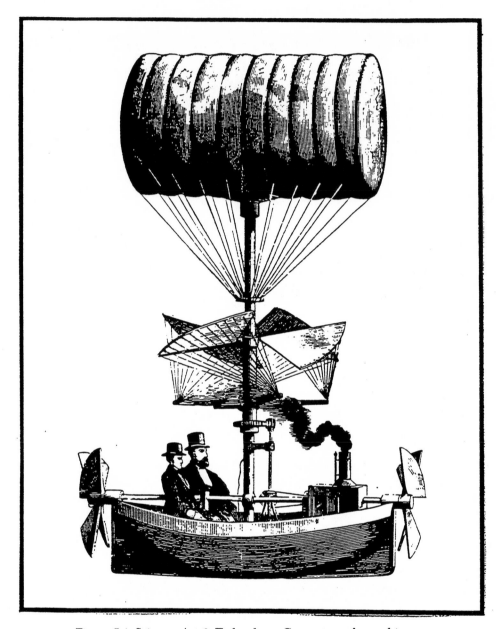

Figure 5.4. Science, Art & Technology. Computer enhanced image.

RESOURCES AND REFERENCES

National Science Education Standards

Principles
- Science is for all students.
- Learning science is an active process.
- School science reflects the intellectual and cultural traditions of contemporary science.

Selected Overview of the Science Curriculum Content Standards
- Students should understand the unifying concepts and processes in science.
- All students should become familiar with modes of science inquiry.
- Students should know and use science subject matter: physical, life and earth/space sciences.
- Students should understand the relationship of science and technology and make connections between them.
- Students need the opportunity to understand and practice science in a personal and social perspective.
- Students should identify with the history and nature of science.

Bybee, R., & DeBoer, G. E. (1994). Research on goals for the science curriculum. In D, Gable (Ed). *Handbook of research in science teaching and learning.* New York: Macmillan.

Bybee, R. (1998). *Reforming science education: Social perspectives and personal reflections.* New York: Teachers College Press.

Duckworth, E. (1987). *The having of wonderful ideas and other essays on teaching and learning.* New York: Teachers College Press.

Kahle, J. B. (1997). Systemic reform: Challenges and changes. *Science Educator, 6*(1) Spring 1997 1-6.

Kuhn, T. (1962). *The structure of scientific revolutions.* Chicago: University of Chicago Press.

Maddox, J. (1998). *What remains to be discovered?* New York: The Free Press.

Martinello, M., & Cook, G. (1994). *Interdisciplinary inquiry in teaching and learning.* New York: Macmillan.

National Assessment of Educational Progress. (1995). Washington, DC: US Publications.

National Science Education Standards. (1996). *National Science Education Standards.* Washington, DC: National Academy Press.

National Science Teachers Association.(1982). *NSTA Position Statement On School Science Education for the 1980s.* Washington, DC:NSTA.

Shamps, M. (1995). *The myth of scientific literacy.* New Brunswick, NJ: Rutgers University Press.

TIMSS International Study Center. (1997). *Third International Mathematics and Science Study (TIMSS)*. Boston: Boston College.

Weld, J. (1999). Achieving equitable science education: It isn't rocket science. *Phi Delta Kappan, 80*(10), 756-58.

Chapter 6

AESTHETIC LITERACY
Dance, Music, Theatre, and the Visual Arts

Because meaning is at the core of literacy, we can (and I believe we ought to)
conceive of literacy in terms broader than is customary. Literacy can be
conceived of as the ability to decode or encode meaning in any of the
social or aesthetic forms through which meaning is conveyed.
— Elliot Eisner

Aesthetics is the branch of philosophical inquiry in which we address beauty, culture, and what we know about the significance and meaning of artworks. Appreciating the sensations and emotions evoked by dance, music, theatre, and the visual arts are keys to aesthetic literacy. This includes being familiar with an array of knowledge and skills in each medium. Creation, performance, production, criticism, history, and technology are all part of the mix. Achieving competence in the arts involves having capabilities with artistic elements and understanding of their interdependence. This includes the ability to combine the content, perspectives, and techniques to achieve specific artistic and analytical goals.

The arts may well be the oldest human information and communication technology. Cave paintings are but one example. For all of recorded history people used the arts to get in touch with concepts, spirits, themselves, and other people. The arts have served to connect our imaginations to the deepest questions of human existence. In many respects, they have been everyone's first language. Around the planet educators have long recognized the arts as central to literacy, understanding, and functioning in today's world. The arts can change people's minds and show them what it means to be alive. Without dance, music, theatre, and the visual arts, education would be an impoverished enterprise.

Like the scientist, the artist moves between two worlds. On the one side, there are thoughts, beliefs, and imagination. On the other side is the media and materials available for fashioning works of art. Success in any art form requires both clever ideas *and* mastery of the medium. Art without imagination is sterile; art without technical skill is bound to abort its image. Like any serious subject, it requires imagination in the medium being used.

143

The skills of literacy operate within the social and aesthetic contexts within which people receive and send messages. Recognizing the connections between students' experience with mass media and the essential themes of the arts can be energizing. The same can be said for connecting to a world in which media and technology play a major role.

STANDARDS AS AN ADVOCATE FOR ARTS EDUCATION

The artist is the antennae of a nation.
— Ezra Pound

The *National Standards for Arts Education* spell out what every young American should know and be able to do in the arts. They suggest that the arts can challenge educational passivity and play a major role in the education of children. National identity has always been connected to the arts. European countries, for example, see the arts much like a public utility that is worthy of significant financial support. France now has the equivalent of five billion dollars in the federal budget for the arts. Even in the most difficult of times, Germany supports art galleries, dance troupes, theatrical productions, school programs, and symphony orchestras in its larger towns and small cities. With parents, teachers, and the rest of the community so involved, it is little wonder that arts education shines. From Europe to Asia, informed encounters with the arts has long gone hand in hand with enlightened literacy.

The best American dance groups, orchestras, theater, and visual arts are as good as anything found anywhere. The problem here is that there are fewer of them and they do not connect to a significant percentage of the general population. American popular culture rules the day here and corrodes the edges of culture elsewhere. A high quality arts education program is needed as a balance. A major goal of the *National Standards for Arts Education* is to elevate cultural understanding in this country and contribute to the imaginative life of the nation.

When the Goals 2000: Educate America Act was passed in 1994, the arts were identified as one of the core content areas in which students should show competency at grades 4, 8, and 12. Testing in the arts makes use of performance exercises to measure student ability in dance, music, theatre, and the visual arts. For example, students might be asked to use a computer to rearrange a piece of music. A performance assessment example in theater would be asking students to identify elements of a scene, assume characters, and act out a scene from a story. Sample question: "What would you change in the characters if you could restructure the scene and do it again?" Other items would assess the student's ability to perform, create, and critique various art forms.

Encouraged by Goals 2000, the U.S. Office of Education initiated the federal government's first written prescription for reversing the decline of instruction in the visual arts, dance, drama, and music. The result was the *National Standards for Education in the Arts.* This publication suggests, among other things, that the knowledge and practice of the arts is fundamental to the healthy development of children's minds and spirits (National Standards for Education in the Arts, 1994).

The Standards build on many sources, including Howard Gardner's theory of multiple intelligences, to suggest how the arts can incorporate the whole range of "intelligences" to reach students and therefore more comprehensively teach students. The Goals 2000 report makes it clear that there is a strong relationship between the quality of education and the quality of arts instruction. The best schools usually have the best arts program, and in the weakest schools, programs have often been weak or nonexistent.

Can the national standards for arts education make a difference? To begin with, the process itself requires educators to think about priorities in arts education. Second, setting standards in the arts can help combat the idea that the arts are "soft" and expendable. They give a level of accountability and demonstrate that knowledge and skills in the arts matter, countering the widespread idea that the arts don't contribute to a child's "real" education. Standards also support the notion that the arts present a range of alternate paths to learning so that the uniqueness of each child can be attended to. The arts can also help connect the mind and the senses, uniting the cognitive and affective dimensions of learning. Finally, national standards serve as an advocate for arts education, acting as a lever on public awareness and a stimulus to teacher training.

Encounters with the arts are crucial to pursuing a curriculum that releases the young to pose their own questions and look for solutions. Skills associated with learning about the arts include that elementary school children should be able to understand how to use symbols in visual art, that middle school students should be able to master harmony and improvisation, and that older students should be able to analyze cultural influences in dramatic works. As the new national standards make clear, the arts are not cut-out turkeys, color-the-numbers, or connect-the-dots bunny rabbits. *The arts are serious disciplines.*

Figure 6.1. Computer enhanced image.

We depend on the arts to remind us of who we are, what we are, what we can become, what we're becoming...they are essential to us as humans.

– Gish Jen

A BRIEF OVERVIEW OF ARTS EDUCATION

*Understanding the relationships between the various art forms
and other disciplines is part of aesthetic literacy.*

Movement Elements and Skills in Dance

Dance education begins with an awareness of the movement of the body and its creative potential. Along with basic movement, students learn choreographic skills in musical and rhythmic contexts. As they progress, students can do Internet searches for the likes of Isadora Duncan, Martha Graham, and dance steps from other cultures. As they learn and share dances from around the world, they can gain knowledge that will help them deal with diverse cultures.

To move towards production, students can work out some expressive movement with a partner or two. As they learn to use elements of time, space, force, and energy, they can work out a short dance that demonstrates moving to a musical beat and changing movements as the tempo changes. Kinesthetic awareness, concentration, and focus are major goals. Larger groups can observe and describe the movement elements and tell what they like–and one thing that might make it better.

Children enjoy moving and learning through bodily-kinesthetic engagement. As they become literate in the language of dance, they can use their bodies as a means of self-expression and communication. If 80 percent of human communication is nonverbal, interpreting the kinesthetic expression of others is a crucial skill. Whatever the percentages, dancing and creating dances provide students with the understandings necessary for future learning in dance–and give them a way to celebrate their humanity through movement.

Creating, Performing, Listening to, and Analyzing Music

It is painful to admit that the icons of MTV carry vastly greater cultural resonances for most of our students than even the most revered masters of musical history. Putting music squarely in the domain of learning opens doors to a deep understanding of and response to the full range of music. By singing, playing instruments, and composing, students can express themselves creatively and learn how music enriches their environment. Using musical instruments can help students learn how to improvise melodies and read music. Working alone and with others allows students to cover a varied repertoire of music. What they can do together today, they can do alone tomorrow.

There are many computer programs that are particularly helpful for composition and exploring music from a broad cultural and historical perspective. Skills in analysis, evaluation, and synthesis are important because they enable students to recognize and pursue musical experiences. Practice evaluating the aesthetic qualities of music and musical performances help students figure out what makes a work of music interesting, unique, and expressive. The home and school environments are enriched when students learn to listen with understanding. And life-long musical appreciation is enhanced when we can all apply the skills, knowledge, and habits of the mind acquired through the study of music.

Theatre and the Content of Drama

Creative drama often cuts across the curriculum and sometimes takes up residence in the language arts. Theatre is the imagined world of human beings. It can serve as a way for children to learn about academics and about life. Through their social pretend play, children can learn how to make sense of the world at an early age. By interacting with peers, they can bring their stories together and respond to the creative drama of others. They arrive at school with thousands of hours of time logged watching television and film. Their experience with media at home strongly influences the ability of upper grade students to integrate various aspects of the art form: script writing, acting, designing, directing, and critiquing.

Teachers help by setting up the environment and coaching students to select movement, music, and visual elements to enhance the mood of classroom dramatization. In the early grades, there is usually no memorization of lines, few props, group support, and short skits. Older students can compare how visual, aural, and kinetic elements come together to express emotions and ideas. Memorization of lines and long plays are counterproductive. An example of creative drama: doing their own advertisement for a product might contain only sixty seconds of action, or after sharing life experiences for sixty seconds per child, students can pick out one for a brief skit. (Older students might pick their ideal actors and director.) The teacher can clap their hands to start and stop the action. Camcorders can record the skits. If the results are good enough, it can probably be run on your local cable company's public access channel—or put out on the Internet.

Fluency in the Visual Arts

The visual arts range from painting, sculpture, drawing, and graphic design—to the folk arts, architecture, film, and video. All of these visual tools, techniques, and processes can be used as the basis for critical analysis, cultural investigations, and creative activity. Looking at art is like having a conversation. Art can powerfully visualize and textualize your experience with the world. It allows you take in an emotion in a new way and let go of what you're used to. A major goal of art education is to help students become willing and intelligent viewers, listeners, producers, and thinkers about art in all of its manifestations.

All students can develop enough sensitivity and knowledge to perceive that something is art. To become functioning adults in a technology-mediated society, children need to be able to distinguish among different media forms and know how to ask basic questions about them. One approach to aesthetic criticism involves coming up with answers to questions such as: What beliefs are behind this work? What is being expressed? What does it imply about the world? What is being omitted from the message? If it doesn't sensitize us to something in the world, clarify our perceptions, or make us aware of the decisions we have made, it's entertainment, not art.

Discussing their own art with peers and teachers can help students think critically about art and its relationship to the world. Besides help in choosing a range of subject matter, symbols, and ideas, teachers can help students relate their understandings to the visual world in which they live. However, the conversation has to go beyond counterproductive gratuitous praise to an informed discussion of aesthetic character and qualities. Have the techniques and processes been executed with sufficient skill, confidence, and sensitivity to carry out their intention? Along the path of self and peer evaluation, students can reflect on nature of human involvement in art as viewer, creator, and participant.

TEACHING THE ARTS IN TOMORROW'S SCHOOLS

The arts and all their related subtlety are being woven into the national vision of education in tomorrow's schools. Our personal, social, economic, and cultural lives are shaped by the arts—from the songs on the car radio, to TV drama, to a Saturday dance, to the enduring influence of the classics. Arts education can make us intelligent consumers by cultivating the whole child—building many kinds of literacy while developing imagination and dexterity with many kinds of media.

By studying the arts children stimulate their natural curiosity and learn to learn in situations where there is no standard answer. However, subtlety, intelligent decision making, and ambiguity do not play to the strength of our adolescent culture. Yet it is in the "vague" where creative things and a great deal of important decision making happens. As William James said, "We need to restore the vague to its proper place in our mental life." This is unsettling for some, but if you provide too much structure for your students, they will miss the chance to learn many critical thinking and collaborative skills. Clearly outlining exactly how something should be done can also interfere with transferring what is learned to new situations. An exaggerated structure actually prevents students from learning the important intellectual tools of *subtlety, imagination,* and *insight.* All three are at the heart of most subject matter.

Suggestion: Have students practise the following reading in pairs. Each one reads it once and gets some praise—plus suggestions. The next step is to change the stress, volume, pause point, and expression for a second reading.

Don't tell people how to do something.
Tell them what to do and they will surprise you with their ingenuity.

Although quality programs in the arts come in a wide variety of shapes, the research suggests the following as common keys to success:
  • An integrated arts program throughout the curriculum—at all age levels.
  • Regular arts classes of comparable length to other academic disciplines with art specialists to enhance the curriculum.
  • Effective teacher training and professional development in the arts.
  • Artists involved as teachers, coordinators, or as resources for arts specialists and non-arts teachers.
  • Inclusive arts education that makes sure that all students have a chance to study and practise the arts.
  • Involvement by the community, business, and local arts organizations in helping students learn about the arts.
  • Regular assessment and evaluation to determine what works best in arts education.

For the teacher, the arts are a vehicle for teaching critical thinking and collaborative skills across the curriculum. The Standards have helped schools take a significant step toward ensuring the study and practice of dance, music, theatre, and the visual arts. Now it will be left to the educational community to make it happen.

CONNECTING TO THE GLOBAL COMMUNITY
AND TO OTHER SUBJECTS

How do the arts fit into a shared vision of American culture and schooling? Dance, music, theater, and the visual arts transcend language barriers and have long served the dual function of building common values and a respect for diversity. From Puerto Rican *Nyorican* poems to Asian music, the very attributes of the arts can give them a credibility in creating a sense of shared public space across subcultures. As one of the great civilizing aspects of human nature, the arts give human dimension to our society.

Artists around the world use symbols in ways that create thought and feeling and you cannot comprehend the symbolism without some education in the arts. From the media and architecture to fashion and advertising, the arts are basic to human expression and understanding the world around us. Schools can get a boost for arts education by connecting to the resources of that world. For example, you can tour the Louvre on the Internet. And by reaching into the schools and into the community, the arts can play a major role in providing a solid foundation for our future as a democratic society.

Experience has shown that the arts have a potential for engaging all students and connecting to a variety of curriculum areas. For example, geometry can be studied through the graphic and visual arts. To connect music and science, teachers can have students write a jingle about the human skeleton or compose a song for an endangered species. The circulatory system can be explored through a dance performance and choreography. Students could also write some songs or poems that practise moving as the song is sung or as the poem is read. Thus the arts can reach across learning modalities, subjects, and cultures, providing tools for interdisciplinary dialogue and connecting the emotions with discipline in a manner that is essential to developing a full and empowering literacy and numeracy.

The arts attend to the human spirit in a manner often missed by other subjects. They provide a way of understanding the world and are valid in helping us tell stories and develop a critical aesthetic. The arts can also teach divergent and convergent thinking. Along with these thinking skills, they show that there are many "right" answers. As in the real world, in the arts, there is rarely one way to do a problem. Education in the arts encourages skills needed for tomorrow's workplace: vision, imagination, critical thinking, persistence, and a deeper appreciation of who we are as individuals and as a society. Far from being viewed as an expendable luxury, national goals and standards place the arts at the center, keeping America competitive, creative, and civilized.

MULTIPLE PATHS TO KNOWLEDGE

The National Standards for Teaching the Arts are beginning to influence other subjects and general curriculum writing at state and local levels. The

Standards hold exciting promise for helping teachers reshape the arts curriculum and how it is taught. Emphasized at each grade level are communication through arts disciplines, arts performance, analysis of artworks, growing awareness of exemplary works, and the ability to connect art knowledge across disciplines. These emphases, as well as the other content-specific standards, are briefly highlighted in the activities that follow.

1. ***Spatial/Visual Arts*** (Standard 2: Communication)
   After reproductions of paintings, sculptures, or drawings are made made available to students, thinking can be generated by asking questions like the following
   • Which painting really speaks to you and what does it say?
   • What in your own life reminds you a little of the painting?
   • What people, places, and things does it bring to mind?
   Write down some words and phrases that explain some of your feelings about the art. This work might start out in pairs and later be   shared in small groups or with the whole class. Obviously students need enough background in art to know what to recognize and what to ignore.

2. ***Music and Beginning Literacy*** (Standard 2: Communication)
   • Find a song that your children like that contains words with rhyme, rhythm, and repetition.
   • Link the words to print by writing the lyrics on a song chart. Lead the group in singing the song one phrase at a time, and help the children sound out words.
   • See if musical notes can be matched with syllables to build the rhythm (you can use the old bouncing ball of community singing). Encourage the creation of new lyrics by matching new words that have the right number of syllables to the rhythmic structure of the song.
   • For children in grades 2 and up, you can introduce the concept of ascending and descending melody by directing singing with up or down hand motions.
   • Students can also explore the similarities between composers, writing notes on a staff for singers and authors writing words for readers.

3. ***Linguistic Patterns and Intrapersonal Connections:*** (Standard 1: Communicate in four arts disciplines; Standard 2: Communicate proficiently in at least one art form; Standard 5: Be able to relate various types of arts knowledge and skills across the arts disciplines)
   • Whether it is exhilarating or disturbing, art can be enlightening giving us insight into humanity and self-understanding. Older students, for

example, might view a videotape of Hamlet's "Alas poor Yorick" speech to gain insight into human foibles.

• Students could read the Langston Hughes poem *The Dream Keeper* and rewrite the poem using the best dream (or daydream) they have ever had. Poems can be read in pairs, alternating the reading of lines.

Dreams and Creative Drama: Give students overnight to come up with a dream from anytime in their life. For those few who cannot remember their dreams a daydream will do. Students can bring in their own dream and tell it to their small cooperative group. After each student has shared a dream or a daydream, the group picks one dream that can involve everybody in a 60-second bit of creative drama. After some minutes of practice, each group can put their skit on for the class, and the whole class guesses whose dream it is. Next, the "dreamer" explains the dream to the class. Remember that it is best that you not try to interpret the dreams, because it ensures misinterpretations and inhibits the children.

4. *Dancing to poetry:* To create a magical atmosphere with dance and poetry, darken the classroom and allow two students to use a flashlight to alternate in reading the lines of the poem. It works just as well to have one student read loudly. As the poem is being read, four or five students use penlights to move to the poem. It obviously helps if the poem lends itself to active movement. If it is dark, and there are strobe lights available near the school stage, the flashing adds a stunning effect. If you cannot get a darkened room, you can choreograph the dancing to poetry with long silk scarfs or long ribbons like those used with movement during the Olympic games. Small groups need to practice their routine for 15 or 20 minutes. After the choreography has been worked out the group performs for the entire class. In order for the audience get the full effect, you may want to run it by them twice. Three examples that worked well for us: *Eel-Grass* by Edna St. Vincent Millay, *Fireworks* by James Reeves, and *Engine on the Track*.

Engine on the Track
Klickety-klick, klickety-klack,
Klickety-klick, klickety-klack,
Whoo-whoo, engine on the track,
Klickety-klick, klickety-klack,
Hey, hey! Stand back!
Whoo-whoo, engine on the track,
Klickety-klick, klickety klack
Klickety-klickety, klack, klickety, klickety klack
Whoo-whoo, engine on the track!

Encourage students to pretend to be the Engine on the Track as they move their hands and arms in circles as they read the poem.

Shorter poems may have to be read twice through for full effect.

5. ***Music, Dance, Performance Art, and Drama*** (Standard 1: Communicate in four arts disciplines; Standard 2: Communicate proficiently in at least one art form; Standard 5: Be able to relate various types of arts knowledge and skills across the arts disciplines).

Movement Activity: This experience is designed for younger students. It draws on students' creative imaginations. Movement plays a major role. Play some soft music. Explain to students that you are going on an imaginary journey. Have students imagine what it is like at the end of the winter season. Ask questions about their image. What does it look like around you? What does it feel like? Now imagine that you are a seed buried under the snow. You start to sense the light. You begin to feel the warmth of the sun. You feel the hard earth around you loosening up.

You begin to stretch yourself inside the seed. The sun beats down more intensely. You like the warm feeling. After awhile, you hear raindrops falling above you. Pitter-patter, pitter-patter, pitter-patter. You feel scared. You notice that your seed shell is getting softer. You stretch again. This time you begin to feel more room inside the shell. You start to wiggle. You wiggle so much that the seed begins to pop open.

You recognize your roots wiggling out of the seed. The ground feels so good. It feels warm. You sense the warmness, the brightness. You feel yourself stretching and growing under the ground. You keep on stretching. It feels wonderful.

And quite suddenly you are blinded. You notice that you've developed tiny sprouts, and the sun is hitting these small sprouts. Oh no, it's raining again! It feels great. You're not at all scared. You feel yourself expanding, stretching, growing. Your tiny sprouts are sprouts no more. Instead they have changed and grown into leaves. You hear them rustle in the wind. You feel them absorbing the raindrops. Other things are changing too.

You feel very alive. You keep stretching and growing. Suddenly your leaves pop open to reveal a tiny bud hiding underneath. The bud slowly starts to open. Move and show how you feel. You are now a beautiful soft yellow flower. You feel happy and proud. You dance to the wind. The sun and rain don't bother you at all. But over time you're still growing and stretching. Act out the photosynthesis process. Pretend your feet are roots, and burrow your roots deep into the soil. Stretch your arms wide, and pretend they have leaves to gather the sun and rain.

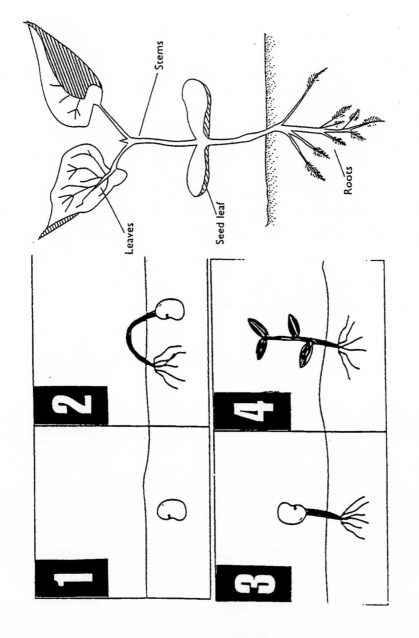

Figure 6.2. Using your imagination: Pretend you are a seed. Dance performance art and drama (life cycle of a seed) [Think of this as a science storyboard]

Next, you begin simulating that you are drinking through a straw, modeling the plant drinking. Your soft yellow flower eventually turns white and feels lighter. They've turned into seeds. The wind is blowing harder now. It sets the seeds free and blows them away. The seeds scatter. They dance, and dance, and dance and finally drop back down to earth. You'll begin your journey yet again another day.

At the end of this performance students explain their feelings, explaining how they changed, and end with an art activity like movement and drama. Encourage students to reenact some of the scenes for the class. Did anyone do it differently? Students may wish to hear it again, moving differently. Children may wish to draw a picture, paint, write a story or poem, keep a dialogue journal, make up a song, or write a play that captures the experience.

MAKING EDUCATION IN THE ARTS HAPPEN

High quality arts education programs don't just happen; they require broad-based and sustained support. Unless the arts are specifically included in a state's education goals and curriculum content laws, then most students and teachers will not come to recognize the integral role of the arts as a vehicle of human expression, communication, and cultural identity. America needs more than standardized answers in a world that increasingly demands critical thinking and creative analysis. The arts teach students divergent thinking, craftsmanship, and the notion that there are many paths for solving a problem. The Standards in arts education can be viewed as an important tool for keeping America both creative and competitive.

The arts expand our world and provide us with multiple entry points to knowledge and meaning. They challenge as many people as much as they soothe. They help us make better use of the world, others, and our self. As an important language of human communication, the arts can provide insights into subtle corners of the human imagination and aspects of life missed by other subjects. The arts are much more than cute bunny rabbits, personal therapy, and frivolous entertainment. By opening our eyes and touching our humanity they replenish our spirit and inspire us.

As the national arts standards make clear, quality education in the arts elevates and gives structure to creative expression and cultural understanding. If educational reform at the local level neglects the arts, our culture, our schools, and our lives will be more desolate places. Art, in all its distinct forms, defines those qualities that are at the heart of education reform—creativity, perseverance, a sense of standards, and, above all, a striving for excellence.

The arts have always provided a space, a sense of opening, a loving of the question, and a unique communal resource. Today's school reform process should not push aside such a basic aspect of social consciousness and interdisciplinary knowing. If there are no arts in a school, there are fewer alternatives to exploring subjects by the spoken and written word. The arts can open some collective doors of the mind and provide new spaces for the active construction of knowledge. What a powerful tool for countering the tendency toward standardization! At the classroom level it will take the skill of collaborative teachers to move forward and use the arts to shape the interconnected exuberance of learning.

USING THE ARTS TO CONNECT DISCIPLINES

Children without knowledge of the arts are as ignorant as children without knowledge of literature, math, or science. The Standards suggest a broader curriculum using the arts to connect such subjects as math, literature, science, physical education, and social studies. Connecting the arts to other subjects adds depth and excitement. Instead of being taught as a separate set of skills, arts education is taking its place as an exciting and powerful way of knowing.

The arts can serve as the glue that pulls the curriculum together. Connections between subjects are even more vital as the nation implements its national standards in the core subjects in the curriculum The arts are a natural way to connect different disciplines without adding to the mass of nonacademic time burners being piled onto the school day. The arts can provide important intellectual tools for understanding many subjects. They also build on qualities that are essential to revitalizing schooling: teamwork, analytical thinking, motivation, and self-discipline. The arts provide cultural resources that people can draw on for the rest of their lives. Without attention to the substance of the discipline and concerted action, the arts are more likely to be dismissed as expendable in an era of curriculum gridlock and financial difficulties.

The arts can also help get a dialogue going between disciplines that often ignore one another. When knowledge from diverse subject matter areas are brought together, the result can be a new and valuable way of looking at the world. The arts and humanities have proved very useful tools for integrating curricular areas and helping students transcend narrow subject matter concerns. Teachers at many levels have used intellectual tools from the fine arts as a thematic lens for examining diverse subjects. Some schools have even worked out an integrated school day, where interdisciplinary themes based on the fine arts add interest, meaning, and function to collaboration. Mathematics, science, social studies, and the language arts can all be wrapped around central themes in the arts so that rich connections stimulate the mind and the senses.

The Internet now transmits new forms of participatory art that allows viewers to change it at will. Different arts-based tools, different information, different students, and a different world. To thrive in that world, American students must learn how to learn, learn how to think, and have a solid understanding of how technology works and what it can do.

Early experiences in the arts are important, because they produce intellectual as well aesthetic gains. Technology can help or hurt. For example, computer-aided productions are fine if they are coupled with tried-and-true arts materials. But dragging and dropping cookie cutter figures is as bad for creativity as a coloring book.

Education early in life should provide opportunities to think deeply, create, and perform in an authentic artistic medium. As students grow, it is equally important that they gain access to the tools and master works fashioned by real artists. These works of art convey the ideas and feelings of different times and places, express a range of emotions, and incorporate a sense of beauty and harmony that enriches all who have experienced them.

THEMATIC STRATEGIES FOR LINKING SUBJECTS AND STUDENTS

Themes can also direct the design of classroom activities by connecting cooperative classroom activities and providing them with a logical sequence and scope of instruction.

A set of steps for developing thematic concepts is to:
1. determine what students know about a topic before beginning instruction (this is done by careful questioning and discussion),
2. be sensitive to and capitalize on students' knowledge,
3. use a variety of instructional techniques to help students achieve conceptual understanding, and
4. include all students in discussions and cooperative learning situations.

Thematic instruction values depth over breadth of coverage. The content should be chosen on how well it represents what is currently known in the field and its potential for dynamically making connections (Rogoff, 1990).

The design of thematic units brings together a full range of disciplines in the school's curriculum: language arts, science, social studies, math, art, physical education, and music. Using a broad range of discipline-based perspectives can result in units that last an hour, a day, a few weeks, or a semester. They are not intended to replace a discipline-based approach but act as supportive structures that foster the comprehensive study of a topic. Teachers can plan their collaborative interdisciplinary work around issues and themes that emerge from their ongoing curriculum. Deliberate steps can be taken to create a meaningful and carefully orchestrated program that is more stimulating and motivating for students and teachers. Of course, shorter flexible units of study are easier to do than setting up a semester or year-long thematic unit.

Collaborative thematic curriculum models require a change in how teachers go about their work. It takes planning and energy to create effective integrated lessons, and more time is often needed for subject matter research because teachers frequently find themselves exploring and teaching new material. Thematic teaching also means planning lessons that use untraditional approaches, arranging for field trips, guest speakers, and special events (Tebbs, 1991). Contacting parents, staff members, and community resources who can help expand the learning environment is another factor in teachers' time and planning efforts. Long-range planning and professional development for teachers are other important elements of the process.

The fact that the arts are now part of the testing process for American students has helped schools take them seriously. Using such tests for their stated purpose of informing students, parents, and teachers how their children are doing relative to national standards in each subject is fine. But using test results for high-stakes purposes, like teacher evaluation, is a mistake. High standards cannot be established and maintained simply by imposing them on teachers and students. Accountability for educational outcomes in the arts —or anything else—should be a shared responsibility of the government, the mass media, school districts, public officials, educators, parents, and classroom teachers.

SHARING A SENSE OF WONDER

The arts have a power beyond aesthetics or making us "see." They can help us view ourselves, the environment, and the future differently, even challenging our certainties about the arts themselves. In connecting the basic concerns of history, civilization, thought, and culture, the arts provide spatial, kinesthetic, and aesthetic skills that are the foundation to what it means to be an educated person. Such understandings do not occur spontaneously. They have to be taught.

The process of understanding or creating art is more than unguided play, self-expression, or a tonic for contentment. The arts can serve as tools for shattering stereotypes, changing behavior, and building a sense of community, and as a vehicle for sociopolitical commentary. There is a connection between productive citizenship, academics, and the arts. For students to make these connections, it will take more than a specialist in the art class for one hour a week or an inspirational theater troupe visiting the school once a year. These brief experiences can help and inspire, but it takes more sustained work in the arts to make a real difference.

Cheating on daily arts education denies students a vital quality of life experience expression, discovery, and an understanding of the chances for human achievement (Schubert & Willis, 1991). The arts can open up a sense of wonder and provide students with intellectual tools for engaging in a shared search. This won't occur if children are having fewer experiences with the arts at school and in their daily lives. Certainly some grasp of the discipline is needed if the arts are going to awaken students to the possibilities of thoughtfulness, collaboration, and life.

Why Teach the Arts?

• The arts can provide for alternative ways of knowing.
• Visual art, music, dance, and drama can be integrated with other subjects to enrich the curriculum.
• The arts invite student inquiry into the "big ideas" that link several areas of knowledge.
• The arts can enhance multicultural understanding.

AN OVERVIEW OF SUGGESTED SKILLS AND POSSIBLE ACTIVITIES

Dance

Identifying and demonstrating movement elements and skills in performing dance.

Sample Skills and Activities:
• Demonstrating movements like bending, twisting, stretching, galloping, skipping, and swinging.
• Demonstrating the ability to define and maintain personal space.
• Demonstrating accurately in moving to a musical beat.
• Creating a sequence with a beginning, middle, and end (rhythmic accompaniment).
• Demonstrating partner skills like copying, leading, and following.

- Observe and discuss how dance is different from other forms of human movement.
- Present their own dances to peers; discuss their meanings.
- Explore, discover, and realize multiple solutions to a movement problem.
- Perform folk dances from various cultures and discuss the elements of dance.
- Identify personal goals for improvement and discuss how exercise helps.
- Respond to dance using another art form; explain the connections.

Music

Performing, creating, and responding to music requires a balanced and comprehensive program of study.

Sample Skills and Activities:
- Singing alone and with others, on pitch and in rhythm.
- Singing expressively, with appropriate dynamics, phrasing, and interpretation.
- Singing in groups, blending vocal timbres, matching dynamic levels, and responding to the cues of a conductor.
- Improvising rhythmic and melodic embellishments on familiar melodies.
- Improvising songs and instrumental pieces using a variety of sound sources.
- Reading and notating standard symbols in simple patterns presented.
- Listening to, analyzing, and describing music and music performances.
- Understanding the relationship between music, the other arts, and core subjects.
- Understanding music in relation to history, culture, and daily experiences.

Theatre

Theater is the imagined and enacted world of human beings. It is one of the primary ways for children to learn about actions, consequences, customs, and beliefs. It involves scriptwriting, acting, designing, directing, playing, and comparing art forms.

Sample Skills and Activities:
- Collaborating on script writing, using dialogue to tell stories, and improvising based on personal experience, heritage, imagination, literature, and history.

- Acting by assuming roles and interacting in improvisations.
- Designing by visualizing and arranging classroom environments for classroom dramatizations.
- Researching by finding information to support classroom dramatizations.
- Comparing and connecting art forms by describing theater, dramatic media (such as film, television, and other electronic media), and other art forms.
- Analyzing and explaining personal preferences and constructing meanings from classroom dramatizations from theater, film, and electronic media productions.
- Understanding context by recognizing the role of theater, film, television, and other media encountered in daily life.

Visual Arts

The visual arts include drawing, painting, sculpture, design, architecture, film, video, and folk arts. As children begin to understand the visual world in which they live, they also learn to unravel the essence of artwork and appraise its purpose and value.

Sample Skills and Activities:
- Knowing how different materials, techniques, media, and processes cause different effects.
- Knowing the differences among visual processes and how visual structures communicate ideas.
- Identifying specific works of art as belonging to particular cultures, times, and places.
- Being able to reflect upon and assess the characteristics and merits of their own work and the work of others.
- Making connections between the visual arts and other disciplines.

The standards document defines the terms used in each of the four areas and provides sequential detail about what can be expected at various grade levels.

COOPERATING AND REFLECTING

Reflecting is a special kind of thinking. Reflective thinking is both active and controlled. When ideas pass aimlessly through a person's mind or someone tells a story that triggers a memory is not reflecting. Reflecting means focusing attention. It involves considering the possibilities and imagining alternatives. The following examples are designed to encourage higher-order thinking and provide a collaborative vehicle for arts education.

Looking at the Familiar Differently

Students are asked to empty their purses and pockets on a white sheet of paper and create a face using as few of the items as possible. For example, one case might be simply a pair of sunglasses, another a single earring representing a mouth, a third could be a profile created by a necklace forming a forehead, nose, and chin. It gives students a different way of looking at things. It is also an example of a teaching concept known as aesthetic education.

Figure 6.3. Taking a different look at the familiar. Big Julie, a painting by French artist Fernand Leger.

Exploring Collage Photo Art

Students at all levels can become producers as well as consumers of art. We used a videotape of David Hockney's work from Art in America.

Hockney, one of today's important artists, spoke (on the videotape) about his work and explained his technique. Students then used cameras to explore Hockney's photo collage technique in their own environment. Student groups can arrange several sets of their photos differently telling unique stories with different compositions of the same pictures. They can even add brief captions or poems to make more connections to the language arts, social studies, or science. Photographers know that the meaning of their pictures depend to a large extent on the words that go with them.

Note: Teachers do need to preview any videos before they are used in the classroom, because some parts may not be appropriate for elementary school children. Teachers can also select particular elements and transfer them from one VCR to another so that only the useful segments are present on the tape used in class.

Painting with Watercolors and Straws

In this activity, students simply apply a little suction to a straw which is dipped in tempera paint Working in pairs, students then gently blow the paint out on a sheet of blank paper to create interesting abstract designs.

Creating Paintings with Oil-based Paints Floating on Water

Working in groups of three, have students put different-colored oil-based paints on a flat dish of water. Apply paper. Watch it soak up the paint and water. Pull it out and let it dry.

Examining Similarities in Folklore and Literature

Have student groups explore myths, folk tales, legends, and fairy tales to look for similarities and differences between people, times, and cultures. Construct a group list, concept map, collage, visual image, or writing that shows these group findings. Students can even take photocopies of major works, paste them down on a large piece of tag board, and paint on top of them.

Understanding Images of the Past Through Oral History

Oral history is a systematic way to obtain from the artifacts, music, photographs, and lips of living Americans a record of their participation in the political, economic, and cultural affairs of the nation. It is a process of collecting reminiscences, accounts, and interpretations of events from the recent past that are of historical significance. As small cooperative groups of students gather information from an elder who grew up in a time and manner different from theirs the students can delete, compile, select, and organize data. This activity works best if you have an elder for each small group. You really need five or six elders there at the same time. If you get more, just make the student groups smaller. A student in each group can give a 60-second explanation of their visitor to the whole class just before the end of the activity. Avoid having one elder stand alone at the front of the class for a lecture-style presentation.

Other Possibilities

• Bring in veterans of World War II to explain that time period and their role in the war. Be sure to ask them to bring visuals, artifacts, and possibly newspapers from that time period. If you do this a little before Veterans Day, for example, it might even be possible to notify the media and get some press coverage. Do we sometimes hear echoes of ideas about art from the 1930s and 1940s ?

• Student groups can be re-formed so that each group has someone who has interviewed several elders. The new small group can construct and compare the experiences of the older Americans from different cultural, ethnic, or racial backgrounds.

The Process:

a. Prior to the interview, students identify topics of interest and do some preliminary research on the topic they are going to discuss.

b. Students identify individuals to interview, contact these individuals to arrange an interview, giving the purpose, time, and place.

c. Working in groups, students prepare some questions for the interview and review with the class the questions they have chosen.

d. Students and the teacher then prepare for the interview. Questions should be simple, relevant, and varied. Procedures for interviewing should be reviewed with the class (Let the respondent do the talking, don't interrupt a story, etc.).

e. During the interview, students should take notes or record (audio or video) the data.

f. Following the interview, students transcribe their notes or recorded data to prepare material for publication or oral presentation.

g. Students then interpret and edit materials, verify dates and obtain written release from respondent for "publication" to the whole class.

The Preparation That Is Needed Before Students
View Modern Art

Pablo Picasso once said, "I paint things as I think of them, not as I see them."

You do not want students to be surprised when they go to a museum and find that the "old masters" may have no more status than a modern artist who spattered or poured paint onto an abstract canvas. An example of a response by an unprepared fifth-grader: "I can't understand what's in it because it doesn't look like it's from real life." Now that photography, videotape, and film capture realistic images, painting and sculpture have moved on to a different "reality." In the twentieth century, it became redundant for visual artists to simply repeat what the technology can usually do better and always do much quicker.

The response of an adult who hasn't done her homework: "The perspective is all wrong; my four year old son could do that!" This is not as great an insult as you may think. Many artists consider art done by many children as having an intensity and spontaneity that breaks the traditional "rules" of composition. As Henri Matisse said, "We must see all of life as if we were children." Overemphasizing technique can stifle the imagination. Now we might look for things like evidence of originality and how the work of art helps us see today's world, the past, or the future differently. Does it open new spaces for understanding?

When we accompanied a fifth-grade class to an artist's work area at the nearby university, two children came up close to a painting that the artist in residence was doing. They asked, "What does it mean?" The artist replied, "What do you think it means?" There is rarely one "right" way to interpret a work, but it helps to have at least an idea of the artist as a person and the social context within which the work was created and a little historical background and some understanding of the arts community today.

Artists rarely conceptualize their work in a vacuum; influences come from every direction. As they experiment with new styles and techniques, they may gather in groups to talk about their ideas or work together on a project. The coming together of artists with similar aims has generated most of the modern art movements of this century. Such movements have helped create a sense of solidarity. By being part of such a group, artists may be taken more seriously than working alone.

Working with a Partner in the Art Museum

In an art museum, students might focus on a few paintings or pieces of sculpture. Have students make up a question or two about some aspect of the art they wish to explore further, and then have them respond to five or six questions from the list in a notebook or writing pad they take with them.

Possible Art Museum Questions for Reflection

- Compare and contrast technology and art as vehicles for viewing the past, present, or future differently.
- How is the visual put together?
- How are images used to communicate?
- How did the creator of the visual image expect the viewer to actively engage the image? Is content more important than form?
- How does your social background affect how you receive (or construct) the message?
- Visuals are authored in much the way print communication is authored. How does the author of a picture or piece of sculpture manipulate the viewer through such things as point of view, size, distortion, or lighting?
- What are the largest or smallest artistic elements of the work?
- What is the main idea, mood, feeling, or intent conveyed by the image?
- When you close your eyes and think about the visual what pictures do you see? What sounds do you hear? Does it remind you of anything a book—a dream, television, something from your life?
- How successful was the visual in making use of the medium?
- How successful is the sculpture or image? Does it have validity? Is it effective? What is your response to it?
- Where did the visual maker place important ideas?
- How do combinations or organization of elements contribute to an overall mood?
- Does the image tell us about big ideas such as courage, freedom, war, and so on?
- Determine the nature of the image through its style, period, school, and culture. How does it fit in with the history of art?
- What does the work say about present conflicts concerning art standards, multiculturalism, and American culture?
- Estimate the aesthetic value of the sculpture or image as it relates to others.
- How did the work make you feel inside?
- Was the artistic work easy or hard to understand?
- Why do you think it was made? What would you like to change about it?

Figure 6.4. Digitized image of M.C. Escher's "Sky and Water I."

Sharing information, ideas, and insights in the arts can be done with group members within small cooperative groups. In the small group, each member or partnership can share ideas and discoveries. Each group may synthesize its work and present briefly to the entire class. As the small group's "reporter" reports to the whole class, the information could be recorded on a class chart. A variation would be to have one student from each group visit another team to collect and share findings, returning to their original group for a discussion.

Children frequently have the innate ability to do creative work in the arts. What is frequently missing are basic artistic understandings and the opportunity for expression and group analysis. When students do have the chance to explore the discipline and express themselves, there is the excitement of producing in their own way, conveying their personal aesthetic experience through the use of figurative language (metaphors, similes, etc.) in their song lyrics, expressive movement, and symbolism in their painting. There is a world out there that students must explore with the arts if they are to be broadly educated. The challenge is to provide the necessary background and opening doors so that meaningful concepts and images will emerge.

ARTS EDUCATION CULTIVATES THE CHILD AND THE NATION

Human societies have always depended on the arts to give insight into truths, however painful or unpopular they may be. Today, in many countries, there is wide agreement that the arts can aid children in developing creativity, becoming good citizens, and being productive workers. The basic notion is that the person, the world, and the nation are poorer without the arts. As Argentine artist Nicolas Urburu has suggested, "A country without culture is like a person without a face."

Americans have generally not paid much attention to the arts. Little is expected of our citizens or our leaders when it comes to knowledge about artistic forms. This is due, in part, to not having a long tradition of prizing artistic expression beyond the cute and the comfortable. As far as the schools are concerned, the arts have often received more attention as a form of therapy than as a serious discipline. It is little wonder that if the arts are found at all, they are most often found on the fringes of our curriculum and when a budget crunch hits, arts education is one of the first things cut.

Teachers can create a space for the arts to flourish, freeing students from the predicted and the expected. Using the arts to inquire and sense openings results in what Emily Dickinson called "a slow fire lit by the imagination." As America moves into the new millennium, we need all the imagination we can get. Advancing the understanding, culture, art, creativity, and human values has everything to do with the life and quality of this nation. Successful education in the arts can come about when students and their learning are at the center, which means motivating and enabling them to meet the standards.

A future worth having depends on being able to construct a vital relationship with the arts. Literacy, enlightenment, richness of knowledge, and enduring resources for thoughtfulness are diminished when artistic endeavors are diminished. The arts are much more than self-expression, filling in the coloring book turkeys, soothing sounds, or visual wallpaper. One of the functions of the arts is to stir up debate, to make people question things in life, and to make people see situations from a different viewpoint. Discipline-based art education (DBAE) is a good example of a new approach. It involves not only creating art but learning how to appreciate it, respond to it, and how to make judgments about what constitutes quality in art. This is all quite a change from the school art of yesteryear. Art in school used to be thought of as kind of nonconsequential fluff designed to make you feel good. Today, literacy in the arts involves everything from discipline-based national tests to a specific body of knowledge that connects to the rest of the school day and to the real world.

Around the world serious education in the arts is one of the most integrating and significant features of the school curriculum. It is widely believed that the passion, vision, and imaginative life generated by the arts has real significance for the quality of national culture. The *National Standards for Arts Education* provides a foundation, gives direction, and enhances the possibilities in America. At every age level, being creatively engaged in the arts plays a major role in broadening literacy, opening new horizons, enriching the spirit, and encouraging bold visions. As with any other subject, making powerful instruction happen depends on well-prepared teachers who can help children understand the arts and use them as a vehicle for seeing what can be but isn't yet.

VIDEO PRODUCTION ACROSS THE ARTS

Students affirm their understanding of the arts when they can apply the arts skills in creative video production. Planning, visualizing, and developing a video allows students to sort out and video techniques to relay meaning. Movement, music, theatre, and the visual arts can all be involved as they learn to redefine space and time, and use media attributes such as structure, sound, color, pacing, and imaging. Easy-to-use camcorders make everything easier.

Suggestions:

- Have students create their own music videos based on a favorite song.
- Assign students to write, record, and shoot a poetry video.
- Use closeups, panning, tilting, and zooming techniques to shoot one scene from many different perspectives.
- Have students build their own story or TV ad from selected short TV or movie segments. They add their own soundtrack and change the dialogue.
- Give students 10 to 12 short segments of video and have them arrange each clip under the following headings: setting, problem, solution, and ending equals a coherent story.

• Use flashbacks, cuts, and dissolves to create a 60-second TV ad. Explore how these techniques are used to lure consumers. Comedy works well here.

Student productions should build on a wide range of intellectual and technological tools to explore today's reality. Composing with media technologies broadens student understanding of meaning making in the arts and invigorates the curriculum. Creating media messages also provides opportunities for problem solving in a manner that promotes deeper analysis. From video to performance art, we can teach our students to ask the following questions about media messages:

• Who created this message and why?
• What techniques are being used to attract my attention?
• What values and points of view are represented?
• How might different people understand this message differently?

The ability to make sense out of the various forms of representation gathered from the arts is a way of securing meaning that can enhance other cognitive skills. The richness of interpretive thought that can be evoked in students by asking engaging questions about works of art that they have made. Clearly, the manner in which the arts are taught strongly influences the forms of thinking that children are able to use.

Quality arts education is not a hit-or-miss effort but a sequenced and comprehensive enterprise of learning that builds on the disciplines of dance, music, theatre, and the visual arts. The world of arts education is not static. New technology changes things, because the convergence of television, computers, and the Internet allows students to enter and communicate in art worlds beyond their classroom. Digital artists are but one example. They are using the Web as a global distribution system for art. The diversity is amazing: illustrated stories, video art, animations, hypertext novels, and digital paintings the viewer can enter, change, and experience like a visual narrative.

For educators to reach for a mobilizing vision, they must have some understanding of the arts and the available technology and, most importantly, they need a thorough knowledge of the characteristics of effective instruction.

GREAT EXPECTATIONS FOR ARTS EDUCATION

Artistic vision and scientific skill
are both the art of seeing things invisible.
— Jonathan Swift

A quality arts education program can come about only when students and their learning are at the center, which means motivating and enabling them to meet the goals of a quality education in the arts. Competency in the arts can expand and deepen the kinds of meaning that people can bring into their lives. The meanings that stem from music, for example, have no identical counterpart in any other form. The ability to understand such forms is not innate, it is developed. And this development is helped or hindered by the school curriculum.

Knowing and practicing the arts disciplines are fundamental to the healthy development of children's minds and spirits. The same can be said for the powerful presence and participatory formats of digital media. After all, new technology has as much potential to diminish aesthetic quality as it does as an enriching tool. Everyone must have a solid academic background in the arts if our technology-intensive educational future is going to contain the enduring power of the imagination that our children bring to it.

Arts education cultivates the whole child and helps bring discipline, imagination, sensibility, and insight to many literacy building activities. All children must have the opportunities and the tools (at every grade level) to create in dance, music, drama, and the visual arts. The goal is not to make miniature experts in each of these disciplines but to enable students to draw on cultural habits of the mind as they explore their world. The primary goal of student production in any medium isn't self-expression or vocational job readiness. It is the fact that hands-on production informs analysis that really matters. Arts-based media education includes hands-on production *and* the cognitive analysis of media. It may be viewed and taught as an aspect of all subjects. The arts and media technology go hand-in-hand in rethinking and broadening literacy in an array of contexts.

The success of any country depends on creating a society that is literate and imaginative, competent and creative. To make their contribution to these critical social objectives, the schools can do more to provide children with an understanding of the world. By attending to arts education, they can stimulate the natural curiosity and creativity of students in ways that meets the needs of an increasingly competitive, complex, and technological society.

Teachers are still struggling to integrate technological tools and aesthetic thinking into the day-to-day life of the classroom. And they are only beginning to envision what they will do when they have access to multimedia digital networks. Of one thing we can be certain, future citizens will have to draw on technological tools and aesthetic understandings to shape tomorrow's world. And they will need competency in both areas to make their way in that world.

Any future worth having depends on being able to
construct a vital relationship with the arts.

RESOURCES AND REFERENCES

Selected Overview of the National Standards for Arts Education

Students Should Be Able to:

- communicate at a basic level in the four arts disciplines dance, music, theater, and the visual arts;
- communicate proficiently in at least one art form, including the ability to define and solve artistic problems with insight, reason, and technical proficiency;
- develop and present basic analyses of works of art;
- understand the historical development in the arts disciplines and have an informed acquaintance with exemplary works of art from a variety of cultures; and
- relate various types of arts knowledge and skills within and across arts disciplines.

See the standards document for detail. The specific goals contained in the Standards were unanimously approved by representatives from the U.S. Office of Education, the National Endowment for the Arts, the National Endowment for the Humanities, and the Music Educators National Conference. Classroom teachers, artists, musicians, dancers, actors, and business leaders also played an active role the process

Association for Supervision and Curriculum Development. (1994). ASCD Conference Report, Fowler *ASCD Update.* Author.

Bruner, J. (1990). *Acts of meaning.* Cambridge, MA: Harvard University Press.

Bruner, J. (1985). Paradigmatic and narrative modes of knowing. In *Teaching and learning the ways of knowing.* 84th Yearbook of the National Society for the Study of Education, E. W. Eisner (Ed.). Chicago: University of Chicago Press.

Calkins, L. (1991). *Living between the lines.* Portsmouth, NH: Heineman.

The College Board. (1985). *Academic preparation in the arts: Teaching for transition from high school to college.* New York.

Dissanayake, E. (1992). *HomoAestheticus.* New York: Free Press.

Eisner, E. (1991) *The enlightened eye.* New York: Macmillan.

Eisner, E. (1998). *The kind of schools we need.* Portsmouth, NH: Heinemann.

Fowler, C. (1992). *Understanding how the arts contribute to excellent education.* A study prepared for the NEA.

Fraser, J.T. (1990). *Of time, passion and knowledge.* Princeton, NJ: Princeton University Press.

Gardner, H. (1983). *Frames of mind.* New York: Basic Books.

Gardner, H. (1993). *Creating minds.* New York: Basic Books.

Gardner, H. (1999). *The disciplined mind: What all students should understand.* New York: Simon & Schuster.

Getty Center for Education In the Arts. (1989). *Education in art: Future building.*

Kaagan, S. (1990) *Aesthetic persuasion: Pressing the cause of arts education in American schools.* A Monograph for the Getty Center for Education in the Arts.

Maeroff, G. (1988). *The empowerment of teachers.* New York: Teachers College Press.

National Art Education Associates (1992). *Elementary art programs: A guide for administrators.* Reston, VA: National Art Education Association.

National standards for education in the arts (1994). *The arts and education reform Goals 2000.* Washington, DC:U.S. Office of Education.

National Standards for Arts Education. (1994). *What every young American should know and be able to do in the arts.* Reston, VA: Developed by the Consortium of National Arts Education Associations.

Nesbitt, J. (1986). *International directory of recreation-oriented assistance.* Venice, CA: Lifeboat Press.

Novel Unit Themes. (1990). *Fly high with novel units.* P.O. Box 1461, Dept. RT, Palatine, IL 60078.

Report of the National Commission on Music Education by the Music Educators National Conference. (1991). *Growing up complete: The imperative for music education.* Reston, VA: MENC.

Rogoff, B. (1990). *Apprentices in thinking: Children's guided participation in culture.* New York: Oxford University Press.

Schubert, W,. & Willis, G. (1991). *Understanding curricula and teaching through the arts.* New York: State University of New York Press.

Sharan, S. (1990) *Cooperative learning: Theory and research.* Westport, CT: Bergin & Garvey and Praeger Publishing.

Smith, R., (Ed.). (1990). *Discipline-based art education: Origins, meaning and development.* Champaign, IL: University of Illinois Press.

Snow, R. (1997). Aptitudes and symbol systems in adaptive classrooms. *Phi Delta Kappan, 78*(5): 354-60.

Tebbs, T. (1991). *Art, collaboration, and gifted education.* Unpublished manuscript.

Viadero, D. (1993). *Draft standards for arts education: Knowledge performance, and disci-*

pline-based learners. Washington, DC.: U.S. Education Department, the National Endowment for the Arts, and the National Endowment for the Humanities. National Panel for the Development of Standards for Arts Education.

Wlodkowski, R., & Jaynes, J. (1990). *Eager to learn.* San Francisco: Jossey-Bass.

Chapter 7

TECHNOLOGICAL LITERACIES
INTEGRATING A MIX OF MEDIA INTO THE CURRICULUM

The prediction that I can make with the highest confidence
is that the most amazing discoveries will be
the ones we are not wise enough to foresee.
– Carl Sagan

The information revolution is playing itself out faster and with higher stakes than any other media onslaught. Our democracy depends on having citizens who can engage in the debate and accelerate the positive possibilities. It is little wonder that America's embrace of the digital age has created a need for new educational visions. If we just sit back and let the technology wash over us, our future will be defined by others.

Of course, there is only so much we can do to channel technology in positive directions. Taming beasts like film and television is particularly difficult. Like it or not, violence, gross-out humor, and obnoxious ads reach a wider young audience than programming that is culturally uplifting. In all its forms, media has a powerful ability to process thought and change how we perceive reality. Networked computers are just the latest problem, with strangers having access to children at home and at school. This is one thing we can do something about by simply being *with* children when they are on-line. Still, we live in a wired and mediated society that makes constant companionship difficult. When it comes to broader patterns of media abuse, parents, the schools, the media, and our society are all responsible for protecting children. It really does take a village—or a caring neighborhood—to get it right.

RECONCEPTUALIZING LITERACY AND LEARNING

The successful educational use of any medium is highly dependent on the context in which it is used. Linking technology with standards-based reform involves clarifying educational goals and reconceptualizing how literacy and learning activities are orchestrated. The best approach is to establish clear educational goals, then use the best mix of available media to achieve those goals. To be intelligent consumers of programming, for example, students need to know that television is a business whose purpose is gathering audiences, and they need to recognize how even the news seeks out the easiest avenue to our emotions. Television, computers, the Internet, and integrated information systems are all things that students need to understand and master. Comprehension skills matter, but the content of the curriculum is more important than mastering specific software or hardware.

When children grow up with computers at home, they are less inclined to accept instruction that is less interesting than what they can experience outside of school. The role of the teacher is bound to change along with media changes in the home and school environment. But after all is said and done, learning will still depend on what humans do best: role modeling, nurturing, and lighting intellectual fires. Technology can assist us with project-based learning and give us exciting access to information, but it takes good teachers to be sure that it actually amplifies learning. Only by applying our knowledge of effective instruction can we be sure that high-tech tools will actually help children reach new plateaus of thinking and learning.

All of the Standards projects mention technology as a partner in learning subject matter. The science Standards go into the most detail. Science looks to both high and low technology to help students understand the laws of the physical and biological universe. Forming connections between the natural and technological worlds is viewed as important to understanding how technological objects and natural systems interact. In every subject, students can use electronic databases to retrieve information and examine the relationship between variables. From interactive literature in the language arts to digital laboratories in mathematics, each subject in the core curriculum builds on promising high tech possibilities.

Figure 7.1. Continuous flow of computer code.

Technology Samples from the Science Standards

Students Should Have an Understanding of Science and Technology

The science and technology standards connect students to the designed world and introduce them to laws of nature through their understandings of how technological objects and systems work. People have always invented tools to help them solve problems to the many the questions that they have about their world.

Science is one way of explaining the natural world; technology helps explain the man-made (or designed) world. In early grades, students can begin to differentiate between science and technology by understanding the similarities, differences, and relationships between science and technology. Observation, making comparisons, sorting and classifying objects both natural and man-made are skills that can be employed at this level. Just as scientists and engineers work in teams to get results, so students, too, should work in teams that combine scientist and engineering talents.

All Students Should Develop Abilities of Technological Design

This standard begins the understanding of the design process, as well as the ability to solve simple design problems. Children's abilities in technological problem solving can be developed by firsthand experience by studying technological products and systems in their world. Young students should have experiences with objects they are familiar with and find out how the objects work. Experiments might include exploring simple household tools or kitchen items. Older students can enrich their understanding by designing something and studying technological products and systems. Suitable design tasks for students should be well defined, based on contexts that are familiar in the homes, schools, and in the immediate community. By the time students reach middle school, investigations using technology can be complemented by activities in which the purpose is to solve a problem, meet a human need, or develop a product.

The science standards list a sequence of five stages that are usually involved in the technology-based problem solving process:

1. Identify and state the problem.
   Children should explain the problem in their own words and identify a specific task and solution.
2. Design an approach to solving the problem.
   This may involve building something or making something work better. They should be able to describe and communicate their ideas.
3. Implement a proposed solution.
   Students should work individually and as a group using tools, techniques, and measurement devices where appropriate.
4. Evaluate results.
   Students evaluate their solutions as well as those of others by considering how well a product or design solved the problem.
5. Communicate the problem, design, and solutions.
   Students should include oral, written, and pictorial communication of the design process and product. Group discussions, written reports, pictures, or group presentations show their abilities.

Technology Samples from the Mathematics Standards

The National Council of Teachers of Mathematics (NCTM) standards include the use of technology in their set of core beliefs about students, teaching, learning, and mathematics.

Using Technology to Investigate Mathematics

The widespread impact of technology on nearly every aspect of our lives requires changes in the content and nature of school mathematics programs. The math standards suggest, in keeping with these changes, that students should be able to use calculators and computers to investigate mathematical concepts and increase their mathematical understanding.

Selected Technology Elements in the Language Arts Standards

Students Use Many Technological and Information Sources

Students use a variety of technological and information resources to gather information and communicate knowledge. Students need to learn how to use many technologies, from computer networks to electronic mail and interactive video. Using computers and video technology empowers students to represent themselves to others. This experience gives them the power of visual representation and enables them to see its importance in enriching a sense of cultural identity.

Students Become Critical Members of a Literacy Community

Students participate in a reflective and critical literacy community. This includes "visual language." Whether students' participation in a community is between classmates or technologically mediated by computer networking and video, it is an essential part of their learning to view themselves as effective users of language and technology. Virtual book clubs represent one of the possibilities. Interactive cinematic narrative is another.

Selected Media Issues in the Arts Education Standards

Students Should Understand the Role of Theatre, Film, Television and Electronic Media in Their Community and Other Cultures

Understanding art media by recognizing the role of theatre, film, television and electronic media in daily life. Students need many opportunities to analyze the role of theatre, film, television, and electronic media in their daily lives. This can be done through discussions, illustrations, drama, or writing.

Understanding and Applying Media, Techniques, and Processes

Students should be able to apply media, techniques and processes with skill, confidence, and sensitivity in their art works. Working in the visual arts with a wide range of subject matter, symbols, meaningful images, and visual expressions, students extend their understanding and express their feelings and emotions. To achieve its positive potential, multimedia requires a solid background in the arts. Otherwise, television, film, video games, and their media associates are more likely to indoctrinate our youth with a lot of tawdry visual trash. Computers make bad art easier to mass produce.

Using Technology to Construct Meaning Across the Curriculum

> *We cannot replace curiosity with
> mechanical memorization
> and call it knowledge.*
> – Paulo Freire

As students gain knowledge and skills they also grow in their ability to apply these skills and knowledge to their widening personal worlds: computers, calculators, science instruments, video cameras, the Internet, Netcams, satellites, and integrated information systems. The list goes on. Whatever the task, digital tools can magnify the ability to think and articulate our thoughts. They can also help us act together on the result. By using a variety of technologies for real-world inquiry, problem-solving, and communicating, students can come to recognize that learning is more than preparing for life; it is life itself.

The language arts standards go beyond information and communications technology and refer to visual and media literacy as central factors in learning about language and communication skills. All of the standards projects have suggested or implied that students should be given opportunities to use a mix of media to construct meaning. In addition, there is general agreement that exploring the world and designing solutions to problems work best when students can use technological tools much the way adults use them.

Student-generated questions provide excellent opportunities to apply a whole range of technological tools to interesting real-world problems. In the early elementary grades, many of tasks can be designed around the familiar contexts of the home, school, and community. Figuring out the best ways to solve problems is what is most important. So don't leave out the low-tech or the nonelectronic possibilities. Although realistic problems usually have multiple solutions, it is often best for lower grade students when there are only one or two possible solutions. This cuts preparation time or complicated assembly. Simplicity and elegance are not contradictory terms.

Whatever the grade level, multidisciplinary analysis of problems is a natural when it connects to the students' day-to-day world. Virtual and face-to-face collaboration makes it more interesting. So do manners. There is no good reason why a digital medium has to encourage rudeness. As in life, when on-line, it is best to respect others, be generous, and not get into silly fights.

To some degree, communication and information technology has always reflected the strengths and weaknesses of the human condition. It creates and it solves problems. Sticking with the problem-solving possibilities for now, it is clear that today's expanding mix of electronic media can serve as passports to an expanding reservoir of dynamic knowledge and communication. For this and other reasons, technology is in the process of redefining how we learn, play, and understand our lives. It is also redefining literacy and reshaping the nature of knowledge acquisition.

SIMPLE OFF-LINE ACTIVITIES

Design a Communications Technology Time Line

Time is often a difficult concept for children to grasp. Throughout modern history, people have recorded the passage of time. This activity gets students involved in time measurement by using a number of old and new technological tools. The ways in which people communicate with each other have changed throughout history.

Materials: reference books, science/language arts journal, communication devices from home, grandparents, community, etc.

Procedure:
1. Have students research the history of communications technology and create a time line in their science/language arts journal.
2. Using as many actual objects or their representations, encourage students to assemble a communications time line project for display.
3. Remind students that each time period needs to have some examples of the actual objects used and a written explanation about these communications devices.

Reading Culture Through Advertising

Take students to the library and have them collect copies of ads from each decade of this century. Much of this may be on microfilm. Some can be found on the Internet. Compare and contrast the images in the ads and relate them to social events in each decade. Ask students to produce their own ads using the production techniques they see pictured at a particular time. Use the style of the period.

Research can also be done on the history of cigarette advertising, misleading claims, and ad campaigns directed towards a specific audience. Zero in on who is responsible for an ad. *The Standard Directory of Advertisers* will tell you the name and address of the advertising agency that created an ad. Ask students to choose an advertisement that they think is offensive, irresponsible, or one that they think represents things fairly. They can write a letter of complaint or congratulate on a job well done.

Technology is changing everything, even itself. The Internet, for example, is changing how we view and use television. Television broadcasting isn't standing still. It is going digital and figuring out ways to work hand-in-hand with the Internet, satellites, computers, and the telephone. This convergence is bound to influence popular culture. And sooner or later, most of these new media mixes will influence the curriculum.

Digital technology is a convenient vehicle for inquiry-based classrooms. The Internet, for example, can give students access to data, experiences, simulations, and dynamic model building. Electronic media continues to change itself and change how we go about teaching and learning. By altering the communication and information environment, our new technological tools even give us the possibility for creating new knowledge. Integrated technology gives us instant access to scattered information that we can use to analyze trends, search out opportunities, and create knowledge. The result is transforming the social and educational environment before we have a chance to think carefully about why we want to use it and what we hope to accomplish. By the time we have one thing figured out, we are in the middle of next version, and no matter what you do, you can't slow it down.

EXTRACTING MEANING FROM ELECTRONIC MEDIA

We are all media consumers and all need to make critical judgments about the quality and usefulness of the electronic possibilities springing up around us. One way for students to become more media literate is to learn to "read" and "write" with media. Children can become adept at extracting meaning from the conventions of producing in any medium. Like print, visual imagery from a computer or TV screen can be mentally processed at different levels of complexity.

Piaget showed how certain notions of time, space, or morality are beyond children's grasp before certain developmental levels are reached. Research on TV viewing has suggested that vocabulary isn't the only thing that impedes children from grasping some adult content (Dede, 1985). Children lack fundamental integrative capacities to "chunk" (group) certain kinds of information into meaningful groups which are obvious to adults. Thus, children who need help in developing strategies for tuning out irrelevancies may be especially vulnerable to unwanted adult content (McKibben, 1992).

The greater the experiential background, the greater the base for the development of technological literacy. The ability to make subtle judgments about what is seen and heard is a developmental outcome that proceeds from stage to stage with an accumulation of critically informed viewing experiences. Thus different age groups reveal varying levels of comprehension when they interact with stories in any medium. Eight-year-olds, for example, retain a relatively small proportion of central actions, events, or settings found in a computer or video program. Even when they retain explicit content, younger children often fail to infer the connections between scenes. In a rich home and school environment, comprehension improves with training and maturity.

Most of the time, children construct meaning for television content without even thinking about it. They attend to stimuli, and extract meaning from subtle messages. The underlying message of most TV programs and many Internet functions is that viewers should consume as much as possible while changing as little as possible. How well television content is understood varies according to similarities between viewers and content, viewers' needs and interests, and the age of the individual using a particular medium. Meaning is constructed by each participant at many levels.

A few notes of caution: Broadcast television and the World Wide Web are providing us with a common culture that tends towards cynicism and selfishness. American mass media responds to the public hunger for community with programming that applies market values and standards to human relationships. It may be hard to tell, but living in community with others requires far more than attention to profits. Try exploring all sides of technology issues. For example, what does e-commerce (Internet sales) do to the local bookstore or the educational programs supported by sales taxes? Go to lunch with a Luddite and listen.

Sorting through the mass media themes of mental conservatism and material addition requires carefully developed thinking skills and social conscience. Building a culture of meaning is an increasingly difficult and varied undertaking. Poetry, literature, and public service are just three ways to temper the desire for personal gain with a little compassion, spirituality, and a few transcendent values. When we can all apply an informed set of analytical tools to media signals, the prospects for our public life will improve dramatically.

Substantial understanding of any medium requires providing information for parents, teachers, and children. Some parents, for example, may have to learn how to effectively encourage their children to critique, analyze, and discuss media messages. Modeling is very important. If the adults in a child's life read and take a disciplined approach to their use of television and the Internet, then children are likely to do the same.

Reflective thought, imaginative play, and peer interaction are important to child development. Technology doesn't always add much to the instructional equation. Still, in a media saturated world, children should be able to do some active work with electronic media—making sense of the contents and utilizing the possibilities. Evaluative activities include judging, assigning worth, assessing what is admired, and deciding what positive and negative impressions should be assigned to the content. Even in the early grades, a little production experience helps.

Students learn best if they take an active role in their own learning. Relying upon a host of cognitive inputs, individuals select and interpret the raw data of experience to produce a personal understanding of reality. Ultimately, it is up to each person to determine what they pay attention to and what they ignore. How elements are organized—and how meaning is attached to any concept—is an individual act that can be influenced by a number of external agents. The thinking that must be done to make sense of perceptions ultimately transforms the "real world" into different things for different people.

LEARNING TO MAKE SENSE OF MEDIA MESSAGES

Parents, teachers, and other adults can significantly affect what information children gather from television, and how the skills learned from analyzing this visually-intensive medium will apply to more advanced multimedia platforms. Students' social, cultural, educational, and family context influences what messages they take from the television, how they use TV, and how "literate" they are as viewers. Becoming adept at reading media messages means being able to:

- understand the grammar and syntax as they are expressed in different forms.
- analyze the pervasive appeals of advertising.
- compare similar presentations or those with similar presentations or those with similar purposes in different media.
- identify values in language, characterization, conflict resolution, and sound/visual images.
- identify elements in dramatic presentations associated with the concepts of plot, storyline, theme, characterizations, motivation, program formats, and production values.
- utilize strategies for the management of duration of viewing and program choices.

Parents and teachers can help by explaining content and showing how a media experience relates to a student's interests. Adults can also exhibit an informed response, point out misleading messages, and take care not to build curiosity for undesirable programming.

The habits of families play a large role in determining how children approach any medium. For example, the reactions of parents and siblings toward programming messages all have a large influence on the child (McLeod et al., 1982). If there are books, magazines, and newspapers around the house, children will pay more attention to print. Influencing how children conduct themselves with any medium requires certain rules about what may or may not be watched or what Web sites are fair game. A simple suggestion is to put the computer in the family room. Turning to a television example, influencing the settings in which children watch TV matters. Turning the TV set off during meals sets a family priority. Families can also seek a more open and equal approach to choosing television shows—interacting before, during, and after the program. Parents can also organize formal or informal activities outside the house that provide alternatives to TV viewing, video games, or Internet surfing.

It is increasingly clear that the education of children is a shared responsibility. Parents need connections with what is going on in the schools. But it is *teachers* who will be the ones called upon to make the educational connections entwining varieties of print and visual media with science, mathematics, or technology. It is possible to use the TV medium in a way that encourages students to become intelligent video consumers.

BECOMING AN INTELLIGENT CONSUMER OF MASS MEDIA

To understand media messages, teachers can capitalize on the information and knowledge that students bring to class. It is important to look more closely at the business side of the media. From all the selling and salaries involved it clear that the mass media is an economically valued storyteller in our society.

Questions:
- What is your favorite Web site, TV show, and movie?
- What kind of information, show, or movie is it?
- What are the formal features of your choices?
- What are the most appealing elements of each?
- What do you know about how each medium constructs their "stories"?
- What are some of the formal and informal structures of the Internet, movie industry, and TV broadcasting?
- What are the values in these mass-produced "programs" and how do they change our shared experiences as a people?

(Fifteen years ago, our shared experiences included books and newspapers. Now, only the more educated members of our society do a great deal of reading.)

1. Help Students Critique What They See

Decoding visual stimuli and learning from visual images requires practice. Seeing an image does not automatically ensure learning from it. Students must be guided in decoding and looking critically at what they view. One technique is to have students "read" the image on various levels. Students identify individual elements and classify them into various categories, then relate the whole to their own experiences, drawing inferences and creating new conceptualizations from what they have learned. Encourage students to look at the plot and story line. Identify the message of the program. What symbols (camera techniques, motion sequences, setting, lighting, etc.) does the program use to make its message? What does the director do to arouse audience emotion and participation in the story? What metaphors and symbols are used?

2. Compare Print and Visual Messages

Have students follow a current event on the evening news (taped segment on a VCR) and compare it to the same event written in a major newspaper. A question for discussion may be: How do the major newspapers influence what appears on a national network's news program? What about the news on the Internet? Encourage comparisons between media.

What are the strengths and weaknesses of each? What are the reasons behind the different presentations of a similar event?

3. Evaluate Viewing Habits

After compiling a list of their favorite TV or computer programs, Web sites, or video games assign students to analyze the reasons for their popularity; examine the messages these programs send to their audience. Do the same for favorite books, magazines, newspapers, films, songs, and computer programs. Look for similarities and differences between the media. Have students look for hints about what is going to come next; this is an example of visual or musical foreshadowing. Limit your use of video to five minutes or so of class time. Remember, if it is short, you can show it twice

BALANCING HUMAN RIGHTS AND COMMUNICATIONS TECHNOLOGY

We have yet to figure out how to balance the two of the most powerful revolutions of the twentieth century, those of human rights and information technology. Colleges and universities have long prized the right to explore any subject in the pursuit of knowledge. Freedom of expression is accorded the highest respect. Public or private, institutions of higher education try to give groups—even those on the margin—a forum for discussion. Still, we as a society must continue to make distinctions between what is and what is not appropriate for children. This can be done without violating the First Amendment or reducing everything to the intellectual level of a seven-year-old.

Voluntary guidelines for violence and gross-out bad manners on television, in film, on the Web and in video games would be a good start. Stop the gratuitous killing and public puking. The media industry must acknowledge its influence and do a better job of producing programming that doesn't follow the lowest gross-out humor or show conflicts consistently resolved with violence. Paying more attention to the movie rating system, the new "V-chip" in television sets, and blocking software for the Internet help, but the family has to provide guidance and discuss what is going on. Schools can help with explicit instruction. After all, one of the major purposes of education is to help the young defend themselves against such attention getting imagery.

How can we go about creating an instructional atmosphere that is enabled by the technology? PC's have been around many of us for a decade or two. But it is only recently that a large number of Americans have learned how to really use them. Computers and their technological associates are rarely used to compute anymore. They *are* used to communicate, gather information, simulate, and explore. Everyday many students are receiving and sending large volumes of text, images, and sound. The next step is to sort through the glut and construct some knowledge.

One of the major goals for any educational innovation is to make subjects more interesting, comprehensible, and connected to everyday life. When it comes to schooling, this means connecting to what the curriculum is trying to accomplish and making sure that students don't mind facing lifelong learning needs. Technology can support real-world concepts with visual imagery and help students actually see and share problems. Something very special happens when students know that their research (images and print) is available to other students around the world. The same can be said of the special appeal of bringing images, text, and sound from the outside world into isolated classrooms. It is important to remember that learning is more about mental models than it is about imagery.

An Example of Skeptical Inquiry with a Mix of Media

1. Give students a one-page scavenger hunt activity where they have to find everything from the atomic number of uranium to DNA research to how to say "hello" to people in Finland.
2. Find some current information that you believe. Explain. Find something about current events that you don't believe. Explain.
3. Examine the validity of something hard to believe—in the newspaper, on TV, or on the Web.
4. Critique a movie, computer program, or web site. Ask some questions about the content. (Come up with some answers. Learn to ask better questions.)
5. How would would the accuracy of information from an advertisement be compared to information found on a Web site like the National Geographic?
6. What Metaphor Would You Pick to Cover TV, movies, or the Internet? For example, is the Internet more like the *telephone company* or is it more like a *TV station* or newspaper? Pick a metaphor and explain. Is education more like a river, the wind, or a tree. Explain your choice. From poetry to physics, subjects are built on their metaphors.

The Web is a large vaguely mapped territory with unusually beautiful scenery, unfamiliar languages and customs, treacherous and technological jungles. For computer explorers, the Web is the most exciting communications medium since people a generation ago listened to explorers of the North Pole on their crystal radios. The Web and other equipment such as portable computers, digital cameras, and satellite telephones enable us to participate in rich adventures as they happen on land, sea, air, and space (Lewis, 1996).

EACH MEDIUM IS DISTINCTIVE

Each communications medium makes use of its own distinctive technology for gathering, encoding, sorting, and conveying its contents associated with different situations. The technological mode of a medium affects the interaction with its users—just as the method for transmitting content affects the knowledge acquired. Learning seems to be affected more by *what* is delivered than by the delivery system itself. In other words, the quality of the programming and the level of interactivity are the keys. All too often, computer games (and the like) encourage children to play alone. Like the television set, computer-based activities are becoming babysitters.

Processing must always take place and this process always requires skill. The closer the match between the way information is presented and the way it can be mentally represented, the easier it is to learn. Better communication means easier processing and more transfer. More than a decade ago, research suggested that voluntary attention and the formation of ideas can be facilitated by electronic media—with concepts becoming part of the child's repertoire (Brown, 1988). Now, new educational choices are being laid open by new electronic technologies.

Some schools are arranging for courses to be taught via the Internet. Whatever form it has taken, distance learning has always had its problems. Using satellites and television may give us the ability to distribute education more widely and meet some very specific needs, like teaching the Japanese language to three students in central Iowa but that doesn't mean doing away with classrooms. The impulse to use technology to somehow increase productivity and reduce the cost of education rarely works out. Neither computers nor anything replaces good teachers. The question is how to use the technology to support these teachers and do something really worthwhile for education, culture, and society.

We are now at a stage where even novices can find their way around global networks—downloading images, messages, audio, and video with the click of a mouse. The Internet has become an example of how a virtual community can connect telecommunicators around the world. It is also an example of frenzied commercialization. Across media platforms, the next few years will be a critical time for building things into communications media that benefit the public. It is time to consciously attend to the role of mass communications in a democratic society.

Educators are increasingly looking to the cyberspace reached by these data highways as they strive to make their classrooms more interactive, collaborative, and student centered. As we put together the technological components that provide access to a truly individualized set of active learning experiences, it is important to develop a modern philosophy of teaching, learning, and social equity. While new communications technology has the potential to make society more equal, it has the opposite effect if access is limited to those with the money for equipment. Schools, libraries, and public-private partnerships can help turn this around. As we enter a world of computers, camcorders, interactive TV, the Web, databases, and satellite technology, the schools are behind the curve. Now is the time to start catching up with the more technologically sophisticated.

Electronically connecting the human mind to global information resources will result in a shift in human consciousness similar to the change that occurred when a society moved from an oral to a written culture. The challenge is to make sure that this information is available for all in a twenty-first century version of the public library. The technology could give us the ability to impact upon the tone and priorities gathering information and learning in a democratic society. Of course, every technology has the potential for both freedom and domination. Like other technological advances, this one can mirror back to us all sides of the human condition. But who can argue with easy access to vast troves of information? And soon this technology will set up possibilities for having our best teachers available for tutoring on the Net.

There is no doubt about the fact that the world is re-engineering itself with many technological processes. The convergence of communication technologies may be one of the codes to transforming the learning process and making people more creative, resourceful, and innovative in the things they do. But don't expect technology alone to turn things around. While learning to use what is available today, we need to start building a social and educational infrastructure that can travel the knowledge highways of the future. Experts may disagree about the ultimate consequences of innovation in electronic learning, but the development of basic skills, habits of the mind, wisdom, and traits of character will be increasingly affected by the technology.

Figure 7.2. Storyboard concept sketches for a TV series entitles "Space Conflict III."

NEW MEDIA REALITIES CREATED BY NETWORKING TECHNOLOGIES

Although the research is thin, there are some studies that point to some potential benefits when students and teachers use new computer-based technology and information networks. For example:

- Computer-based simulations and laboratories can be downloaded and help support national standards by involving students in active, inquiry-based learning (Dwyer, 1994).
- Networking technology, like the Internet, can help bring schools and homes closer together (Hendon, 1997).
- Technology and telecommunications can help include students with a wide range of disabilities in regular classrooms (Woronov, 1994).
- Distance learning, through networks like the Internet, can extend the learning community beyond the classroom walls (TEAMS, 1994).
- The Internet may help teachers continue to learn—while sharing problems/solutions with colleagues around the world (Adams & Hamm 1998).

Everything in the world can't be reduced to the intellectual level of a seven-year-old. Since the "Net" is rarely censored, it is important to supervise student work or use a program that blocks some adult content. We suggest that teachers keep an eye on what students are doing and make sure that the classroom is off-line when a substitute teacher is in. Censorship isn't the answer. There are plenty of computer programs for the Internet that act like the V-chip in new television sets. With adult supervision and good software, we can protect children from the cretins and nasty folks out there. A program like *Internet Nanny* is one way to prevent children from accessing inappropriate material. Just as with libraries and bookstores, it is important not to restrict the free flow of information and ideas, but there is nothing wrong with a children's section.

SAILING THROUGH THE CROSSCURRENTS OF TECHNOLOGICAL CHANGE

Students really like teaching other students how to do these things. The teacher can watch and learn. Even the most experienced computer educator cannot keep up with hundreds of new programs coming out every few months. The solution is to tell students to critique a new program, teach it to other students, and then teach the teacher.

In today's world, children grow up interacting with electronic media as much as they do interacting with print or people. They are engaged, but does this mean that they are learning anything meaningful or that they are making good use of either educational or leisure time? Electronic media can distract students from direct interaction with peers, but it doesn't have to. It can inhibit *or* enhance important group, literacy and physical exercise activities. The future may be bumpy, but it doesn't have to be gloomy. Good use of technological tools depends on the strength and capacity of the person using them. As far as schools are concerned, the best results occur when it is informed educators who are driving change rather than the technology itself.

Sailing through the crosscurrents of a technological age means harmonizing the present and the future more than reinventing the schools. It means attending to support mechanisms. To successfully sail through the crosscurrents of our transitional age requires the development of habits of the heart and habits of the intellect. Thinking about the educational process has to preceed thinking about the technology.

Rapid changes in information technology are resulting in less and less of a difference between the television screen, the computer screen, and telephone-linked networks. In fact, connecting a cable modem to the cable TV line (if the cable company does its part) results in much faster communication and quick acting full-motion video. When "on-line" is "on-cable," it becomes even easier to swap E-mail, participate in electronic chat groups, and quickly roam around the Web. Within a few years, very broad bandwidths will result in much faster connections.

Possibilities for intelligent use of the computer-based technologies may be found in earlier media. For example, when television first gained a central place in the American consciousness, sociologist Leo Bogart wrote that it was a "neutral instrument in human hands. It is and does what people want." The same thing might be said about today's multimedia and telecommunications technologies. The Internet and other computer-controlled educational tools may have great promise, but anyone who thinks that technological approaches will solve the problems of our schools is mistaken.

As we venture out onto the electronic road ahead, we should remember the words of T.S. Eliot: *Time present and time past are both perhaps contained in time future, And time future contained in time past.*

NAVIGATING NEW LITERACIES

The Internet is an example of how linked multimedia computers can help us weave a new community—or waste a great deal of time. If linking the classroom to the Internet is going to have positive results, we need a clear set of educational priorities before we select the technologies to advance those priorities. In addition, teachers need training and sustained support to properly harness the technology to instructional purposes. The notion that positive things happen by simply putting the technology in the classrooms and connecting to the Internet is wrong. The technology only helps children learn better if it is part of an overall learning strategy.

It is important to remember that learning works best within the context of human relationships. When it comes to using educational technology wisely, we would do well to remember that just about everything that happens in the classroom must be filtered through the mind of the teacher. In recognition of this fact, the National Educational Goals project recognizes the need for "the nation's teaching force to have access to continual improvement of their professional skills" (1995, National Educational Goals Project). As technological potential and hazard intrude on our schools, there is general agreement that teachers need high-tech inservice training to deal with the explosion of electronic possibility.

As teachers look for ways to engage students with the technology, they must ask themselves, "What is the problem to which this can be applied?" It may sometimes be a Faustian bargain; something important is given and something important taken away. The quality of the technological content, the connection to important subject matter, and a recognition of the characteristics of effective instruction are central factors in determining instructional success. School is, after all, a place where students should come into contact with caring adults and learn to work together in groups.

CONNECTING TO A NEW
TECHNOLOGICALLY-INTENSIVE WORLD

Technology expands to meet the need for more sophisticated instrumentation and techniques for studying phenomena that are unobservable by other means due to danger, quantity, speed, size, or distance. Subject matter helps drive technology—and technology returns the favor. By providing tools for investigations of the natural world, creating art, and communicating as never before, technology is expanding knowledge beyond preset boundaries. As students use a variety of technological and informational resources, they can gather information, synthesize, create, and communicate knowledge.

Figure 7.3. "Time present and time past are both perhaps contained in time future, and time future contained in time past" (Digitized image).

Since the world is not neatly divided up into disciplines, teachers need all the technological help that they can get to soften calcified subject matter boundaries. A mix of media is bound to play a more important role in the discovery of big ideas that link different areas of knowledge. Clearly, technology can lend a hand in helping teachers reach across disciplines with interdisciplinary themes.

To paraphrase Jane Austen, *when unquestioned vanity goes to work on a weak mind it produces every kind of mischief.* If our faith in technology becomes a powerful ideology, we miss the point. It can be magical, but to be educationally healthy, we have to ask challenging questions about such a powerful social force. Experienced teachers know that educational shortcuts from filmstrips to videotapes have promised a lot and delivered little. A little skepticism will improve the end result. But no matter what we do, it will still take rigorous thought, commitment, social interaction, and hard work to teach and learn.

Simply by causing us to rethink the content of the curriculum, computers and their technological associates will contribute to educational reform. Of course, technology can do much more. It can add power to the curriculum, amplify learning, and give us more possibilities for collaborative engagement. With all of the high-tech explosion of possibilities, it is important to remember that the curriculum connections to the natural world must be filtered through the mind of the student and the mind of the teacher. Investment in "human ware" beats investment in "software" every time. The professional development of teachers needs to be a top priority. In addition, school administrators must pay close attention to the barriers that prevent teachers from using available technology effectively.

As a close relative of standards-based instruction, integrated information technology will dramatically change how teachers go about their work. These tools are are bound to become powerful levers when they are placed in the hands of thoughtful teachers. But, like everything else, it still comes down to the teacher's intellectual curiosity, professional development, sense of humor, character, and ability to relate to young people.

THE FUTURE OF LEARNING IN CYBERSPACE

Harmonizing the educational present and the educational future means reinventing the schools, attending to support mechanisms, and having the courage to be out in front on certain issues. To successfully sail through the crosscurrents of our transitional age requires the development of habits of the heart and habits of the intellect. Every age seeks out the appropriate medium or combination of media to confront the mysteries of human learning. The computer is the representational medium that can be an animated wonderland, an interactive book, a theatre, a sports arena, and even a potential life form. Along with its associates the computer is already providing for the rapid dissemination of ideas and giving us a new stage for participatory experiences. Along with its associates, it is already providing for the rapid dissemination of ideas and giving us a new stage for participatory experiences.

In today's world, children grow up interacting with electronic media as much as they do interacting with print or people. Does being engaged by electronic media mean that children are making good use of leisure time or learning anything meaningful? The future may be bumpy, but it doesn't have to be gloomy. The technology does open up some possibilities. Parents, teachers, and programming are the foundations on which possibilities can be built. In schools the technology can also play a role in reexamining what to teach and how to teach it.

New information and communications technologies can be used to help students understand complex issues, solve problems creatively, and apply these solutions to real life situations. Engaging, yes, but it takes effort and planning to make it meaningful. Having a solid educational agenda is more important than having the greatest technology; but once the education piece in place, it is time to figure out exactly how technology can help you.

A Checklist for Planning with Technology

1. Don't expect change immediately.
2. Keep the focus on specific learning needs; start small.
3. Be sure there is equal access for all students.
4. Invest in technology in the early grades.
5. Pay attention to teachers' needs by providing support and assistance.

Knowledgeable teachers are the key to positive change. For technology to reach its potential means making a substantial commitment to helping teachers learn how to use it effectively. Teachers need sustained professional development, common planning time, and opportunities to talk with colleagues. They also need to be encouraged to attend conferences and participate in on-line teacher networks. By funneling more resources to teachers and classrooms, policy makers can help the schools develop practices that reflect what is known about effective instruction. Once there is a critical mass of teachers sharing ideas electronically—and a higher percentage of students with access to computers—the highly developed textbook industry will shift to providing more high-tech products.

Predicting the future of today's digital media is a little like predicting the future of art. Go ahead; indulge yourself. Just don't be surprised when things turn out differently.

PURSUING UNTAPPED POSSIBILITIES

The future is not some place we are going to, but one we are creating.
The paths to it are not found but made,
and the activity of making them changes both the maker and the destination
— John Schaar

During the next decade, a digital nervous system of communications and information technology could (conceivably) unite all systems and processes under a common infrastructure. This system would release rivers of dynamic information directed towards solving specific teaching and learning problems. This would give teachers powerful tools for solving pressing problems and more efficient ways to reach students. Expanding technology can be integrated in a way that gives instant access to scattered information. The potential for propelling learning into an exciting new era is rapidly coming online.

The next great medium for literacy generating activities and storytelling and is digital. Every effort should be made to help students creatively use and "write" with these new compositional tools. It would be a shame not to put our powerful representational media to the highest tasks of society. Computers and their associates have an immense capacity for creating learning experiences that take us beyond today's games and gimmicks to an interactive experience that probes the important questions of human life.

When pedagogy, technology, and subject matter standards are combined, powerful possibilities arise. The standards are not another effort to tie teachers up with objectives and expectations set by others. Rather, they represent the best current thinking in the basic disciplines. This includes the traditional basics of reading, writing, and mathematics and the new basics of science, the arts, and technology. As new research and refined classroom practices become known, the standards will change and grow. One constant is the fact that education is a human practice for enriching the mind and the soul. Another is the human attribute of creating ourselves in the presence of others.

> *For excellence, the presence of others is always required.*
> – Hannah Arendt

As Dewey has suggested, the self is in continuous formation. This search for identity usually takes place among others. Autonomous private behavior can inhibit the social nature of literacy development. What we can do together today we can do alone or with other groups tomorrow. An impersonal system of media distraction can retard the building of social capacities through genuine human interaction. No matter how dynamic the technology, using it in isolation can leave students sad, lonely, and antisocial.

The communal aspects of cyberspace are growing as group work, conversation, reflection, and critical inquiry begin to take hold. Some interaction can certainly take place on line. But some has to be face-to-face so that learners can work together to control the interpretation of what they see and hear. As students learn to become competent and literate in all media forms, they can open windows on the world and pay attention to other points of view. Like art, our technology can help us to look at the world through the eyes of others.

Figure 7.4. Les balets de Monte Carlos, a poster by Keith Haring December 25, 1989.

REFERENCES

Adams, D., & Hamm, M. (1998) *Collaborative inquiry in science, math and technology.* Portsmouth, NH: Heinemann.

Children Now. (1996). *Children watching television: The role of advertisers. August 1996.* Oakland, CA: Children Now.

Dede, C. J. (1985). Assessing the potential of educational information utilities. *Library Hi Tech, 3*(4), 115-119.

Dwyer, D. Apple classrooms of tomorrow: What we've learned. *Educational Leadership, 51,* no.7 (April 1994): 4-10.

Educational telecommunications: The state-by-state analysis. Henzel Associates, 1201 E. Fayette St., Syracuse, NY 13210

Hendon, R. A. (1997). The implications of Internet usage for innovative education. Unpublished manuscript.

Lewis, P. (1996). Adventures can find company on the internet. *The New York Times,* July 2, 1996.

McKibben, B. (1992). *The age of missing information.* New York: Random House.

National Education Goals Panel, (1994). *The national education goals report 1993: Building a nation of learners.* Washington, DC: Author.

National Research Council. (1995) *National Science Education Standards.* Washington, DC: National Academy Press.

National Registrar of Publishing. (1998). *The standard directory of advertisers.* New Providence, NJ: Readel el Sevier, Inc.

Oppenheimer, T. (1997). The computer delusion. *The Atlantic Monthly, 280.*

TEAMS distance learning, (1994) Los Angeles County Office of Education, 9300 Imperial Highway, Room 250, Downey, CA 90242.

Woronov, T. Assistive technology for literacy produces impressive results for the disabled. *The Harvard Education Letter, Vol.X,* No. 5 (Sept./Oct. 1994): 6-7.

The specific goals contained in the national standards were unanimously approved by representatives from the U.S. Office of Education, the National Endowment for the Humanities, and the Music Educators National Conference. Classroom teachers, artists, musicians, dancers, actors, and business leaders also played an active role in the process (The Report of the National Commission on Music Education, 1991).

Chapter 8

NETWORKING LITERACY
INTERNET RESOURCES AND TOOLS ACROSS
THE CURRICULUM

The moment man first picked up a stone or a branch to use as a tool,
he altered irrevocably the balance between him and his environment...
While the number of these tools remained small, their effect took a
long time to spread and to cause change. But as they increased,
so did their effects: the more the tools, the faster the rate of change.
— James Burke

We are in the process of using digital technology to build a global medium that is as central to people's lives as television or the telephone. New technology has changed how we view the world, making globalization possible. Thanks to converging computer, Internet, satellite, and television technologies we can now see and hear through almost every conceivable wall. This new stage in the "democratization" of the media makes no pretense of filtering information on the basis of accuracy, taste, relevance, or concern for privacy. Such concerns often fly in the face of broader economic, social, and technological forces at loose in the world today. A coherent human balance is needed. Schools can make a contribution by developing a vision of teaching and learning that takes global multiliteracy networks seriously. Besides providing us with tools and utilities, technology gives us a lens for reexamining schooling.

There is always some adventure involved in mixing new technological tools with new subject matter standards. Since the dull end of possibility always remains somewhere out beyond the horizon, a certain sense of excitement is generated. Things never become tediously predictable. Who, for example, could have predicted today's Internet based on what was around in the early 1990s.

Over the past several years, a series of projects have defined standards for science, mathematics, language arts, and the arts. All have called for using the latest information and communications technology. But few have specifically mentioned the Internet because it came along at about the same time as the various standards projects were going to press. The Internet has a 25-year history, but it wasn't until the mid-1990s that millions of people and thousands of schools got involved.

Teachers frequently face many barriers, including school cultures that don't value technology and a lack of opportunities for professional development. The fact that teachers need to do an effective job with a new tool like the Internet must be a top priority. Like any technological intervention, it must be linked to our new academic standards, and it must support the improvement of classroom instruction based on those standards.

Knowledgeable teachers are the key to both the wise use of technology and successful school renewal. Integrating technology into daily lessons in a manner that connects dealing with reforms in teaching and learning is a central concern. As Marcel Proust has suggested, the real voyage of discovery is not just seeking new landscapes but having new eyes. To focus on a moving high-tech landscape requires men and women who take at least some pleasure from perpetual professional development. For teachers to add on-line technologies to their current instructional mix requires going beyond the basics of mastering hardware and software to getting around on the Net in a way that builds on the characteristics of effective instruction.

LEARNING IN THE NEW AGE:
THE ELECTRONIC CLASSROOM

The symbol of the globalization system is the World Wide Web. The Web is a large vaguely mapped territory with unusually beautiful scenery, unfamiliar languages and customs, and treacherous technological jungles. For computer explorers, the Web is the most exciting communications medium since people a generation ago listened to explorers of the North Pole on their crystal radios. The Web and other equipment such as portable computers, digital cameras, and satellite telephones enable us to participate in rich adventures as they happen on land, sea, air, and space (Lewis, 1996).

In the early 1990s, a program to access the Internet, called *Mosaic*, unlocked the Web for ordinary users. Then Netscape Navigator (the latest version is Netscape Communicator) came along and became one of the more popular browser tools for making the Internet even more accessible. With some Web sites, we use Microsoft Internet Explorer. Such "browsers" are now often part of the all-in-one Internet starter kits that are taking the pain out of the process. As Web browsers are finding their way into applications programs, the necessary software for connecting into the Internet is coming already installed in many computers. The basic idea is to get away from the more cumbersome "folder and file" system. Microsoft has woven the Internet's World Wide Web into its current Windows PC operating system. Apple Computer and Netscape Communications are doing the same thing for new Macintosh computers. In both cases, the idea is to make it easier for everybody by arranging for the computer (when it comes out of the box) to plug into the phone line and handle everything as if it were a Web page.

Students can retrieve images and text from information sources arranged as World Wide Web pages by clicking the mouse on highlighted words or phrases. We are now at a stage where even novices can find their way around the global Internet network, downloading images, messages, and audio and video files with the click of a mouse. The Internet has become an example of how a virtual community can connect telecommunicators around the world. Educators are increasingly looking to the cyberspace reached by these data highways as they strive to make their classrooms more interactive, collaborative, and student centered.

USING THE INTERNET TO REFRAME OUR UNDERSTANDING OF THE WORLD

Technology is more or less neutral. Like other technologies, the Internet reflects the strengths and weaknesses of the human condition. A recent United Nations Development Program Report shows that globalization is compounding the gap between the rich and poor nations, and that computer technology is exacerbating this gap even more. A tightly wired world brings into sharper focus questions like whether or not global capitalism is benign or evil.

Since the Internet magnifies human attributes, it has to be tailored for a context that is more or less appropriate. It is clearly at its best when serving well-defined educational goals. On the Internet, the truth often seems relative, but the same might be said of telephones. The Internet is much like other communications technologies there are many good and bad possibilities. One difference is that false information spreads even more quickly through the system, getting amplified along the way. The Internet ups the speed, but it has few uniquely demonic powers. Technology may get us there faster, but you still have to know where you want to go. As Yogi Berra put it, "If you don't know where you're going you'll end up somplace else."

When it comes to learning, the Internet can distort reality and be a colossal waste of time. It can also become a great help in understanding the world. It all depends on how you go about using it. With any technology, one thing is for sure: the curriculum has to drive the way the technology is used. "Surfing" the Internet aimlessly wastes time. You have to have a goal. Once you learn focus on what is important, you have a passport to an ever-expanding reservoir of knowledge and global communication.

We are just awakening to the fact that the computer, the Internet, and the World Wide Web are redefining literacy and reshaping how we learn. For better or for worse, these technologies are weaving themselves inextricably into the life of the school. As recently as 1994, the Internet was too difficult for many. Now we have user-friendly World Wide Web browsers to get around with. Anyone can do it. A browsing program is intended to be a kind of passport to see what the world Wide Web has to offer. Netscape's Communicator and Microsoft's Internet Explorer are the most common browsers, and the price is right. You can get them for free.

For less than $200, WebTV offers Web access with a box on top of the television set. You must also pay a $20-a-month fee for unlimited on-line services, much like America Online. By using Excite (an easy Internet search engine for WebTV), you can click on the word "search," type in the words "music" and "radio" and get dozens of sites to visit. Many foreign radio stations can be listened to over the Internet (http.//www.thedj.com/). Sites often contain video, audio, and data on the subject.

RETHINKING STANDARDS IN AN INTERNET-BASED EDUCATIONAL ENVIRONMENT

Although some benefits from the Internet are undeniable, it will take much more than technology to clearly improve instruction or fundamentally reform American education. A solid strategic plan is crucial. The same can be said for incorporating Internet-based activities into daily lessons that grow out of new academic standards.

Figure 8.1. Connecting Internet resources to our lives.

The Internet is viewed as a natural part of the process reflected in the science and math standards. The standards for the English language arts also refer to visual literacy and information and communications technology as central factors in learning language and developing literacy. Possibilities are also found in the arts standards. For example, student video productions can now be put on the Web, and playful techno-art can be inspired by and even transcend developing technologies. Even before widespread computer use, video artists were the first to suggest that we might make some sense of rapidly shifting images. They were also the first to compose visual collages from mundane images. Now we see such constructions in everything from ads on television to Web sites on the Internet. The visual arts, music, theater, and dance are too important and too profound to be left out of our children's lives. Fortunately, arts education is claiming its place in the core curriculum and the arts standards are setting a vision for the future, and for the first time, a test for the arts is included in the most recent National Assessment of Educational Progress (NAEP), also known as the Nation's Report Card. Certainly much of the future belongs to those who can see and read it.

Whatever the subject, students should be given opportunities to use Internet technology to construct information from around the world as they explore problems and design solutions. Helping students see the human factor and the societal implications is viewed as important if students are to use technology to do something worthwhile for our culture and our society. As the science and math standards point out, the laws of the physical and biological universe are viewed as important to understanding how technological objects and systems work. It is clearly important to connect students to the various elements of our technologically intensive world so that they can construct models and solve problems.

TRANSFORMING THE STUDENTS' LEARNING EXPERIENCE

Internet technology is changing our view of literacy. When used well, it changes the instructional environment and provides opportunities for students to create new knowledge for themselves. Along with its computer-based associates, it can serve as a vehicle for discovery-based classrooms, giving students access to data, experiences with simulations, and the possibilities for interactive storytelling.

At their worst, computers and their Internet associates can turn some subjects into spectator sports. At their best, the same technology allows you to take control, communicate, and observe phenomena that would otherwise remain unobservable. This opens up the possibility of representing ideas and solving problems in multiple ways. A technological tool like the Internet can be fast paced and stimulating. It is one good way to investigate, analyze, inquire, and problem solve.

For teachers to connect the Internet to their lessons requires a substantial subject matter knowledge that is deeper and more flexible than textbooks.

This means understanding the key concepts in a discipline and the important debates in a field. It also means actively engaging students in collaborative inquiry. *The keys to success are teacher preparation, professional development, the content of technology-assisted lessons, and how everything is connected to what is going on in the classroom.*

A good example of technology/curriculum integration can be found at *www.globe.gov*. Thousands of middle and high school students from around the world gather information about the weather that is then posted on this Web site to help scientists from around the globe study climate changes and the weather. Add hydrology, land cover, and soil studies for the more advanced. There are chat lines where students can communicate directly with scientists, telling them about the information they are gathering and asking questions. This program was put into place by Vice President Al Gore as a way to give elementary and high school students hands-on science and computer training. It goes under the ungainly title of "Global Learning and Observations to Benefit the Environment." By connecting to this program students work much like scientists and take responsible ownership of both the on-site weather-measuring equipment and the on-line data that they generate.

STEERING INTERNET USE TOWARDS INTELLECTUAL DISCOVERY

As students and teachers continue to grow professionally with changing technology, they need to balance enthusiasm with skepticism. Print literacy encourages the process of reflective thinking. Looking into a literate inner space with print is more likely to result in more secure inner voices and a more reasoned public discourse. Print literacy may create hierarchies of literates over illiterates, but it is still the cornerstone of democracy. Television and film, by contrast, make fewer demands on the intellect. Much of the narrative storytelling found in these visually intensive media has the staying power of comic books. Adolescent demands for pleasure are gratified without taxing the ability to think. Being fun to watch is one thing. Intellectual stimulation is quite another. The Internet has the possibility of building on the best elements of previous media.

As Internet technology has moved beyond the margins of school life, it is being linked to subject matter standards and broader school reforms. The result is often a powerful synergism that contributes to widespread school reform. In our survey of school districts, we found that districts that made the most significant progress in integrating Internet technology into their curriculum were also the ones that had made a substantial investment in teacher training. Our conclusions: Make teachers a top priority, pay attention to equity, and invest in the elementary grades.

As technology has become more powerful and intrusive, our society has become evermore infatuated with communications and information technology. The public and the politicians seem sure that simply connecting the schools to the technological juggernaut will take care of fundamental problems. Good luck. As many teachers will tell you, there has to be a pedagogical plan. A technology like the Internet works best when it is driven by instructional plans. Once clear educational goals and subject matter standards are in place, technology can enable important changes in the curriculum and even help you move down the reform trail. But remember, *put the education piece in place first.*

POSITIVE SKEPTICISM: SEPARATING SUBSTANCE FROM FLUFF ON THE INTERNET

Are you caught between technological cheerleaders and neo-Luddites? There is a middle ground between the technophiles and the technophobes. "Technorealism" is a useful label for this position. The idea here is that it is prudent to embrace Internet technology but with care and critical thoughtfulness. Injecting a little healthy skepticism into the discussion doesn't mean rejecting the possibilities but applying a critical perspective. This will help balance the wonders of the information highway with the dangers of information overload. A full discussion of these issues is available online *(http://www.technorealism.org)*.

How do you sort out what is valid from what is foolish? Here are suggested classroom activities:

1. Give students a one-page scavenger hunt activity where they have to find everything from the atomic number of uranium to DNA research to how to say "hello" to people in Japan.
2. Find some current information that you believe. Explain.
3. Finding something about current events that you don't believe. Explain.
4. Have students find something on the Internet that is funny and clearly false, something that is without question true, and something that could be taken either way. A bit on the foolish side, fifth-grade students are quick to point to unusual Web sites like the one that maintains that one human in three is a werewolf.
5. Examine the validity of something that you find.
6. Critique a Web site.

7. Go through some Web sites and ask some questions about the content. Come up with some answers. Learn to ask better questions.

8. How would the accuracy of information from an advertisement be compared to information found on a Web site like National Geographic's?

New ways of connecting to the Internet keep springing up. Along with WebTV, there are wireless systems that bring the Net to your television. The latest in this technology lets you do just about anything on the television that you can do on a computer: surf the Web, download, print, and save. Like everyone else, teachers and students are consumers of technology and they need to be able to judge critically the quality and usefulness of the electronic choices growing up around them.

ADVICE FOR SCHOOL DISTRICTS: remain skeptical of sheer boosterism, realize that change is accelerating, develop an educational plan for using the Internet, and do more to encourage the professional development for teachers.

DEFINING THE ETHICAL BOUNDARIES OF INTERNET USE

There are moral consequences to being able to tailor the information that reaches us. Without much reflection or assessment, we embrace new technologies and amplify the production of data. We are now awash with less than private e-mail messages, Internet-based news, advertising, infotainment, trash, and even telephone calls on the Internet. Image and instant reaction overwhelm meaning and careful deliberation. Truth is increasingly elusive in such a media-saturated world.

As the Internet mixes print with video, visual art, and film clips, it shows its potential for growing up with the joys and values of artistic achievement, but that's the upscale Internet neighborhood. Across the tracks, it descends into the abyss of instant gratification; sordidness knows no bounds. As a society, we must continue to make distinctions between what is and what is not appropriate for children. We have limits to what children can see in the movies and on television. Without censorship or reducing everything to the intellectual level of a seven-year-old, we can put barriers in the way of the inappropriate on the Internet. More mature use of technology is part of the future. It is as natural as a child growing up. Or at least it had better be, or we should find a new way to communicate and gather information.

Someone has to keep track of the addresses for the Internet to work. Early on it was the U.S. Defense Department. Recently, created as a joint venture with the federal government, the Internet Corporation for Assigned Names and Numbers or ICann now oversees the registration of domain names of Web sites. Domain names are unique names assigned to a collection of computers connected to the Internet. Censorship has always been out, but we may see more of a connection between the name of the site and what's on it.

There is little doubt that schools must continue to hold up before the young the spectacle of greatness in literature, history, and life. The only question is the technological means for going about doing it. Clearly, the ability to understand, evaluate, and integrate information delivered by electronic media like the Internet will be an important part of what it means to be literate in the twenty-first century.

THE WORLD WIDE WEB: RESOURCES FOR TEACHING AND LEARNING

There are many good Internet Web sites for teachers and students. On-line resources include access to discussion groups, virtual classrooms, research tools, free software, and many other tools to help teachers and students integrate the Internet into their daily work. We have chosen a sampling of sites that work across a number of subjects and grade levels. Some are just for the teacher and, as far as we know, everything listed here is free.

The intent of this section is to give you a good sample of good Internet Web sites for teaching and learning. Things are shifting like sand on the beach. So don't be disappointed if an address or two has been changed.

But first, a review of basic search concepts.

A Word on Search Engines

Just how do you find and create information on the Internet: serendipitous discovery, links found at a Web site, subject guides (like Magellan), and software programs that search the index for words found in the user's query (search engines). *Search engines* are programs designed to help information seekers find information on Web pages and sound, video, graphics, and text files available on the Internet. There is no one search engine that will find everything on the Web. The three elements needed to fulfill the information search are the "spider," the index, and the search engine software. A "spider" is a special kind of software that searches Web pages and other information stored on the Web servers in order to find text that is new or modified since the last time it visited those servers. Its findings are then organized into an "index", which is a logical list of text-only records of pages, sounds, and graphics. The search engine often provides you with the electronic form through which you can enter your search word or phrase. After you do this, the search engine searches its databases for documents that best match your query and assigns levels of relevance to the results they generate.

Figure 8.2. Enhanced image of a painting by Roy Lichtenstein.

Search engines are different from Web directories (like Yahoo) or subject guides, which are tools that present you with a menu of broad subjects such as "educational innovations," "special education," and "technology and learning." Web directories will present you with a menu of broad subjects generally assembled from smaller databases compared to those that house search engine indexes. These directories are usually assembled by teams of editors who are experts in a special field of interest. The results you will get, therefore, are more likely to be relevant to what you're looking for as compared to what search engines might turn up for you.

This is not the place for a detailed "how-to" on using specific search engines. However, a few smart guidelines on how to approach the search process could be helpful.

Identify the topic of your search. Start with a rough sketch idea of what you want. Then, write down what you already know about the topic and what else you need to know about it. List ideas and questions you might have about this topic. If you have difficulty doing this, consult reference books and encyclopedias for fresh ideas.

Constantly hone your vocabulary. Arm yourself with a rich vocabulary. Even for what appears to be a simple topic, you should be able to work with only a few selected keywords. Consider synonyms: If you're doing research on "cancer," for instance, you might work with the clinical equivalents, "neoplasm," or "carcinoma." Or, think of antonyms: A good way to find material on "peace" would be to find pages on "war" and "violence." Variant international spelling of words might lead you to unexpected places: "colour" instead of "color" or "labour" instead of "labor."

What are you looking for general ideas or specific details? Are you stopping for information about a general topic ("educational reform") or are you look for specific information (e.g., "collaborative classroom software")? Web directories are more useful when you're looking for general information or working with a broad topic or keywords that are too common on the Web. However, if you know exactly what you're looking for and use rather precise search terms, it is more appropriate to work with search engines.

Help yourself with a list of keywords. Before embarking on the use of a number of search engines, draw up a list of potential search terms, words, and phrases. Experiment and use items from this list with various search engines. Add new words and phrases to your list as you gather search results from these search engines. In the process of collecting search results, you will eventually have a better sense of which search engine serves your purposes best.

Use Boolean searches to the max. Not all search engines offer Boolean search syntax, but the better ones do. These are extremely powerful tools for constructing fairly sophisticated queries in the most compact form.

Know the syntax of the search engines you're working with. Different search engines operate in their own unique way, so learn their peculiarities even if something like Boolean search syntax appears to be universal. Words like "AND," "OR," "NOT" are boolean search operators. If you were to use "AND," for instance, using the search phrase "airplanes AND cars," your search results will show Web pages that have both the words "airplanes" and "cars" in them. If you were to use "NOT," using the search phrase "airplanes NOT cars," your search results will show Web pages that have the word "airplanes" but not "cars." The search engines implement Boolean conventions differently, so consult the extremely valuable on-line search help that is available with each search engine.

The following are the more highly recommended search engines on the Web: Excite, Alta Vista, Hotbot, Lycos, Infoseek, and Metacrawler. A word about metacrawlers: These are search tools used to perform a search using a combination of search engines in a single operation. The obvious advantage in using them is that you get to activate a number of search engines in a single keystroke. The disadvantage is that the search tends to be superficial rather than thorough across the search engines that are used because simple as opposed to advanced search features are being implemented (Angeles, 1998). The value of metacrawlers was reaffirmed after two scientists of the NEC Research Institute found out after a six-month long experimentation that of the 11 search engines covered in their study not one of them indexes more than 16 percent of the Web. Also, these search engines seem to be biased towards more well-known information. They believe this is the consequence of the rapid explosion in the number of web sites daily, so much so that search engines could not keep up with them. The scientists involved in the research study estimated a total of 2.8 million sites and 800 million pages as of July 1999 (Guernsey, 1999).

Another device that is being suggested instead of search engines is the "web ring" (Kelley, 1999). "If using a search engine can be like drinking from a fire hose, Internet surfing using a Web ring is like sharing a cup of tea with a group of strangers who are batty about a favorite hobby, like collecting Australian emergency-squad insignia....[A web ring]...allows all the people who are interested in the same topic to move in next door to each other, click on an icon, go to their neighbors' houses and see what's doing in there...." A "web ring" is organized this way: A webmaster joins a ring by adding a code to their pages that is found at the home page of a particular ring. This embedded code enables surfers to move through different sites within a ring by clicking the forward or back buttons, they show next five sites button, or a button that will activate a site at random again from within the ring. Depending on the topic, a web ring could actually provide more content per click than search engines. Why don't you look up a few rather prominent web rings so that you could see for yourself: Web Ring (www.webring.org), Looplink (www.looplink.com), The Rail (www.therail.com), a business-related site, and (www.execulink.com/wstout).

GENERAL INSTRUCTIONAL RESOURCES

Language And Cultural Resources

Human Languages Page

http://www.june29.com/HLP/
At this single URL, you can find out something about almost every language spoken on earth. Check out the "easy" ones first, such as Spanish or French, and then try any other language that you can think of. Middle English is spoken here.

Geography Resources

MapQuest

http://www.mapquest.com/
At this Web site, you can get map directions to just about anywhere in the world. Want to go to Ogunquit, Maine? This Web site has the ability to help you get there and find a place to stay.

National Flags

http://155.187.10.12/flags/nation-flags.html
If your students are doing reports on nations around the world, they need this site. You can get images of flags from at least 190 countries. More flags are being added on a regular basis.

National Geographic Online

http://www.nationalgeographic.com/main.html
This Web site has excellent resources and collections for teachers and students. It is as good as the venerable magazine that so many of us have grown up with. A useful documentary page can be found at: *http://www.nationalgeographic.com/kids.*

History Resources

American Civil War Home Page

http://funnelweb.utcc.utk.edu/~hoemann/cwarhp.html
The American Civil War is studied in the fifth, eighth, and tenth or eleventh grades in most districts. Sometimes the battles are re-created, and history lessons have come to life thanks to a PBS documentary by Ken Burns. Here you will find maps, documents, diaries, pictures, and more. This site has proven itself with middle-school teachers.

American Revolution to Reconstruction

http://grid.let.rug.nl/~welling/usa/revolution.html
Part of a series on American History, this is an interesting site with lots of color and good history.

The Invention Dimension

http://web.mit.edu/invent/
This is a Web site for the history of science. The people and the stories behind the inventions help bring things to life. A different inventor is featured each week.

Language Arts Resources General Collections

The Children's Literature Web Guide

http://www.ucalgary.ca/~dkbrown/index.html
This Web site offers all sorts of links to good children's literature. There are also links for teachers, parents, storytellers, and children. Elementary teachers really like this one.

Roget's (1911) Thesaurus

http://www.thesaurus.com/thesaurus/
It is kind of fun to go back in history and use an early version of Roget's Thesaurus. Language does change. New words are always coming into play, and old words continue to take on new meanings.

Direct Link to Publishers on the Web

http://www.theslot.com/
This site offers scores of leading book publishers from around the world. It features catalogs, backlist offerings, upcoming books, and the possibility for ordering the books on-line.

Specific Collections

The World of Mark Twain

http://marktwain.miningco.com
This subsite within Mining Co.'s home site is dedicated by Jim Zwick to Mark Twain. This Mark Twain site is a collection of useful links about the famous author himself. There are links, for instance, to exhibits, electronic texts, scholarly studies, syllabi, and other related resources of interest to teachers. Read excerpts from Twain's autobiography, access quotations and maxims, and discover comprehensive guides to his major works.

Arthur C. Clarke Unauthorized Homepage

http://www.lsi.usp.br/~rbianchi/clarke/ACC.Homepage.html
This Web site is great for science fiction enthusiasts featuring Clarke's biography, body of works in print and film, an Internet-based fan club, among others. Arthur C. Clarke, celebrated science fiction writer of over sixty novels, is featured on this Fan Club homepage. Named Grand Master by the Science Fiction Writers of America, visitors to this site can refer to Clarke's numerous awards, publications, and laws of nature. He is the author of more than sixty books with more than 50 million copies in print, winner of all the field's highest honors. He was named Grand Master by the Science Fiction Writers of America in 1986.

The Internet Classics Archive

http://classics.mit.edu
This Web site has been developed partly through the sponsorship of the MIT Program in Writing and Humanistic Studies. Teachers and students may select from a list of 441 works of classical literature by 59 authors, including user-driven commentary and "reader's choice" Web sites. Mainly Greco-Roman works (some Chinese and Persian), all in English translation. Works of such beloved thinkers as Aeschylus, Euripides, Homer, Machiavelli, Plato, Plutarch, and Virgil are featured.

The New York Times Book Review Section

http://www.nytimes.com/books
Feast on the latest and most informed reviews of recent fiction and non-fiction titles. For instance, biographer Michael Reynolds writes an introductory essay for Hemingway's book, *True at First Light,* a posthumous novel based on an unfinished manuscript. The Web site also features reviews of other Hemingway books, interviews, nine of his dispatches from the Spanish Civil War, audio clips, and a photo collection.

Technological and Informational Resources Online Catalogs with Webbed Interfaces

http://www.lib.ncsu.edu/staff/morgan/alcuin/wwwed-catalogs.html
Hunter Monroe has accomplished the impossible task of bookmarking the labyrinth of numerous academic, corporate, and public libraries in existence. In this Web site, he has created a master page of links to libraries with Web-capable search interfaces. Used as a research tool, one may explore browser accessible online public access catalogs.

ZDTV.COM Web Site

http:www.zdtv.com
This is a super site for children and young geeks who would like to develop a passion for information technology. With cleverly assembled programming at a tempo that will keep anyone from being bored, the ZDTV producers and writers make available enticing shows like "Silicon Spin," "Call for Help," "Fresh Gear," "The Money Machine," "Digital Avenue," "ZDTV News," and others to feed us with a daily dose of must-know high-tech stories and news, so very essential to being wired nowadays. Children and young viewers are encouraged to link up with the studio through a netcam network.

NOVA's Special Effects Homepage: Filming "Titanic"

http://www.pbs.org/wgbh/nova/specialfx2/real.html
Learn about the amazing technologies behind the creation of the movie "Titanic." Filming "Titanic" was an epic technological feat not unlike the building of the ill-fated ship about 86 years ago. Sixteen companies including Digital Domain created over 450 effects shots for the movie. State-of-the-art computer-generated imagery and classical techniques in the visual effects tradition are combined to produce dazzling footage for the movie.

Little Planet Times

http://www.littleplanet.com
Children and their parents will find this fictitious newspaper entitled *Little Planet Times*, which is written for and by children, not only entertaining but also extremely informative as well. Stories in the paper urge readers to write to the editor with their suggestions. The target is to enhance the reading, writing, and communication skills of grades K-5. An interactive forum exists to encourage children to make contacts and develop long-distance friendships. Children can also find out about the latest movies and can say hello to the Little Planet Times' librarian, who always has a good word about the latest books for children. There are also books online for children to read and review the latest books for children. There are also books online for children to read and review the latest books for children. It quickly involves children in fun activities and encourages them to respond.

KidNews

http://www.kidnews.com
Children could check out the latest current events at *KidNews*, which is also written for and by children. Through the Internet, children worldwide are welcome to submit stories they have written and teachers, likewise, are encouraged to use these stories in their classes. Find feature stories like "What the Hay-Go for a Ride!" "How to Have Fun in the Snow," and "How to Build Your Own Birdfeeder."

Candlelight Stories

http://www.CandlelightStories.com/
Here is a collection of favorite stories and fairy tales from all over the world. Students can even "publish" their own stories at this site.

Internet Public Library Story Hour

http://www.ipl.org/youth/StoryHour/
This is a link from the larger Internet Public Library Web site. You will find good on-line stories to read and illustrations to view.

Animals, Myths, and Legends

http://www.ozemail.com.au/~oban/
A collection of recently written myths and legends that look at the relationship between man, animals, and the universe. The Web site is recommended for three-to eight-year-olds.

Shakespeare Headquarters

http://the-tech.mit.edu/Shakespeare.html
If you are studying Shakespeare, this Web site is very important. Students can see complete copies of comedies, tragedies, sonnets, and poems. In addition, there is an interactive glossary. If students are reading the text and comes across a word they do not know, they can click on it, and the glossary will appear that explains what the word meant in Shakespeare's time.

Science And Mathematics

The Discovery Channel School

http://school.discovery.com/
Every semester the Discovery Channel School offers lessons that you can use with your students. When you visit their Web page, click on "How to Set Up a Classroom Newspaper (on the Web)."

The Eisenhower National Clearinghouse for Math and Science

http://www.enc.org/nf_index.htm (no frames)
http://www.enc.org/ (frames)
Here you can find wonderful activities to use in your classroom that have been written by teachers for students. Try visiting the math sites, the best school sites, and Internet tools for parents.

Fractals in Nature

http://cps-www.bu.edu/~mkm/museum_project/Main.ian.html
This Boston University site uses still and moving images to show how fractals develop in nature. These random branching patterns can be caused by everything from soil erosion to termite activity. Sometimes they behave in predictable ways. The pictures alone are worth the visit.

Frank Potter's Science Gems

http://www-sci.lib.uci.edu/SEP/SEP.html
This Web site is a collection of thousands of science sites. They are annotated and categorized according to grade level.

The Why Files: The Science Behind the News

http://whyfiles.news.wisc.edu/
This on-line newspaper tries to explain the science behind the headlines. Web walk here and click on previous issues. There are good science images and a question/answer forum.

SAMI (Science and Math Initiatives)

http://www.learner.org/sami
Math-related sites are a little hard to find, but SAMI has some. The "chatback line," "mathematics and science curricula," "other resources," and "rural resources" are all worth viewing. Click on Lesson Plans and Projects and find a list of links to math and science lessons.

Useful Science Web Sites

http://www.hkstar.com/~hkiedsci/de-web.htm
This Hong Kong Web site includes twenty-four links to other science sites. It is part of a larger site called Digital Electronics, which has a tutorial lesson for high school electronics. You can find it at *http://www.hkstar.com/~hkledsci/home.html.introductory*

Figure 8.3. Keith Haring's smiling monster "to incorporate [art] into every part of life."

Planets, Space, and Web Sites

NASA (National Aeronautics and Space Administration) Home Page

http://hypatia.gsfc.nasa.gov/NASA_homepage.html

NASA offers a wealth of possibilities for teachers and students along with links to other sites of scientific interest. There are other busy NASA sites on the Web, including the recent Mars exploration. You can get to all of them from this home page. They are all worth the wait.

The New York Times Science Section

http://www.nytimes.com/science

Find the most recent coverage of significant scientific breakthroughs. For instance, a recent Science Section edition featured an in-depth look at 30 years of lunar exploration, from the first euphoric successes to the later doubts and failures, including coverage of the Apollo missions, and the scientific merits of the expeditions to earth's closest neighbor.

The Messier Science Page

http://seds.lpl.arizona.edu/messier/Messier.html
From 1758 to 1782, Charles Messier, a French astronomer, compiled a list of a hundred diffuse objects that he thought were comets. As it turned out, the "comets" were many things: nebulae, star clusters, and other objects found in the night sky. The study of these objects by astronomers has led to important discoveries, such as the life cycles of stars, the reality of galaxies as separate "island universes," and the possible age of the universe. Excellent graphics enhance this site.

The Nine Planets: A Multimedia Tour of Our Solar System

http://seds.lpl.arizona.edu/billa/tnp/
At this comprehensive examination of our solar system you will find links to just about everything now known about the planets in our solar system: moons, orbits, the Hubble Telescope, photos from space, and much more.

Ocean Planet Smithsonian Home Page

http://seawifs.gsfc.nasa.gov/ocean-planet.html
This Smithsonian exhibit looks at the power of the ocean.

Welcome to the Planets

http://pds.jpl.nasa.gov/planets/
A tour of our solar system from the Jet Propulsion Lab and the California Institute of Technology. Just a little on the difficult side.

Stars and Galaxies

http://www.eia.brad.ac.uk/btl/sg.html
This site explains how stars and galaxies behave, their life cycles, and how they generate energy. An audio portion at the beginning will take about two minutes to download.

Life Science Web Sites

WISE Curriculum Projects in Science (University of California-Berkeley)

http:wise.berkeley.edu

Funded by the National Science Foundation, the WISE Curriculum Project has created a Web-based learning environment and curriculum library addressing the need to capitalize on the synergies between the Internet and integrated science learning. While encouraging the participation of as many schools as possible, WISE seeks to create curricular projects and assessments, design and implement WISE software, create a teacher professional development programs, and help teachers develop science programs.

The Cow's Eye Dissection

http://www.exploratorium.edu/learning_studio/cow_eye/

This site includes a step-by-step lesson on the anatomy of a cow's eye. The purpose of this anatomy lesson is to learn more about how the eye works. While you are here, click on the Eye Primer.

Virtual Frog Dissection Kit

http://george.lbl.gov/itghm.pg.docs/dissect/info.html

The University of California at Berkeley and the Lawrence Livermore Labs offer a good way to familiarize your students with the anatomy of the frog. The Dissection Kit shows gives you a hint of how virtual reality might relate to classroom learning.

Forum on the One-Legged Frog

http://scope.educ.washington.edu/frogs/index.html

This is an excellent online forum for discussion over the deformed frog controversy. Since about 1992, scientists have observed an increase in the incidence of physical deformities among frog populations in many parts of North America. Expectedly, scientists have advanced competing hypotheses involving possible causes such as parasites, environmental chemicals, and ultraviolet exposure to try to explain what has happened. They also think that the frog problem is a precursor of an unseen environmental danger that would eventually affect other animals and humans. The deformed frog dilemma encourages complex, multidisciplinary dialog involving students and teachers of the environment, genetics, and biochemistry. The Web site offers a range of educational resources to keep the discussions alive.

Mathematics Web Sites

Fractals

http://math.rice.edu/~lanius/frac/
This site has fractal units for elementary and middle school math students that is fun and informative.

The Math Forum Home Page

http://forum.swarthmore.edu/index.js.html
Located at Swarthmore College, the Math Forum has a compendium of lists for students, teachers, and researchers. It also features an interesting approach to new ideas and debates in the world of mathematics. Here you can join a Math Forum, and gather valuable resources at *http://forum.swarthmore.edu/~steve/*, as well as the Forum Internet Resource Collection. You can also try "Ask Dr. Math" while you are there. *http://forum.swarthmore.edu/dr.math/drmath.*

The Math Virtual Library: General Resources

http://euclid.math.fsu.edu/science/
There are over sixty math and science links at this one. Some of them are just fair, others good. This is part of a larger Virtual Library site at URL http://www.w3.org/pub/datasources/bysubject/overview.html

Welcome to Mega-Math

http://www.c3.lanl.gov/mega-math/menu.html (text)
http://www.c3.lanl.gov/mega-math/index.html (image map)
The Los Alamos Lab has devised and collected Web sites that will help explain mathematical phenomena such as graphing, machines, infinity, knots, and ice cream.

Physical Education And Sports Resources

PECentral

http://pe.central.vt.edu

This site is one of the most comprehensive pages for the physical educator. PECentral was developed by the Health and Physical Education Program at Virginia Tech to provide teachers with the latest information about appropriate physical education programs for children and youth. This site contains instructional resources like lesson plans, assessment, and links to other Web sites in physical education.

The New York Times Sports Section

http://www.nytimes.com/sports

Be informed of the latest sports events at this New York Times site. This week's edition, for instance, features the biggest cycling race in the world as it tries to recover from last year's scandal-ridden competition. The site includes daily coverage of the results, a full team-by-team listing of race participants, photo slide shows, and a discussion forum for avid spectators.

Sport Quest

http://www.sportquest.com

This virtual resource center includes the best information on sports, coaching, statistics and results, sports training, sports science, sports medicine, and physical education. You can find information on professional sports, disabled sports, Olympic sports, and more. Make sure that you visit this site if you want to know about the world of sports.

The Science of Hockey

http://www.exploratorium.edu/hockey/

The sports fans in your room might be interested in the science behind the game. Learn facts about ice, fitness, the mechanics of skating, reaction time, shooting a puck, and energy. This multimedia Web site uses video clips and interviews of scientists and San Jose Shark hockey players, all talking about their craft. Many lessons can be derived from this Web site.

Women's Sports Pages

http://fiat.gslis.utexas.edu/~lewisa/womsprt.html#issues
This one should be examined by anyone (with a low budget) interested in good Web site design. Amy Smith has also done a good job of providing links by sport. Gender issues and sports festivals can also be found here.

Social Studies Resources

History Social Science K-12 WebPage

http://www.execpc.com/~dboals/boals.html
It would take decades to go through all the Web sites at this URL.

Social Studies Lesson Plans for Teachers

http://www.csun.edu/%7ehcedu013/index.html
This site offers links to lesson plans, resources, on-line activities, and current events.

Web Sites to Publish Work by Children

Kid's Space

http://www.kids-space.org/
This is a place where children can show off their writing, painting, and thinking to others. This is a good place for publishing student work.

KidPub WWW Publishing

http://www.kidpub.org/kidpub/
This is another place where children can publish the stories they have written. Seems like a natural for many elementary classrooms. Good writing suggestions are given.

The Virtual Classrooms

CyberSchool

http://cyberschool.4j.lane.edu
The CyberSchool program based in Eugene, Oregon, was designed for high school students. This site provides on-line courses for K-12 students. It is fairly easy for teachers to adapt the lessons found here.

CU-SeeMe Project

http://www.fortune.org/cuseemebasics.shtml
Many schools are using CU-SeeMe video conferencing to communicate with each other using live video and sound.

Teaching without Walls: A Course in Meteorology

This is a virtual course delivered by Alistair Fraser at Penn State University. The course uses interactive multimedia presentations to help the students visualize the concepts of meteorology. The students have access to the course material anywhere on the Internet. This is a good site for learning about things like the origin of hurricanes and the formation of clouds.

World Lecture Hall

http://www.utexas.edu/world/lecture/
This site contains links to pages created by faculty worldwide to deliver class materials. This site lets you can explore different lessons and courses.

THE INTERNET CONTRIBUTES TO ACCELERATING EDUCATIONAL CHANGE

The impulse to use technology to somehow increase productivity and reduce the cost of education rarely works out. Neither computers nor anything else replaces good teachers. The question is how to use the technology to support these teachers and how to do something really worthwhile for education, culture, and society.

The trouble with the future is that there are so many of them, and they are all moving around quickly. Harmonizing the educational present and the educational future means reinventing the schools, attending to support mechanisms, and having the courage to be out in front on certain issues. To successfully sail through the crosscurrents of our transitional age requires the development of habits of the heart and habits of the intellect. Every age seeks out the appropriate medium or combination of media to confront the mysteries of human learning (Angeles, 1998).

New communication technologies can be used to help students understand imagery, solve problems creatively, and apply these solutions to real-life situations. But it takes effort and planning to make the engaging meaningful. Having a solid educational agenda is more important than having the greatest technology. Whatever the curriculum, it ultimately comes down to the teacher's intellectual curiosity, sense of humor, character, and ability to relate to young people.

Figure 8.4. The future belongs to those who can see it. Op-Art, computer enlarged image by Barbara Kruger.

REFERENCES AND RESOURCES

Angeles, R. (1999) Mining information on the Web using search engines. Unpublished manuscript.

Bennett, S. J. (1998). *The plugged-in parent: What you should know about kids and computers.* New York: Times Books.

Burgstahler, Sheryl E. New Kids on the Net: Internet Activities for Young Learners. New York: Prentice Hall, 1998.

Buyens, J. (1998) *Stupid Web Tricks.* New York: Microsoft Press.

Cassel, P. & Bolton, R. (1998). *Sam's teach tourself the internet in 10 minutes.* New York: Sams.

Chorowsky, J., et al. *The parents' pocket guide to kids & computers.* Family Computer Workshop.

Einstein, D. (1998). *America Online for busy people: The book to use when there's no time to lose.* New York: Osborne/McGraw-Hill.

Gralla, P. (1999). *Online kids: A young surfer's guide to cyberspace.* New York: John Wiley & Sons.

Guernsey, L. (1999). Seek–But on the web, you might not find. *The New York Times,* July 8.

Harper, C. (1998). *And that's the way it will be: News and information in a digital world.* New York: New York University Press.

Hoffman, A. (1998). *50 fun ways to internet.* Career Press.

Hughes, D.R. & Campbell, P. (1998). *Kids online: Protecting your children in cyberspace.* Fleming H. Revell Co.

Kaufeld, J. & Kaufeld, A. (1998). *America Online for dummines.* (4th ed.) IDG Books.

Kelley, T. (1999). Surfing in circles and loving it. *The New York Times,* January 21.

Leebow, K. et al. *300 incredible things for kids on the internet.* Mass Market Paperback, 1998.

Levine, J.R., Baroudi, C., & Young, M.L. (1998). *The internet for dummies* (5th ed.). IDG Books.

Lewis, P. Adventures can find company on the internet. *The New York Times,* July 7, 1999.

Morton, J.G., & Cohn, A.L. (1998). *Kids on the 'net: Conducting internet research in K-5 classrooms.* Beeline Books.

National Assessment of Educational Progress. (1995). Washington, DC: U.S. Government Publications.

Norell, G.T. (1998). *95 Windows: An unofficial poetry collection from Microsoft network.* Dandelion Press.

O'Hara, S. (1998). *Official netscape beginner's guide to the internet.* Ventana Co.

Owen, B.M. (1999). *The future of television in the internet age.* Harvard University Press.

Pedersen, T., et al. (1998). *Make your own web page!* Price Stern Sloan Publishers.

Ray, E.J., et al. (1998) *Alta Vista search revolution* (2nd ed.). New York: Osborne/McGraw Hill.

Snell, T. (1998) *Teach yourself the internet in 24 hours.* Sams.

Trumbauer, L. (1999). *Free stuff for kids on the net (cool sites).* Millbrook Pr Trade.

Trumbauer, L. (1999). *Super sports for kids on the net (cool sites).* Millbrook Pr Trade.

Vega, D. (1998). *Learning the internet for kids: A voyage to internet treasures.* DDC Publishing, Inc.

Wang, W. (1998). *Steal this computer book: All the stuff they never tell you about the internet.* No Starch.

Ziff-Davis Education. (1998). *Internet search techniques: Student manual.* Ziff-Davis Education.

Ziff-Davis Education. (1998). *Using the internet and www, level 1.* Ziff-Davis Education.

We would like to thank the following teachers and librarians for their contributions:

Shari Alboum   Helen Machleder
Meg E. Brandt   Lynn F. Mackwell
Laura S. Coburn   Millicent Petrullo
Donna L. Cohen   Jeanne Rotolo
Helen Flynn   June M. Wolff
Sharon Holster

This chapter was edited, updated, and revised by Rebecca Angeles, Information & Decision Sciences Department, Montclair State University, New Jersey.

INDEX

EFFECTIVE RESPONSE TO SCHOOL VIOLENCE

To be published 2001, 266 pages
Tony L. Jones
$61.95, hard
$39.95, paper

EXCEPTIONAL LEARNERS

Education and Research from a Global Perspective

Published 2001, 260 pages
Ivan Z. Holowinsky
$59.95, cloth
$38.95, paper [displayed]

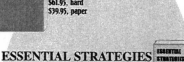

ESSENTIAL STRATEGIES FOR SCHOOL SECURITY

A Practical Guide for Teachers and School Administrators

To be published 2001, 268 pages
Richard A. Haynes & Catherine L. Henderson
$54.95, hard
$36.95, paper

RESEARCH WRITING IN EDUCATION AND PSYCHOLOGY—FROM PLANNING TO PUBLICATION

A Practical Handbook

To be published 2001, 176 pages
Herbert J. Klausmeier
$40.95, hard
$25.95, paper

MEDIA AND LITERACY

Learning in an Electronic Age - Issues, Ideas, and Teaching Strategies (2nd Ed.)

Published 2000, 244 pages
Dennis Adams & Mary Hamm
$43.95, hard
$31.95, paper

TEACHING THE ENGLISH LANGUAGE (2nd Ed.)

Published 2000, 166 pages
John H. Bushman
$29.95, paper

ISSUES IN SOCIAL STUDIES

Voices from the Classroom

To be published 2000, 222 pages
Cameron White
$46.95, cloth
$31.95, paper [displayed]

HUMAN SERVICES AND THE FULL SERVICE SCHOOL

The Need for Collaboration

Published 2000, 128 ages
Robert F.Kronick
$18.95, paper

AUTISM AND POST-TRAUMATIC STRESS DISORDER

Ending Autistic Fixation

Published 2000, 136 pages
Kenneth Lenchitz
$36.95, cloth
$19.95, paper [displayed]

SPECIAL EDUCATION, MULTICULTURAL EDUCATION, AND SCHOOL REFORM

Components of Quality Education for Learners with Mild Disabilities

Published 2000, 280 pages
Cheryl A. Utley & Festus E. Obiakor
$63.95, hard
$ 41.95, paper

THE SIMPLIFIED CLASSROOM AQUARIUM

A Teacher's Guide to Operating and Maintaining a Small Classroom Aquarium

Published 1999, 150 pages
Ed Stansbury
$25.95, spiral (paper)

TEACHING AND TESTING IN READING

A Practical Guide for Teachers and Parents

Published 1999, 164 pages
Charles H. Hargis
$40.95, hard
$28.95, paper

THE NEW EDUCATIONAL TECHNOLOGIES AND LEARNING

Empowering Teachers to Teach and Students to Learn in the Information Age

Published 1999, 322 pages
Ibrahim M. Hefzallah
$65.95, cloth
$50.95, paper [displayed]

HANDBOOK FOR LITERACY TUTORS

A Practical Approach to Effective Informal Instruction in Reading and Writing

Published 1999, 204 pages
Arlene Adams
$35.95, spiral (paper)